ENGLISH AS A LINGUA FRANCA IN THE INTERNATIONAL UNIVERSITY

In this book, Jennifer Jenkins, one of the leading proponents of English as a Lingua Franca, explores current academic English language policy in higher education around the world.

Universities around the world are increasingly presenting themselves as 'international' but their English language policies do not necessarily reflect this, even as the diversity of their student bodies grows. While there have been a number of attempts to explore the implications of this diversity from a cultural perspective, little has been said from the linguistic point of view, and in particular, about the implications for what kind(s) of English are appropriate for English lingua franca communication in international higher education.

Throughout the book Jenkins considers the policies of English language universities in terms of the language attitudes and ideologies of university management and staff globally, and of international students in a UK setting. The book concludes by considering the implications for current policies and practices, and what is needed in order for universities to bring themselves in line linguistically with the international status they claim.

English as a Lingua Franca in the International University is an essential read for researchers and postgraduate students working in the areas of Global Englishes, English as a Lingua Franca, and English for Academic Purposes.

Jennifer Jenkins is Chair of Global Englishes and Director of the Centre for Global Englishes at the University of Southampton, UK. She is author of *World Englishes*, second edition (2009, Routledge).

"This book puts the spotlight on the nature, role and consequences of 'English' in the 'international' university. It provides a welcome focus on debates about what kinds of language and literacy policies should be informing contemporary higher education. An important book for researchers and practitioners alike."

Theresa Lillis, *The Open University, UK*

"On reading this book, people will wonder why native English remains so entrenched as the sole standard. The author's call for a complete change of mind-set is compelling … this is a timely and important book."

Andy Kirkpatrick, *Griffith University, Australia*

"Jennifer Jenkins offers us a comprehensive and incisive analysis of the complexities of higher education in the global world, with a welcome focus on the burning issues of linguistic and intercultural complexity involved."

Anna Mauranen, *University of Helsinki, Finland*

ENGLISH AS A LINGUA FRANCA IN THE INTERNATIONAL UNIVERSITY

The politics of academic English language policy

Jennifer Jenkins

Routledge
Taylor & Francis Group

LONDON AND NEW YORK

First published 2014
by Routledge
2 Park Square, Milton Park, Abingdon, Oxon OX14 4RN

Simultaneously published in the USA and Canada
by Routledge
711 Third Avenue, New York, NY 10017

Routledge is an imprint of the Taylor & Francis Group, an informa business

British Library Cataloguing in Publication Data
A catalogue record for this book is available from the British Library

Library of Congress Cataloging in Publication Data
Jenkins, Jennifer, [date]
English as a Lingua Franca in the International University : the politics of academic English language policy / Jennifer Jenkins.
pages cm
Includes bibliographical references.
1. Language policy–English-speaking countries. 2. English language–Political aspects–Foreign countries. 3. English language–Social aspects–Foreign countries. 4. Intercultural communication. I. Title.
P119.32.E54J46 2013
306.44'9–dc23
2013004966

ISBN: 978-0-415-68463-7 (hbk)
ISBN: 978-0-415-68464-4 (pbk)
ISBN: 978-0-203-79815-7 (ebk)

Typeset in Bembo
by Taylor & Francis Books

MIX
Paper from
responsible sources
FSC
www.fsc.org FSC® C013604

Printed and bound in Great Britain by
CPI Group (UK) Ltd, Croydon, CR0 4YY

CONTENTS

ILLUSTRATIONS

Figures

Tables

ACKNOWLEDGEMENTS

Although this book was researched and written during the two years prior to publication, it was several years in conceptual evolution, and the first person I would like to thank is Andy Kirkpatrick who, several years earlier, had first stirred my interest in exploring English Medium Instruction within the ELF paradigm. Many others have influenced my thinking on the subject since then and/or have had direct input into the book in various ways. In these respects I am particularly grateful to Jiannis Androutsopoulos, Will Baker, Jill Doubleday, Constant Leung, Theresa Lillis, Felix Maringe, Anna Mauranen, and Ursula Wingate. I would also like to thank all the members of the Centre for Global Englishes at the University of Southampton for many stimulating discussions, and especially Lanxi Hu and Melissa Yu for helping me get my facts right, and Sonia Moran Panero and Ying Wang for helping directly with aspects of the research process. As well as this, a number of colleagues generously gave me access to their publications and presentations that were either difficult to obtain or still in press at the time I was writing: Jim D'Angelo, Alessia Cogo, Jim Coleman, Martin Dewey, Helen Fraser, Rebecca Hughes, David Lasagabaster, Enric Llurda, Constant Leung, Anna Mauranen, and Barbara Seidlhofer.

I am also heavily indebted to all those around the world who distributed and took (rather a lot of) time to respond to my questionnaire, to those who identified international student participants to take part in my interview study, and to the interview participants themselves. Because of the demands of ethical approval I am unable to mention any of their names specifically, but they know who they are, and I hope they realize that without their contribution, this book would not exist.

It is also important to acknowledge the part played by psychological support and encouragement. In this respect, my heartfelt thanks to the colleagues from afar and not so far who kept in touch by email and skype during those three final months of near isolation as I struggled to finish the book on time, and to Ros Mitchell, Gabi

Budach, Laura Dominguez, and Julia Hüttner in Southampton for their very welcome visits – and cakes!

Finally, at Routledge I would like to thank Louisa Semlyen, for her belief in the project and her support from beginning to end, Sophie Jaques for all her practical help and advice, Sarah Douglas for her extensive help and reassurance during the production process, and Kate Reeves for her careful copyediting.

This book is dedicated to all university students around the world who do not speak English as their first language and are studying in English medium.

1

ENGLISH, THE LINGUA FRANCA OF THE GLOBAL ACADEMY

Setting the scene

In March 2009 during a research strategy seminar held by the Centre for Applied Language Research at the University of Southampton, one speaker, the multilingualism scholar Gabriele Budach, posed the following question:

> How do we respond in our teaching to an academic culture that is becoming more and more globalized, and the needs of students with diverse linguistic and cultural backgrounds?

The "we" in the question referred, presumably, to the members of the Centre and perhaps also to all our colleagues in the wider University. But it could equally well be taken to include all academics in the UK and, indeed, all globally, given that academic culture "is becoming more and more globalized" around the entire world.

In essence, this book is an attempt to answer Budach's simple but profound question. She herself would no doubt have approached the issues it raises from a multilingualism perspective, particularly the implications for generating and disseminating knowledge in languages other than English, and for their mother tongue speakers (see, e.g., Ferguson 2007 in relation to Europe); and she would very likely have focused on the cultural aspects of the question as much as the linguistic. While I would not want to minimize in any way the critical importance of such concerns, my own interest is in the linguistic issues raised by the question. Specifically, given that globalization has gone hand-in-hand with the globalization of English, I am interested in what globalization means for *English* language use and users in Higher Education settings around the world. And while the prime focus of this book is on the implications of the globalization of English for its *non-native* speakers, particularly so-called 'international students' studying in Anglophone contexts, the chapters that follow also consider the question in relation to other kinds of English users, be they home students and staff at Anglophone universities, students and staff at so-called 'offshore' or 'branch' universities of Anglophone universities in overseas settings, or native and non-native English speakers at English medium instruction (EMI) universities in mainland Europe, East Asia, and Latin America.

The chapters of this book, along with the research underpinning them, combine my two main academic preoccupations: English as a Lingua Franca, and the international student language experience. English as a Lingua Franca (henceforth ELF) refers, in a nutshell, to the world's most extensive contemporary use of English, in essence, English when it is used as a contact language between people from different first languages (including native English speakers). I have been working on ELF since the 1980s when I began investigating phonological accommodation in ELF communication for my PhD. Since then, empirical research into ELF and academic ELF (ELFA) has grown dramatically, and in the process has demonstrated numerous ways in which English is used effectively by its (majority) non-native lingua franca speakers but often differently from ways in which it is used among native English speakers (see Chapter Two for a fuller definition of ELF and discussion of empirical ELF research, Chapter Three for a discussion of ELFA specifically).

My interest in the international student[1] language experience has developed in parallel with that in ELF as a result of my role as supervisor to large numbers of postgraduate, particularly doctoral, students for whom English is not their mother tongue, and the majority of whom come from Asia. At exactly the same time as ELF research has been questioning the validity of the current widespread insistence on native English norms for non-native English speakers, I have thus had the opportunity to observe at first hand the often negative impact of this insistence on non-native English students studying at university through the medium of English. And increasingly, the findings of empirical ELF/ELFA research and the experiences of my students as well as those of others' students (see, e.g., Hyland, Trahar, Anderson, and Dickens 2008, Montgomery 2010, Trahar 2011), have combined to feed a conviction that university students and staff, including native English speakers, are poorly served by the linguistic status quo, and that academic English policies and practices need to be brought into line with, and better reflect, the sociolinguistic reality of international university life, to which I turn next.

The changing global landscape of Higher Education

The terms 'globalization' and 'internationalization' are often used interchangeably. However, in many areas of life, Higher Education being a prime example, it makes far better sense to distinguish the two. Starting with globalization, Maringe and Foskett (2010) point out that while there is no single agreed definition of the concept, it is generally understood to mean "the creation of world relations based on the operation of free markets" (p. 1). Internationalization, they continue, is a key strategy by which universities have responded to the influence of globalization and is, itself, widely taken to mean "the integration of an international or intercultural dimension into the tripartite mission of teaching, research and service functions of Higher Education" (ibid.).

Foskett (2010: 44–45) categorizes universities globally into five groups: Domestic universities, which focus on their own local (regional and national) context and are therefore largely outside the interests of this book; Imperialist universities "which have strong international recruitment activities to draw students from overseas, but have done relatively little to change their organization, facilities or services 'at home'" (p. 44); Internationally aware universities "which are changing their organization and culture to have a profile that is international ... but have not yet engaged with 'overseas'" (p. 45); Internationally engaged universities which are "driving an internationalization agenda 'at home'. This typically includes curriculum review to make the teaching programmes global in perspective and to provide an international experience" as well as "encouraging staff to seek research and education partnerships overseas"[2] (ibid.); and finally Internationally focused universities, "a small number where the level of progress and achievement in internationalization is strong in many dimensions, and where the cultural change within the university has been transformational" (ibid.).

Foskett's categories are derived from the analysis of a survey of 23 universities, 7 within the UK and 16 in Asia. The universities surveyed were found to spread across all five categories, but with only three being in the 'Internationally focused' group, revealing in the other 20 cases a gap of some sort "between strategic aspiration and strategic reality" (Foskett 2010: 45). In the 'Imperialist' group, for example, a primary (although not explicitly stated) interest seemed to be in the economic rewards of international student recruitment rather than in promoting an international culture. This, Ferguson (2007) argues, is a prime feature of international universities in mainland Europe, where universities have introduced English medium courses in order firstly, "to attract fee-paying international students", secondly, "to enhance the university's international prestige and contacts" (again, likely to bring financial rewards), and thirdly, "to develop the English language skills of their staff and students" (p. 13). Their actions, he believes, are conditioned by "the globalization and commodification of higher education in a competitive, market-driven world characterized by the increased mobility of academics and students, and by the increased ease of international communication" (p. 14). Thus, when any university around the world advertises itself as 'international' or 'global', as increasing numbers do,[3] we cannot be at all sure what this entails in practice. Whether this same ambiguity extends to English language policies and practices, or whether international universities around the world adopt a more uniform approach to English language issues regardless of differences in other respects across Foskett's five categories, is an empirical question, and one which this book goes some way to answering.

Central to the internationalization of Higher Education (henceforth HE), as Ferguson (ibid.) points out, is student (and to a lesser extent, staff) mobility, which is leading above all to a massive increase in the number of international students. The English mother tongue countries, particularly the US, the UK, and Australia, along with France and Germany, currently account for the largest number of students from outside their own borders. According to the OECD (Organization for Economic Co-operation and Development) (2010: 314), in 2008 these countries were responsible for just over 50 per cent of such students, with the US taking 18.7 per cent, the UK 10 per cent, Germany 7.3 per cent, France 7.3 per cent, and Australia 6.9 per cent, although figures vary according to source. For example, while Maringe and Foskett (2010), put the total market share of these five nations at 56 per cent, close to the OECD's figure, Woodfield (2010) considers that it may be as high as 70 per cent. But whatever the precise figure, it is clear that these five nations accounted in 2008 for the education of over half the total of foreign students in tertiary education globally, while, according to the OECD (2010: 314), the mother tongue English countries (US, UK, Australia, Canada, and New Zealand) together accounted for just short of 43 per cent.

However, there have also recently been growing transnational flows within both mainland Europe (e.g. into Denmark, Sweden, and the Netherlands) and the Asia-Pacific region (e.g. into China, Hong Kong, and Malaysia), as universities start teaching in English medium in order to attract more students from outside (Woodfield 2010). According to the OECD (2010: 315), while "an increasing number of institutions in non-English-speaking countries now offer courses in English to overcome their linguistic disadvantage" vis-à-vis the dominance of English medium in attracting foreign students, "this trend is particularly noticeable in countries in which the use of English is widespread, such as the Nordic countries", as can be seen from Table 1.1 below. At the time of writing, it is not yet clear whether this trend will continue, while a further complicating factor is the

TABLE 1.1 OECD and partner countries offering tertiary programmes in English (2008)

Use of English in instruction	OECD and partner countries
All or nearly all programmes offered in English	Australia, Canada, Ireland, New Zealand, United Kingdom, United States
Many programmes offered in English	Denmark, Finland, the Netherlands, Sweden
Some programmes offered in English	Belgium (Fl.), Czech Republic, France, Germany, Hungary, Iceland, Japan, Korea, Norway, Poland, Portugal, Slovak Republic, Switzerland, Turkey
No or nearly no programmes offered in English	Austria, Belgium (Fr.), Chile, Greece, Israel, Italy, Luxembourg, Mexico, Portugal, Russian Federation, Spain

Source: OECD, compiled from brochures for prospective international students by OAD (Austria), CHES and NARI (Czech Republic), Cirius (Denmark), CIMO (Finland), EduFrance (France), DAAD (Germany), Campus Hungary (Hungary), University of Iceland (Iceland), JPSS (Japan), NIIED (Korea), NUFFIC (Netherlands), SIU (Norway), CRASP (Poland), Swedish Institute (Sweden) and Middle-East Technical University (Turkey) (OECD 2010: 316).

substantial growth in the number of offshore branches of local (mainly Anglo-phone) universities, particularly in the Asian region, where English is again the usual medium of instruction.

The mobility of people involved in HE has meant a far greater degree of contact and interconnectedness across borders than has been the case hitherto (Held, McGrew, Goldblatt, and Perraton 1999). Accompanying this, on the one hand, there have been new homogenizing discourses and activities across global HE, such as the Lisbon Strategy and Bologna Process in Europe, and a global increase in the use of uniform international English language tests for university entry. In Gibbs's view, the result is that "distinct forms of higher education have become homo-genized in a collusion of mediocrity based on immediacy, hedonism and financial return" (2010: 251). On the other hand, mobility has also meant a substantial increase in the diversity of individual university populations, as people from various parts of the world, often with very different linguistic and cultural backgrounds, converge on the same university site to learn, teach, and research either partly or entirely through the medium of English. The globalization of English is thus par-ticularly well exemplified in HE, where it has become a key aspect of the strategic response to globalization of many universities. In other words, the English language is playing a major role in the internationalization of global HE.

Furthermore, the existence of growing numbers of universities teaching some or all of their courses in English in addition to the large numbers of international students studying in Anglophone universities means, in practice, that for the first time there are probably more non-native than native English speakers using Eng-lish for at least some purposes on university campuses around the world. Mauranen and Ranta (2008) argue that this situation "calls for a better understanding of the way English is used in the new circumstances where the native speaker may not be present, and where Standard [i.e. native] English may not be the most relevant norm" (p. 199). Seidlhofer (2011) puts it more strongly: "it is important to realize that native-speaker language use is just *one* kind of reality, and one of very doubtful relevance for lingua franca contexts" (p. 19). International universities are prime examples of such "lingua franca contexts", and yet these universities have not even begun to consider the possible linguistic implications of their diverse student and staff make-up. What does it mean, for example, for the kind of English that is required in entry tests, or that is acceptable (or not) to those who assess students' content work, or that is the focus of the teaching of English for Academic Purposes?

Attempts to address such questions are likely to exacerbate existing tensions between those who favour the homogenization of English and those who take a broader ELF-oriented view. This is particularly likely in Anglophone countries, where even those academics who acknowledge the appropriateness of different kinds of English in non-Anglophone HE settings tend to adopt a proverbial 'when in Rome, do as the Romans do' position at home. And in my experience this also applies to many non-native academics working in Anglophone contexts as well as to those commenting on Anglophone contexts from outside. For example, Klitgård (2011: 185) argues that this approach "does not have to be the norm in a non-English-speaking educational system" but is "obviously" so in English-speaking settings.

In adopting this stance, academics ignore not only the needs of non-mobile home students for 'internationalization at home' (Jackson 2010, Turner and Robson 2008; and see the penultimate section of this chapter), but also the fact that international students in Anglophone countries, especially at postgraduate level, tend to be taught and to socialize largely in English lingua franca groups where the majority of their peers are also non-native English speakers. As an example, my own experience of teaching at different UK universities has been that at masters and doctoral levels, and increasingly also at undergraduate level, the vast majority of my students (postgraduate) and a sizeable minority (undergraduate) have been international students from different language backgrounds who speak English mainly among themselves for both academic and social purposes, and do so happily and successfully as well as using their mother tongues with each other where appropriate. However, this 'grassroots interconnectedness' is of a very different order and status from the 'homogenizing from above' tendency in HE to which I referred above, and seems to support Preece and Martin's claim that "there is a mismatch between the monolingual ethos and the ideology of English-medium tertiary education and the needs and identities of multilingual students" (2010: 3).

Others have reported similar experiences. Durant and Shepherd (2009), for example, state that the student community in their faculty of the University of Middlesex reflects "recent trends in British higher education. Most speakers are bilingual or multilingual; in communication they combine pragmatic strategies, cultural schemata and general knowledge derived from many different backgrounds." They go on to say that:

> overlap between members of the community is also evident, for example in the degree of access they share to a body of international cultural forms carried by contemporary global media and the Internet, as well as by their *proficiency in English as an international language*, and by familiarity with given bodies of educational subject matter.
>
> *(p. 159; my italics)*

They conclude that their student population "provides an interesting case of what would have been called, in an older vocabulary, a multicultural 'melting pot'" and that it "offers potentially important observations about intercultural contact and globalization" (ibid.).

For the purposes of this book, the most relevant aspect of Durant and Shepherd's description of their intercultural student community is their reference to its members' "proficiency in English as an international language", in other words, their proficiency in ELF. We will return to this later in the chapter when we consider ELF, ELFA, and the deficit discourses around the English of 'bilingual' university students who, given the small number of bilingual native English speakers, are predominantly non-native.

While the make-up of student communities in HE is becoming increasingly intercultural, the institutions in which they study are not by any means necessarily so. For though there is much talk by universities of 'internationalizing the curriculum', 'internationalization at home' (see p. 16), and the like, in practice the process seems not yet to have gone very far. Indeed, according to many of those participating in the research for this book, there is, as Bash (2009) puts it, "a continuing presence of national academic cultures contextualized in national higher education systems" (p. 476). Bash goes on to argue that the fact of internationalizing HE does not of itself ensure interculturality because:

> [t]he globalized marketization process is premised upon a capacity for transnational economic *contractual* engagement without necessarily taking into account the complexities of the process of *intercultural* engagement. In the quest for increased international student business, interculturality issues tend to be subordinated to economic issues of supply and demand – and, in commercial terms, issues of profit and loss. Thus, the increased 'internationalization' of higher education, while superficially seen as a sign of increased intercultural engagement, is frequently viewed as yet another aspect of the perpetuation of western dominance, contributing to an overall cynical perception of globalization.
>
> *(ibid.; his italics)*

This seems to be particularly so in Anglophone contexts, as well as in Anglophone offshore university campuses, whose aim may be to replicate what is on offer at the home campus. To take just one of many possible examples, Nottingham Ningbo's website, www.nottingham.edu.cn, claims that: "[a]ll undergraduate and postgraduate programmes in Ningbo are conducted entirely in English with the *same teaching and evaluation standards* as at Nottingham UK" (my italics). And in an article in *Times Higher Education* about Nottingham's two offshore campuses (the other being in Malaysia), Vincenzo Raimo, director of Nottingham's international office, is quoted as saying "[t]here is only one University of Nottingham – it just happens that we've got campuses in three countries" ('Be quids in at our branches abroad, Nottingham tells students in the UK', 25 August 2011, p. 11). Even the Nottingham Ningbo university buildings are the same as those in Nottingham UK (see Chapter Five for further discussion of this and other offshore campuses).

The offshore university campus appears to bear a good deal of resemblance to another recent phenomenon, the 'English village'. So-called English villages are replicas of parts of England that have been set up in East Asian countries such as Japan and Korea and where only English is spoken (see, e.g., Seargeant 2005). Their HE counterparts are, in effect, 'academic English villages'. And while offshore campuses may present a worst case scenario in terms of promoting Anglophone (academic) culture, the need for the promotion of genuine interculturality applies to all universities that wish to claim international status. As Bash concludes, all institutions "may need to address possible changes in their policies and practices in relation to the process of acculturation and crossing boundaries. ... New ways of engagement with students from diverse national/cultural backgrounds ... might be sought to encourage the further growth of globalized higher education" (op.cit.: 481). We turn now to consider these issues in relation to the English language specifically.

Globalization and ELF

While ELF will be explored in detail in Chapter Two and ELFA in Chapter Three, it will be helpful at this stage to signal their broad implications in relation to globalization and the globalization of English. We therefore consider ELF in this section and ELFA in the section that follows. For while ELF researchers would argue that those working in the field of globalization should take notice of ELF, the same is also true vice versa, that is that those studying ELF should "pay close attention to the intellectual discourse on globalization", given that "ELF is simultaneously the consequence and the principal language medium of globalizing processes" (Jenkins, Cogo, and Dewey 2011: 303).

ELF in practice represents one side of the globalizing phenomenon of inter-connectedness that was discussed above and which I termed 'grassroots inter-connectedness' in order to contrast it with what I called 'homogenizing from above'. In other words, ELF represents how the majority of English speakers actually *use* the language in their daily lives (and ELFA how many use it in their academic lives), while a homogenizing approach represents how the linguistic homogenizers *wish them* to use it. Thus, whereas ELF fits in with a view of globalization as "neither fixed nor certain" (Dixon 2006: 320) producing "a dynamic, hybrid environment" (Jackson 2010: 3), the conventional approach to English (i.e. standard native English, known as English as a Foreign Language, or EFL, when taught to non-native speakers) fits in with a view of globalization as "standardization across cultures" producing "greater levels of sameness" (McCabe 2001: 140). Of course it is not simply the case that one of these two orientations to globalization in general and the globalization of English in particular exists in practice and the other only in theory: both orientations can be instantiated in real world practices such as those discussed in the previous section in respect of HE. The question, then, as far as the globalization of English goes, is whether it is ELF or standard native English/EFL that provides the more appropriate response to globalization and its concomitant interconnectedness.

In tackling this question, Dewey (2007) takes as his starting point Held et al.'s (1999) framework in which they identify globalization as being conceptualized according to three different perspectives: the hyperglobalist, the sceptical, and the transformationalist.[4] Dewey explains:

> For the hyperglobalizer, globalization is the key defining force of the current epoch, an era where traditional nation states have given way to a global market economy in which most networks are transnational, and where

globalization is driving a construction of new economic, social, and political world orders, leading ultimately to greater overall *homogeneity*. The sceptics, on the other hand, maintain that the current level of interdependence has precedence in earlier periods of ... internationalization. Their argument holds that national governments retain the power to regulate trade, commerce and politics, and that any interdependence operates only at surface level. In contrast, the transformationalist defines the current epoch as a period of significant and rapid economic, social and political change, where globalization is regarded as the driving force responsible for fundamental *socio-political transformations*.

(p. 334; my italics)

As Dewey observes, these three perspectives on globalization can be mapped onto orientations towards English. Hyperglobalizers, regardless of whether they regard the globalization of English as beneficial or as a form of linguistic imperialism (Phillipson 1992, 2009),[5] believe that the English language is the property of its native speakers. Thus, for them, it is – or should be – distributed in its native form (by which they mean either standard North American or standard British English), unchanged around the globe (see Widdowson 1997 on the distinction between distribution and adoption as contrasted with spread and adaptation). Even Phillipson, in a chapter in which he talks of the global spread of English in HE in terms of a "pandemic" (2009: 195), nevertheless speaks of "*the* global standard form of English". He goes on to say that the learning of English "must be based on the lexis, grammar and much of the pragmatics of *the* global form" (2009: 206; my italics), implying that he believes such a form exists in the first place. His "must", however, is ambiguous. The text that follows this sentence implies that it does not reflect his own position, whereas his critique in the same book of a German scholar's English (see p. 14 below) implies otherwise. But either way, this is not at all dissimilar to the position of those hyperglobalizers who take a positive view of global linguistic developments. Crystal, for example, believes that a new "neutral global variety" of English, which he calls World Standard Spoken English (WSSE), is emerging, and that English speakers are becoming bidialectal in their own local variety and this new 'world' variety, albeit that, he thinks, it is likely to be heavily influenced by US English (2003: 185–89).

The sceptics of Held et al.'s (1999) framework translate into orientations towards English as a belief – common in the English Language Teaching industry – that the findings of ELF research are trivial, that there is nothing particularly new about them, and/or that there is no need to move away from the teaching of English according to standard (i.e. native English) norms (e.g. Maley 2009, Mollin 2006, Prodromou 2006). By contrast, those who take a transformationalist position on English "perceive the need to address the considerable reshaping that movements in the socio-political world order have produced" (Dewey 2007: 334). This is where ELF enters the frame. According to the ELF school of thought and supported by extensive empirical ELF research, innovative English features are emerging in intercultural communication not because speakers are unable to 'master' the forms of native English, but as a result of their desire (whether conscious or unconscious) to promote effective communication in interactions that are characterized by a far greater degree of diversity among English users than has been the case until recent times. Non-native-led transformations in the English language, according to this position, are inevitable.

Brumfit (2001) talks of a shift in the role of English education. By this he means:

> a shift … away from English as part of an education that inducts you into a humanistic tradition, to an education that facilitates your communication *for whatever you want with whoever you want*: a shift therefore towards a notion of communicative competence where the communication is defined by *the capacity of individuals of different cultures to interact.*
>
> *(p. 120; my italics)*

The notion of communicative competence in English is by no means unproblematic given the continuing tendency of English language teachers and applied linguists to focus on 'what the natives do' and to ignore "real-world social, cultural and language developments in contemporary conditions" (Leung 2005: 119). By contrast, Brumfit's observation points to the possibilities not only for English language education, but also for subsequent English use, which, after all, is (or should be) the primary purpose of language education. This leads neatly to ELFA, the kind of English most widely used (if not currently acknowledged, let alone accepted) in HE, where the default communication is among "individuals of different cultures".

Globalization, Higher Education, and academic ELF

As discussed earlier, the response of HE to globalization has been one of inter-nationalization which itself refers to the integration of an international or inter-cultural dimension into one or more areas of university life, be this teaching and/or research and/or service functions (Maringe and Foskett 2010). The issue as far as language is concerned is the extent to which English is seen as a bona fide part of this new international or intercultural dimension. For despite the burgeoning literature on the internationalization of HE, language is rarely mentioned at all other than in a passing reference to the fact that the internationalization process is accompanied by the use of English as the global academic lingua franca (e.g. Altbach and Knight 2007), and to non-native students' consequent need to gain the (taken for granted) levels and skills in standard (i.e. native) English seen by those in control as necessary to be able to operate successfully in the academic lingua franca (see, e.g., Yumei 2010 on how this is being approached in China). And while there are occasional comments on the hegemony of English in HE (e.g. Gibbs 2010), concerns over potential domain loss for other, especially smaller, languages (e.g. Phillipson 2009), and investigations into the role of multilingualism in HE (see, e.g., several contributions in Haberland, Mortensen, Fabricius, Preisler, Risager, and Kjærbeck 2008,[6] and the website of the CALPIU network),[7] there is little discussion of the implications for *academic English* per se in light of its new lingua franca role. Thus, the writings in which the language issue is taken seriously in relation to the internationalization of HE, are primarily the work of scholars whose research is not within HE studies as such, but within language-focused fields of enquiry such as Academic Literacies, Critical EAP (English for Academic Purposes), and of course ELFA itself, all of which will be discussed in Chapter Three.

However, if the aim of an international education is to provide students, wherever they come from and wherever they study, with the "knowledge, attitudes and skills [they] need in order to be globally and interculturally competent" (Jackson 2010: 11), such sidelining of English language is unacceptable. English can no longer be cast aside in the internationalization literature as though it was merely a practical problem to be 'fixed' in university EAP units. If the complexities involved in English being the global academic lingua franca are to be explored effectively, then the subject needs a full airing in the HE literature and some searching language-related questions need to be asked. For example, why, in an *international* institution, should it be acceptable to require non-native English speakers (NNESs) to replicate the *national* academic English norms preferred by native English speaker (NES) staff and students? If not, what are the alternatives? Similarly, why is it so often assumed that NES students possess, by definition, the relevant English language skills they need for their studies (and afterwards) at both academic and intercultural levels? After all, academic language, as was observed long ago (Bourdieu and Passeron 1977), is nobody's mother tongue; and by the same token, nobody is a native speaker of ELF, academic or otherwise. And given the international nature of academic life, what other kinds of skills do NESs need to equip them for intercultural communication? These are questions to which I will return in later chapters.

In addition to the literature on the internationalization of HE, there is also a burgeoning related literature on the subject of international students, especially (but not exclusively) those studying in Anglophone contexts. Even here, however, language is generally a marginal consideration if mentioned at all, or is treated as a (native) skill to be mastered, and approached in terms of the difficulties students encounter in the process (e.g. Jackson 2010).[8] More often it is cultural factors and/ or practical issues such as financial problems, feelings of isolation and the like, that are foregrounded (e.g. Marginson, Nyland, Sawir, and Forbes–Mewett 2010, Montgomery 2010). And even here, the discussion tends to lack any problematizing of the widespread assimilation approach in Anglophone HE, and of cultural issues such as what international students can (or should) expect culture-wise in an international university (e.g. Wildavsky 2010).

And it is not only scholars researching the internationalization of HE who marginalize the English language issue. Perhaps in part because of the gap in the literature, it also seems to be regarded – according to the research underpinning this book – as a rather marginal, or at least a technical, issue by many members of university faculty. This appears to be especially so in Anglophone countries, where the teaching of academic English "is routinely sidelined in the institutional discourse of higher education ... in order to focus on what is considered more 'important', namely ideas or content" (Turner 2011: 3). Meanwhile, academics in Anglophone as well as many other settings tend to take it as given that appropriate academic English means standard *native* academic English, while "the cultural values inscribed in these expectations have themselves received little attention" (op.cit.: 2). The only issue, from this perspective, is to ensure that international students acquire standard native academic English, or at least something sufficiently close to it, either before arrival or by attending a pre-sessional EAP course prior to starting their studies, and subsequently, in in-sessional training if need be. However, international students, at least according to the research reported in this book, see the situation rather differently. For them, language "is a central rather than peripheral player in the work of higher education" (op.cit.: 1). They are well aware that English has a major impact on their university experiences and outcomes as well as – for those who desire academic careers – their future international publishing prospects.

All this, of course, assumes that international students survive the high-stakes English language entry tests that they are obliged to take before they can be admitted to university. If students wish to study in HE not only in Anglophone countries, but also in English medium in Mainland Europe, East Asia, and the like, they need to gain an acceptable score in one of the 'international' tests such as IELTS (International English Language Testing System), TOEFL (Test of English as a Foreign Language), TOEIC (Test of English for International Communication), or PTE Academic (Pearson Test of English Academic), all of which test their proficiency in native British or American English. Some even need to pass an English examination for entry into HE within their own countries. For example, a quarter of the Gao Kao, or 'High Test', the obligatory examination for university admission *within* China, tests Chinese L1 candidates' English language skills.

International students not only regard language issues as central rather than peripheral, but also tend to have more nuanced understandings of these issues than, it seems, do many faculty members and researchers into the internationalization of HE. For one thing, as the interview study reported in Chapter Seven demonstrates, these students may be more perceptive than the latter in their critiques of 'standard' academic English. They observe, for example, that there are no unambiguous sources available to inform them of what it actually is. One participant in a separate focus group study (Maringe and Jenkins in preparation) described standard English as existing "just in the air".[9] The interview participants also point out that EAP books and courses focus in the main on surface level details such as the use of topic sentences, passive versus first person, and British versus American English; and even in basic matters such as these, they find inconsistencies among EAP teachers. Again the participants report that their content tutors tend to comment on language only when students write (or, less often, speak) in a way that a NES would not do: in other words, they can only tell them what the standard *is not*, and not what it is. And again, there are inconsistencies across academic staff, even sometimes within a single discipline. And to make matters worse, they note, NES academics do not necessarily conform in the ways they expect of international students, but allow themselves poetic licence in their own academic English.

Another difference language-wise between international students and university staff is their approach to linguistic creativity. As just noted, NES academics assume the right to be creative in their use of English. International students, on the other hand, risk being told their English contains errors if they, too, are creative with it. They therefore generally accept the demand made on them to defer to conventional standard English, at least in so far as they can, given the vagueness of the notion itself. But while recognizing the need to conform so as to achieve a successful outcome, they may also see this as something of an ideological imposition. Even if they know nothing about ELF, as in the case of almost all the international student participants in my research, they may still believe they should have the right to be creative in their academic English and not be constrained by the culture-specific frames of reference of native English, a point made by several of my interview participants.

Indeed, if these participants are typical, it seems that international students may be rather more international than the NES staff that teach them, at least as far as lingua-cultural issues are concerned. For despite the fact that academics generally consider themselves to be internationally minded, very few outside the fields of Academic Literacies, Critical EAP, and ELFA itself see international academics (students or staff) as entitled to legitimate input into academic English, let alone accept the diversity and hybridity this would entail. Instead, there is a trenchant deficit orientation towards non-native English, which Flowerdew (2008), drawing on Goffman (e.g. 1963), describes as an example of stigma. In HE, this deficit orientation leads, as Turner argues, to a "relentlessly remedial representation of language issues" (2011: 3), though finding out how widespread it is globally was one of the objectives of the research for this book.

According to the "remedial" perspective, "the language adopted for intercultural communication is effectively owned by one or other party in any interchange" (Durant and Shepherd 2009: 149) which, in the case of international HE, inevitably means the NES party. The result is that "[l]anguage use can be referred back to authoritative, standard forms and patterns" (ibid.), in other words, to British or American academic English. Intercultural communication, from this position, is seen as "a problem to be addressed, rather than that of a neutral social phenomenon to be investigated, or even that of a possible source of creativity and communicative innovation to be encouraged" (ibid.). NNES students' 'problem' – that is, their English 'errors' – are therefore at best sometimes tolerated (provided that the outcome is intelligible to a NES reader or listener), but never seen as legitimate forms of expression. Thus, NNES students in HE, who should be entitled to feel that they "have the identity of a legitimate university student" and that "they have left behind the difficult years of doing ESL [English as a Second Language] and *being* ESL", are forced back onto an ESL identity by being required, or at least made to feel they need, to take EAP courses to improve their English

(Marshall 2010: 45; his italics). And like Flowerdew (2008), Marshall (ibid.) sees this as a form of stigmatizing.

This orientation to NNES students leads, in turn, to the relentless negative stereotyping of NNES university students' and staff's academic English in the HE and ELT press. The following are but a few of the many similar examples I could have quoted:

- A recent piece in the *EL Gazette* (an ELT newspaper) reported without comment a claim made by a Dr Daniel Guhr of the US company Illuminate Consulting Group that "most international students use a type of 'pidgin academic English'" (July 2011, p. 2).
- In a similar vein, *Times Higher Education* carried an article by the Oxford University emeritus professor of general linguistics, Roy Harris, with the title 'Mother tongue twisted by drive for global gains' (30 March, p. 12). In the article, Harris depicted any lenience towards international students' English as political correctness, and asked: "How can anyone learn a hotchpotch in which it does not matter how the words are spelt, whether or not singulars are distinguished from plurals, and which syllables are stressed in speech and which are not? Chinglish, Singlish or Schminglish: take your choice".
- Again, in a piece with the title 'Trips and falls of the tongue', also in *Times Higher Education* (21 October 2010, p. 19), Brian Bloch, a lecturer in management and economics at the University of Munster, described the English of German academics as "Denglisch", meaning "English that remains shackled with German structures and idioms", and went on to argue that "[n]on native speakers are generally unable to write an acceptable level of English for academic purposes", and that "[t]heir work needs to be edited by fellow academics" which "generally entails changes in almost every sentence".
- Finally, an example from a less expected source, Robert Phillipson. As was observed above (p. 9), on the one hand, Phillipson opposes the spread of English as the language of global HE, while on the other hand, he seems to believe in the existence of a global standard form of (academic) English that is determined by its Anglo users. This leads him to object when NNESs appropriate the language and use it in their own way. For example, in his review of a collection edited by the German scholar Ammon (2001), he criticizes "countless German-influenced forms that disrupt, without perhaps impeding, comprehensibility" (Phillipson 2009: 250; and see Seidlhofer 2011 for several other examples of this kind of contradiction in Phillipson's writings). In other words, Phillipson's concern for language rights does not extend to NNESs' *English* language rights. Their 'choice', as far as Phillipson is concerned, seems to be either to use their mother tongue (his preference) or to use English in a native-like way.

Common to all four (and numerous other) commentators on NNES academic English is the apparent perception of English as being in the ownership of its NESs and by the same token, of academic English as being owned by NES academics. They also reveal an astonishing lack of awareness of the facts of the global spread of English and of the processes of language contact, accommodation, and change that such language spread entails. For as the Creolist scholar, Mufwene, notes, "[t]he agency of [language] change lies definitely within the behavior of individual speakers, and causation partly in the mutual accommodations they make to each other while they are more intent on communicating effectively than in preserving idiolectal, dialectal, or language boundaries" (2001: 24). Mufwene's observation was echoed in a response to Bloch by Morán Panero, then a PhD student at the University of Southampton. She pointed out that "[l]anguages continually develop as speakers reshape them in innovative ways", that English "no longer belongs solely to native speakers. Proficient international users can also develop ownership by appropriating the language while respecting intelligibility", and that "[i]n order for English to work as an international lingua franca, accommodation is crucial ... as opposed to expecting other users of English to maintain UK norms or standards instead of their own perfectly valid, creative and intelligible productions" (Letters, *Times Higher Education*, 18 November 2010, p. 33).

Stereotypes of non-native academic English such as those quoted above continue in part, as Turner (2011) notes, because "the workings of western academic culture, as it relates to how language is used and evaluated in higher education pedagogy and assessment" have tended not to be "available to critical reflection and transformation" (p. 3). This, she observes, is "in marked contrast to the prevailing institutional discourse, whereby discussion of language issues circulates in a deficit discourse and language work is marginalised" (ibid.). It is, in fact, a current irony of Anglophone HE that the very faculty who criticize international (particularly East Asian) students for a perceived lack of criticality are often the very same faculty who lack critical skills themselves when it comes to reflecting on the linguistic correlates of internationalization.

Preisler (2011) describes the current situation as a "clash" between native and non-native norms in which diversity is seen as needing to be discouraged and standard native academic norms preferred, particularly in the case of written academic English. This, he argues, misses the point:

> the internationalization of universities represents a new cultural and linguistic *hybridity* based on cultural interdependence, with the potential to develop new forms of identities unfettered by traditional 'us-and-them' binary thinking, and a new open-mindedness about the roles of self and others, resulting in new patterns of communicative (educational and social) practices.
>
> *(p. xiv; his italics)*

Preisler has here, in effect, provided a description of an ELF(A) perspective, and we return to his points about hybridity, new forms of identity, problems with the traditional binary NES–NNES divide, and the like in Chapter Two.

Internationalization and native English speaking students in HE

So far, my discussion about students has focused mainly on NNESs. However, this is not to suggest that NES students are unaffected by current approaches to the internationalization of English in HE. Indeed, two things have always puzzled me about the term 'international student' as it is used in the UK at least: firstly, that the only students who are referred to as 'international' are those from overseas (sometimes including mainland Europe); secondly, that these same students are required to assimilate culturally and linguistically to the home institution's preferred (national) way of doing things and problematized where they 'fall short'. This implies that the word 'international' — as far as students are concerned — is a euphemism for 'non-native' (when applied across the board) and for 'high-fee-paying non-native' when applied to non-Europeans. If this were not the case, why is it not used for home students too? Do they not want to see themselves — and be seen — as international? In today's 'globalized' world, this can only be an asset and is fast becoming a requirement.[10]

The problem is that many NES university students seem unaware that being a NES doesn't bring with it, by default as it were, an international aspect to their make-up. They are often aware that 'their' language has become the international lingua franca of HE and many other areas of life, hence perhaps the increasing unwillingness to learn foreign languages. However, they do not understand what it means to be a lingua franca. They are therefore unaware that the English used as an academic lingua franca around the world is not the same as the English they use to communicate with other NESs, but a kind of English in which they, too, need to acquire skills. Thus, they may complain if they find the accent of a NNES lecturer or ITA (International Teaching Assistant) unfamiliar, rather than treating it as an opportunity to find out about other ways of speaking English than their own local British or American variety.[11]

I referred earlier (p. 7) to the notion of 'internationalization at home' (IaH), a term coined by Nilsson (1999). This involves "the embedding of international/intercultural perspectives into local educational settings" (Turner and Robson 2008: 15). As Jackson (2010) points out, it aims "to raise the global awareness and intercultural understanding of faculty and 'non-mobile' students ... to prepare individuals for life in an interconnected world whereby contact with people from other cultures (e.g., face-to-face, e-mail) is increasingly the norm" (p. 13). Jackson describes various initiatives that have been developed to promote IaH at institutional, faculty, and programme/course level. These initiatives involve intercultural collaborations across and within institutions, faculty workshops focusing on intercultural communication, the building of an international element into curricula, and the like (see, e.g., Clifford 2011 and the other articles in *Higher Education Research & Development* vol. 30, no. 5, which is dedicated to internationalization at home from a global citizenship perspective). But what seems to be missing in all of this is any initiative to explore intercultural awareness in relation to the English language. It seems that while there may be a growing acknowledgement of the need to incorporate IaH at the cultural level, the same is not true at the linguistic level, where a strong native English ethos still appears to pervade HE.

When I tried to explore the issues in my own institution at a departmental staff workshop on whether and how to correct PhD students' writing, it was made clear to me by all colleagues present, both NES and NNES, that my (international) orientation to academic English was unwelcome. And when a group of PhD students in my institution's Centre for Global Englishes pursued the same issue in two seminars on the subject of 'appropriate English for PhD theses', the NNES participants reluctantly came to the conclusion that in order to be passed by the external examiner, they would have to adhere to British academic English. As an aside, however, given that an increasing number of countries are now offering courses and even entire degrees in English medium,[12] Anglophone universities may be at risk of losing international students to non-Anglophone countries if the latter are, or become, more international in their orientation to English than the former, whether by design or by default (see Chapter Five for further discussion).

Yet it is NES students as much as, and possibly more than, the NNES students (and staff) in Anglophone contexts who may ultimately be the losers in all this, even if they do not yet recognize it. In the HE press over the past two or three years there has been a small but steady stream of articles disparaging NES students' (and sometimes staff's) lack of intercultural skills, including their lack of languages other than English, their lack of awareness of cultural difference, and, most relevant in terms of the present discussion, their inability to use English in a way that is internationally intelligible. Although many NES students study alongside NNES students, especially (but not only) at postgraduate level, the expectations concerning linguistic accommodations seem to be one-way: that is, NNES students are expected to adapt their English to make it easily intelligible to the NES students (and staff), and not vice versa. Wherever this is normal practice, NES students are missing an important opportunity to acquire skills in the lingua franca use of English, skills that they are likely to need in any international career in their futures.

Ironically, the best hope for British NES students in this respect may be to study for their degrees in an offshore Anglophone university, which to a great extent can be regarded as another kind of 'internationalization at home' – except that the 'home' in question is a branch of (usually) a US or UK university that has been set up in another country. At a time when UK university home undergraduate fees have tripled, offshore universities such as Nottingham Ningbo in China (see p. 7) offer a cheaper alternative. While native English is still the medium of teaching, NES students in such universities are in a very small minority and therefore exposed daily to other kinds of English, those of both local Chinese students and (mainly NNES) international students from around the world, whom they need to understand and to whom they need to make themselves understood. In other words, NES students are acquiring ELF through experiencing it directly and rather more so than they would do in their home country, where they tend to study and socialize in NES groups rather than mix with their NNES peers (Montgomery 2010; and see Chapter Seven).

Summing up and moving on

In this first chapter, I have signalled the main themes of the book, all of which will be explored in greater detail in the chapters that follow and in some cases with the support of new research. Two overarching and overlapping themes have emerged, both of which relate directly to Budach's question that I presented at the start of the chapter: firstly, the way in which language is sidelined in the discourses of internationalization and globalization; and secondly, the uncritical tendency of many involved in HE (and other areas of life) to persist in traditional ways of thinking about English that do not take account of the major structural changes in the use and users of English around the globe and their implications for HE settings.

As regards the sidelining of language, this chapter has demonstrated, at least in respect of those scholars working on English from a less traditional perspective, that "[w]hile many people who think about language are thinking about globalization, the people who think about globalization never think about language. Language has not been a category of analysis in the literature on globalization" (Pratt 2010: 9). This is curious given, as Pratt goes on to say, that "language and linguistic difference shape global processes at every turn". We need, she argues, to think about "the redistribution of linguistic competencies", "lingua francas", and "the emergence of new heterolingual practices" (ibid.).

Although Pratt has broader concerns than the English language in mind, what she says is immensely relevant to ELF in general and ELFA more specifically. There is, as I pointed out earlier, a vast literature on globalization, internationalization, and the internationalization of HE, while large numbers of HE institutions around the world are declaring their 'international' and/or 'global' credentials. Yet there has so far been no serious attempt in either case to consider the issues in relation to the (English) language in which international universities and programmes operate, and the implications for HE English language policies and practices. Even the programmes of the annual *Going Global* conference series (see http://ihe. britishcouncil.org/going-global/ for details) include very few talks on language topics, and those few tend to take the remedial orientation towards English that I referred to earlier. This is perhaps not surprising given that the *Going Global* conferences are run by the British Council and sponsored by organizations from among the Anglophone testing industry such as IELTS and TOEFL. Thus, while there is much talk at these conferences of internationalizing the HE curriculum, there is no corresponding talk of internationalizing the language in which the curriculum is taught and studied.

Turning to the other main theme of this chapter, the uncritical tendency to accept traditional orientations to English premised on NES ownership of the language, I will end the chapter geographically where I began by quoting the late Christopher Brumfit, formerly Professor of Applied Linguistics at the University of Southampton. As he pointed out many years ago in words that have since been much quoted:

the English language no longer belongs numerically to speakers of English as a mother tongue, or first language. The ownership (by which I mean the power to *adapt and change*) of any language in effect rests with the people who use it. ... The major advances in sociolinguistic research over the past half century indicate clearly the extent to which languages are shaped by their use. ... Statistically, native speakers are in a minority for [English] language use, and thus in practice for language change, for language maintenance, and for the ideologies and beliefs associated with language – at least in so far as non-native speakers use the language for a wide range of public and personal needs.

(2001: 116)

This leads us straight into a discussion of the English spoken by those who are now statistically in a majority for English language use, in other words, ELF, the subject of the next chapter.

Notes

1 The term 'international student' has a number of overlapping but slightly different meanings. It is conventionally used within Anglophone contexts to refer to students from overseas (having replaced the older term 'overseas student'), and in the UK (but not necessarily other Anglophone regions) it excludes students from mainland Europe. This is primarily because students from mainland Europe pay the same fees as home (i.e. UK) students, rather than the higher 'international' fees, although this is not to deny that there may be other, more nuanced, differences such as cultural between European students and those from Asia, Latin America, the Middle East, and the like. In non-Anglophone contexts, the term 'international student' tends to refer to any student from outside the national border except in the case of offshore Anglophone universities, which continue to refer to students from the native English speaking country of the original institution as 'home' students. This, in theory could be taken to include native English speaking students from other countries, although it rarely does so in practice. While recognizing that there are differences in the meaning of the term as it is used in different contexts, my own use of 'international student', unless otherwise stated, refers to any non-native English-speaking student studying at university through the medium of English. However, the term itself is critiqued and the implications for native English speaking students discussed later in the chapter.
2 However the issue of HE partnerships is a complex one, and it is not clear at this stage whether the rationale for partnerships is a genuine desire to internationalize both partners via mutual engagement, or in order for one partner to promote its perspective in the other's institution and gain some kind of (possibly economic) advantage. While it is impossible to generalize, it would make sense to look closely at the small print in announcements of such partnerships to see whether or not they are partnerships in scare quotes.
3 These are typical examples of headings drawn from the large number of university adverts that I have collected from educational periodicals and newspapers during the period in which I was writing this book: "City University London is a global university", with "global" occurring a further time in the blurb (*Times Higher Education*, April 2011); "A leadership role in a global university", with "global" occurring a further four times, "international" twice, and "internationalization" once (advert for Coventry University, *Times Higher Education*, May 2011); "A degree from the University of New South Wales

in Australia is your passport to global career opportunities", with "global" appearing three further times in the blurb and "international" once (*Education Guardian*, August 2011); "An internationally recognized university located in the heart of Asia" (Hong Kong Polytechnic University, *Times Higher Education*, September 2011); "Xi'an Jiaotong-Liverpool University (XJTLU) is set to become the most international university in China" (*Times Higher Education*, February 2012) with "international(ly)" appearing a further four times; "A world-class university in a world-ranked city" (University of Auckland, *Times Higher Education*, May 2012).

4 Citing Steger (2003), Maringe (2010) uses slightly different terms: "hyperglobalizers, globalizers, and anti-globalizers" he states "have been used to describe the spectrum of opinions, reactions and responses of different people to the phenomenon of globalization" (p. 19), with the first two viewing globalization in a positive light and the third emphasizing its negative aspects.

5 As Blommaert points out, the linguistic imperialism paradigm "subscribes to a sociolinguistics of immobile languages" (2010: 182). It is thus a self-evidently anachronistic perspective that takes minimal account either of global changes over the past few decades or of people's right to choose how they respond to those changes, and their agency when they do so (see also Brutt-Griffler 2002).

6 This edited volume also contains a small number of contributions that focus in part or entirely on the English language issue.

7 Cultural and Linguistic Practices in the International University, http://calpiu.dk/

8 Jackson's (2010) introductory chapter problematizes the language issue in relation to HE, and discusses the implications of the "decentring" effect of globalization "for the learning and teaching of English in non-English speaking countries" (p. 5). However, Jackson does not extend the "decentring" phenomenon to *English-speaking* countries. As a result, her analysis of the language problems of her native Hong Kong study abroad research participants in the UK is premised on the traditional study abroad paradigm, according to which the aim of the sojourn abroad is to acquire the language and culture of the natives. Jackson's analysis thus reflects the 'when in Rome' position that I described earlier, which is at odds with the notion of the globalization of English and the role of English as the lingua franca of HE wherever in the world (including Anglophone countries) an individual HE institution is located. Her analysis also reflects the World Englishes paradigm, which sees English around the world as consisting of bounded varieties, each with its own discrete features, and each appropriate for use *within* the home nation (British English in Britain, Indian English in India, and so on). This contrasts with the ELF perspective, which sees English as a more hybrid and contingent means of communication *across* national boundaries (see Seidlhofer 2009a and Chapter Two below for further discussion of the differences between the two paradigms).

9 Similarly, Lillis refers to students' perceptions of the requirements of academic writing as "an institutional practice of mystery" (2001: 76).

10 The University of Warwick seems to be a rare exception in this respect. On 7 February 2012, they advertised on the BAAL mailing list for their new post of "Internationalisation Officer" as follows: "You will work with colleagues across the University and particularly with the Students' Union (on the joint 'Go Global' project) to internationalise the student experience on campus and increase international integration in line with *the University's strategic objective of making Every Student an International Student*" (my italics). Although I am not claiming a direct link with this development, I found it particularly interesting as I had recently made the point in a plenary I gave at the 14th Warwick International Postgraduate Conference in Applied Linguistics (29 June 2011) that UK home students, too, should want to be seen as international. What the development means in terms of Warwick's language policy and practice, of course, remains to be seen.

11 The same can be true of staff. For example, a Saudi participant in my interview study (Chapter Seven) told me how a lecturer on her master's at a US university had said to

her "now you're here you should speak like us, otherwise you'll sound like a strange person".

12 Those offering subjects in English include China, Finland, India, Mexico, Russia, South Africa, Sweden, and United Arab Emirates, while it is possible to take full degrees in English medium in Finland, Germany, the Netherlands, and Sweden, and others in Asia and Latin America (Jackson 2010: 16–17).

2

THE SPREAD OF ENGLISH AS A LINGUA FRANCA

Lingua francas and the emergence of ELF

When people first come across the term 'English as a Lingua Franca' or its acronym 'ELF', they tend to assume that it refers to a completely new phenomenon. However, this is by no means the case: both lingua francas in general and ELF in particular have existed in various forms for many centuries. On the one hand, as the literature on ELF often points out (e.g. House 2003, Knapp and Meierkord 2002, and more recently, Jenkins, Cogo, and Dewey 2011, Seidlhofer 2011), languages such as Arabic, Greek, Latin, Portuguese, and Sanskrit have performed the function of lingua francas at various times in history. On the other hand, English itself has served as a lingua franca in the past, and continues to do so nowadays, in many of the countries that were colonized by the British from the late sixteenth century on (often known collectively as the Outer Circle following Kachru 1985), such as India and Singapore. And besides ELF's shared background with other lingua francas, it also has much in common with the ways in which all natural languages develop, as will be discussed later in the chapter.

What *is* new about ELF, however, is the extent of its reach. This goes well beyond the relatively narrow spreads, both geographically and domain-wise, of other lingua francas, including, at least geographically, the earlier lingua franca uses of English. And because this extensive spread brings with it, by definition, so much diversity among ELF speakers in terms of their linguistic (and cultural) backgrounds, a further difference has emerged between ELF and other lingua francas: ELF's uniquely flexible nature. As House (2003: 557) notes, the original term 'lingua franca' (which, itself comes from the Arabic 'lisan-al-farang') simply referred to "an intermediary language used by speakers of Arabic with travellers from Western Europe" (see also Kachru 1996). This early meaning, House continues, "was later extended to describe a language of commerce, *a rather stable variety with little room for individual variation*" (ibid.; my italics).[1] This kind of lingua franca is thus of a very different order from ELF, whose speakers in any given interaction are drawn from a vast potential first language pool that encompasses the whole of the Expanding Circle, while not excluding members of the Inner and Outer Circles[2] (Kachru 1996), and who therefore have to be ready at any time to adapt their speech accordingly. This point will be taken up in detail later in the chapter, in discussions of accommodation and other aspects of ELF's flexibility.

ELF in the modern sense of the term was, to my knowledge, first reported by two German scholars, Hüllen (1982) and Knapp (1985, 1987), although they did not conduct empirical research at that time. Instead, their interest, as Knapp later acknowledged, was "mainly conceptual in nature, stressing the importance of ELF as an objective for English language teaching and also postulating the necessity of empirical studies that could identify formal or functional aspects to be taken account of in teaching" (Knapp 2002: 218). While the empirical aspect of that early interest has more recently been taken up extensively, particularly since the start of the twenty-first century, the pedagogical aspect still remains largely to be addressed (see Cogo and Dewey 2012 and Seidlhofer 2011 for lengthy discussions of issues relating to ELF pedagogy). However, the field of ELF as a whole moved on very little in the latter years of the twentieth century, and Hüllen's and Knapp's early leads were not taken up by other scholars. Instead, ELF (also widely known then as English as an International Language, EIL for short) remained a minority interest pursued independently around Europe by scholars who approached it from a range of different perspectives (e.g. Firth 1996, Firth and Wagner 1997, Haberland 1989, House 1999, Jenkins 1996a, 1996b, 1998, Meierkord 1996, 1998).

All this changed early in the new millennium with the publication in close succession of two works that seemed to capture the imagination (or displeasure!) of a number of those engaged in applied linguistics and English language teaching. The first of these was my own book, *The Phonology of English as an International Language* (2000). This was an early empirical study of ELF pronunciation that identified some of the kinds of "formal and functional aspects" to which Knapp had previously referred. It concluded that native English pronunciation was not optimal as a safeguard of mutual intelligibility in international (that is, ELF) communication contexts. This was swiftly followed in 2001 by Seidlhofer's conceptual article, 'Closing a conceptual gap: the case for a description of English as a lingua franca'. In the article, Seidlhofer pointed out that although ELF is "the most extensive contemporary use of English" (p. 133), there is little description of it available, with the result that ELF users are not seen as "language users in their own right" (ibid.). Seidlhofer therefore announced the establishment of her own ELF corpus, VOICE (the Vienna–Oxford International Corpus of English), which now numbers over a million words, and challenged others to follow suit. Soon afterwards, the ELFA (English as a Lingua Franca in Academic Settings) corpus, also now numbering over a million words, was set up by Mauranen, in Tampere, and subsequently Helsinki (see Mauranen and Ranta 2008). And most recently, another large corpus, ACE (the Asian Corpus of English) was set up in Hong Kong by Andy Kirkpatrick (see Kirkpatrick 2010).

During the decade from 2000, there was an explosion of ELF research carried out not only by established academics but also by PhD and even masters students, leading in turn to a proliferation of ELF corpora, published books and articles, special journal issues, and unpublished theses and dissertations on ELF. From 2008, a dedicated ELF conference series was established, with the first five conferences taking place in Helsinki (2008), Southampton (2009), Vienna (2010), Hong Kong (2011), and Istanbul (2012). And in 2011, the *Journal of English as a Lingua Franca* (DeGruyter Mouton) was launched, with the first volume appearing in 2012, and a book series, *Developments in English as a Lingua Franca* (also DeGruyter Mouton) was set up. At the time of writing, the first book in the series, Björkman 2013, has just been published and the second, Kalocsai 2013, is in press. The speed with which ELF has travelled from being a minority interest to becoming a major focus of discussion among applied- and socio-linguists, English language teachers and testers, World Englishes scholars, and those working in many other English language related areas, is little short of phenomenal. Meanwhile, new empirical ELF evidence has been coming in thick and fast over the past few years, causing ELF researchers to make conceptual adjustments in line with new findings about the workings of ELF. It is therefore not at all surprising that the notion of ELF has proved highly controversial. Indeed, ELF seems to have aroused an unusually high degree of concern as well as a good deal of animosity, sometimes as a result of misinterpretation or of assumptions based on out of date information.

Defining ELF

Defining ELF has proved to be problematic and controversial. In the previous chapter (p. 2), I described ELF as "English when it is used as a contact language between people from different first languages (including native English speakers)". But even this simple definition is not uncontroversial. For one thing, some (albeit a small minority) who write on ELF do not include NESs in their definition. Firth (1996: 240), for example, describes situations where "English is used as a 'lingua franca'" (he does not actually use the term ELF) as follows:

> a 'contact language' between persons who share neither a common native tongue nor a common (national) culture, and for whom English is the chosen foreign language of communication.

In fact, it would have been difficult for Firth to include NESs in his 1996 definition, as the focus of his article is on communication between NNESs who manage to communicate with each other despite what Firth describes as the "dysfluencies", "unidiomatic" language choices, and "syntactic, morphological, and phonological anomalies and infelicities" in their English (p. 239), which amount to "extraordinary, deviant, and sometimes 'abnormal' linguistic behaviour" (p. 237). His claim is, in essence, that NNESs using English as their common language manage "to imbue talk with an orderly and 'normal' appearance" in spite of this behaviour (ibid.). While

Firth's more recent publications (e.g. 2009) focus on ELF's variable rather than (what he earlier saw as) its "deviant" nature, his position on NESs appears to be unchanged.

Most ELF researchers, by contrast, do not exclude NESs from their definition of ELF. Nor have they ever made assumptions of NNESs' use of ELF as being by definition deficient where it differs from ENL. Instead, they have been endeavouring to find out "whether and in what ways ELF interactions are actually *sui generis*" (House 1999: 74; her italics). This involves exploring ELF communication *in its own right* rather than against some native English yardstick or benchmark. But it does not mean that ELF researchers are claiming that all English used by ELF speakers, NNES or NES, is by definition acceptable, or that all the processes and features found in ELF communication are different from those of native English. I will return to both points later in the chapter, where we will see that on the one hand, ELF use can be 'incorrect' (although in a very different sense from the way correctness is conceived in English as a Foreign or Second Language approaches), and that on the other hand, ELF and native English have a good deal in common. The crucial factor is that ELF researchers identify the kinds of processes, motivations, features, and so on that typify ELF communication first, and only begin making comparisons and contrasts with native English after that.

However, it is not merely those scholars taking a deficit view of ELF who define it as involving NNESs only. According to House, for example, "ELF interactions are defined as interactions between members of two or more different lingua-cultures in English, for none of whom English is the mother tongue" (1999: 74). Others such as McKay (2009) use the term EIL (English as an International Language) to include NESs and reserve ELF for NNES–NNES communication. But as Seidlhofer (2011: 7) points out:

> While these definitions could be said to highlight a particularly striking feature of ELF, namely that the majority of its users are not native speakers of English, it has to be remembered that of course ELF interactions include interlocutors from the Inner and Outer Circles, and take place in these contexts too, such as meetings at the United Nations headquarters in New York, tourist cruises around Sydney harbour, or academic conferences in Hyderabad.

Seidlhofer argues, therefore, that ELF should be regarded as *"any use of English among speakers of different first languages for whom English is the communicative medium of choice, and often the only option"* (ibid.; her italics). And Mortensen (in press) defines it still more broadly as "the use of English in a lingua franca scenario". Nevertheless, as Seidlhofer observes, given the fact that worldwide there are so many more NNESs than NESs, NESs are likely to find themselves in the minority in ELF interactions (if they are present at all). And this, in turn, means that they will also find themselves decreasingly in their former role of providing the linguistic reference point for the rest of the world. Or, to put it another way, in line with Brumfit's observation about languages being shaped by their majority users (see p. 19 above), NESs are likely to contribute far less than NNESs to the ways in which ELF evolves over the coming years.

TABLE 2.1 English as a Lingua Franca (ELF) and English as a Foreign Language (EFL)

ELF	EFL
1 Belongs with Global Englishes	1 Belongs with Foreign Languages
2 Difference perspective	2 Deficit perspective
3 Its metaphors: contact and change	3 Its metaphors: interference and fossilization
4 Code-switching seen as bilingual resource	4 Code-switching seen as error resulting from gap in knowledge
5 Goal: successful intercultural communication	5 Goal: successful communication with NESs

In the process of defining ELF, it will be useful if I clarify the relationship between ELF and EFL on the one hand, and ELF and World Englishes on the other. Starting with ELF and EFL, the distinctions between the two in terms of their conceptual approaches to English can be summed up in Table 2.1. In other words, ELF belongs with the Global Englishes paradigm, one which recognizes that the majority of the world's English speakers are NNESs and accepts the sociolinguistic implications of this fact, namely that the majority have the right to determine the kind of English they wish to use. This is in contrast to the Foreign Languages paradigm, according to which people learn foreign languages including English primarily in order to be able to communicate with the native speakers of those languages. This leads to the second distinction: that differences from ENL are not automatically regarded as errors in ELF (as they are in EFL), but may simply signal a preference to use English in ways that are different from those that NESs use to communicate with each other. Or, to paraphrase, as Cogo and Dewey (2012) point out, ELF speakers find some forms of ENL communicatively important and others not. This leads Cogo and Dewey (ibid.) to point out that asking what constitutes an error in ELF is the wrong kind of question to ask (see p. 38 below). It is not a case that in ELF, anything goes, but that traditionally narrow views of correctness are irrelevant to discussions of this kind of communication. I will return to this point later on in the chapter in considering the qualities of a skilled ELF user.

Unsurprisingly in view of the contrast between ELF's and EFL's approaches to difference, they are underpinned by very different metaphors: ELF by metaphors of language contact and change, and EFL by metaphors of interference and fossilization. Thus, within the ELF paradigm, code-switching can be seen as a useful resource that is available to bilingual English speakers, whereas in EFL it is normally taken as a sign of a gap in the NNES's knowledge, a lexical gap, for example. Finally, the two have very different goals. Whereas ELF is about intercultural communication in the broadest sense, and this means mainly NNES–NNES interactions, EFL conceives of intercultural only in the sense of communication with NESs. Not surprisingly, then, the focus of EFL teaching is on native English, with the aim of mimicking this as closely as possible. For ELF, on the other hand, intercultural communication skills and strategies are paramount.

Seidlhofer (2011: 18) proposes that we look at the distinctions between ELF and EFL in a slightly different way, which is summed up in Table 2.2.

TABLE 2.2 Foreign language (EFL) and lingua franca (ELF)

	(EFL)	*(ELF)*
Linguacultural norms	pre-existing, reaffirmed	ad hoc, negotiated
Objectives	integration, membership in NS community	intelligibility, communication in NNS or mixed NNS–NS community
Processes	imitation, adoption	accommodation, adaptation

Seidlhofer points out (ibid.) that her table both idealizes and simplifies the distinctions between EFL and ELF, but that she has presented them in this basic form in order to provide a conceptual framework which she goes on to develop in detail in subsequent chapters of her book. The main point that she draws from her framework is the need to acknowledge ELF users' crucial contribution to the development of the English language. Drawing on Brutt-Griffler's (2002) notion of macroacquisition ("second language acquisition by speech communities, that links language change to its spread", p. xi) in respect of post-colonial settings, Seidlhofer argues that:

> at a time when in many parts of the world some knowledge of English has come to be taken for granted as a kind of basic skill, it seems to be reasonable to extend the notion of macroacquisition to contexts where English is a pervasive element in the education as well as in the working lives of a large portion of the population.
>
> *(2011: 18)*

Extending the notion of macroacquisition to ELF, as Seidlhofer's table demonstrates, involves reconsidering traditional (EFL) orientations to the linguacultural norms of English, the objectives in learning and using it, and the kinds of processes involved.

We turn now to the distinction between ELF and the World Englishes (henceforth WE). Whereas ELF and EFL arise from very different ideologies, ELF and WE have much more in common. More specifically, both paradigms share an ideological perspective that sees the kinds of English resulting from the global spread of the language as existing in their own right and as means of expressing their speakers' identities, rather than as failed attempts to emulate ENL and acquire NES identities. Both therefore subscribe to Kachru's position vis-à-vis "myths" about English, such as that it is learnt for communication with NESs or as a means of studying Anglo culture, that NNES varieties are interlanguages, that NES varieties are universally intelligible, and that diversification across Englishes is a sign of decay (see Kachru 2009: 184–85).

On the other hand, whereas WE research primarily involves the study of bounded varieties, that is the nativized Englishes of post-colonial nations such as

India, the Philippines, and Singapore, ELF research operates *across* national boundaries. While recognizing that speakers from different first language groups (in any of the three circles) develop their own ways of speaking English, ELF researchers see English as so bound up with globalization that it is no longer realistic to talk of Englishes, be they native, nativized, or foreign, only in a national sense. So while "the world Englishes framework places nationalism at its core" (Pennycook 2009: 20) and focuses on the nature of discrete English varieties, ELF is concerned with communication across nationalities and aims "to capture the pluricentricity of ongoing negotiated English" (op.cit.: 201) in the fluid, flexible, hybrid, intercultural, and contingent uses of English that occur in ELF interactions (Dewey 2007). For more detailed discussion of the differences between WE and ELF as well as their similarities, see Cogo and Dewey (2012), Jenkins (2006b), Seidlhofer (2011), and the contributions to the WE-ELF symposium edited by Seidlhofer and Berns (2009).

Locating ELF

ELF is used and researched widely in terms of both geographical areas and domains. As regards geographical areas, it will be clear from what has already been said that ELF speakers are spread widely around the world, with the majority coming from Expanding Circle regions, particularly within East Asia, Mainland Europe, and, increasingly, Latin America. However, as was also pointed out, speakers from the mother tongue and post-colonial regions also engage in ELF communication, even though they each form a minority of the totality of ELF speakers globally.

Given the spread of ELF use, it is not surprising to find that ELF is nowadays also being researched widely around the world. As was noted earlier in the chapter, the first ELF research was conducted in western Europe. Subsequently, interest in ELF research has spread across the rest of Europe and researchers are now to be found in northern, southern, central, and eastern European countries such as Finland, Greece, Serbia, and Turkey. During the same period, interest in ELF has grown in East Asia, initially concentrated on a handful of scholars, most notably Deterding and Kirkpatrick and their colleagues (see, e.g., Deterding and Kirkpatrick 2006), and since then has been taken up by increasing numbers of researchers and resulted in weighty publications such as Kirkpatrick's (2010) monograph on ELF in ASEAN.[3] In this respect, it is significant that the fourth international ELF conference was held in Hong Kong in 2011, with many of the papers being given by East Asian ELF researchers.

More recently, the use of ELF has spread to parts of Latin America and the Middle East, both of which, of course, have existing lingua francas of their own, respectively Spanish and Arabic. Accordingly, a research interest in ELF has also emerged in these regions. In the case of Latin America, interest is greatest in Brazil (perhaps in part because of the forthcoming 2016 Olympic Games in Rio and also in part because the Brazilian mother tongue is Portuguese rather than Spanish). Nevertheless, at the time of writing, there have been no major ELF-focused publications emanating from the region, and the few who have so far engaged with

ELF have tended to focus on broader issues (see, e.g., Rajagopalan 2009). As regards the Middle East, again, there is so far little empirical ELF research available, although a small number of publications have begun to document a transition from Arabic to English as the lingua franca of the Gulf States (e.g. Randall and Samimy 2010).[4]

Although I have described the geographical areas in which ELF is used and researched, I would not want to create the impression that geography is itself a major determinant of the kind of ELF communication to be found in any particular area. For while it is likely that ELF spoken among, for example, a group of Chinese, Japanese, and Thai people at a meeting in Seoul will have a flavour of the East Asian region to the extent that the speakers' ELF use is influenced by their local languages (ELF with, e.g., Chinese, Japanese, and Thai characteristics), geography is not the only or even the main factor involved. This is because these same speakers could potentially have the same conversation in a bar in Madrid, at a conference in Rio de Janeiro, and so on. And by the same token, a group of European ELF users from different countries could have a conversation among themselves in Seoul, while in any of these hypothetical situations, it is just as likely that the ELF conversation group will be made up of speakers who come from both within and outside the local region. The point is that in all these scenarios, it is not the geographical location per se that determines the nature of the ELF spoken. Rather, it is the composition of the conversation group and the purpose and setting of the conversation (e.g. seminar discussion in a university, business meeting in a bank), as well as the speakers' orientations towards their use of English. And while there are certain settings, such as meetings of ASEAN leaders in one of the member nations, or of the European Parliament in Strasbourg, where the kind of ELF used is likely to be more local (but not in a narrow national sense), this is not by any means the norm for ELF. We will return to these points later when we consider ELF speakers in relation to the notion of Community of Practice (Wenger 1998).

Turning to domains of ELF use and research, the main ones are: business, primary, secondary, and higher education, academia more generally, diplomacy, tourism, the media, and technology. ELF is also used for intercultural socializing, a point which tends to be forgotten, although this is not a 'domain' in quite the same sense as the others, and often involves sub-groups from within the other domains (e.g. a group of conference delegates or PhD students spending an informal evening together in a bar). In all cases, these domains, and therefore ELF use within them, cut across geographical areas which means, as McGroarty (2003) notes, that domains have become more useful contexts than geographical areas for the study of language contact.

Two of the domains, academia (especially HE) and business, have been characterized by extensive ELF use for longer than the others. Indeed, HE has been identified as one of the driving forces behind the spread of ELF (Bolton 2011), as increasing numbers of universities around the world begin teaching partly or entirely in English medium as a means, often, it seems, primarily of attracting high fee-paying international students. And as was observed in the previous chapter, one main outcome of this process is that campuses are becoming more international in their composition, and in turn that ELF, by default, is being widely used (if not recognized as such), particularly among postgraduate students. We should not be surprised, then, that HE has become one of the main domains of ELF research, particularly from the time when the first corpus of ELF in academic settings was launched (see Mauranen 2003).

Academic ELF, or ELFA as it is often called, is discussed in detail in Chapter Three, so no more will be said about it for the moment. Business ELF, the other most researched ELF domain, has existed even longer than ELFA to the extent that for some decades, English has been the lingua franca of international business. Research into business ELF (henceforth BELF), however, began rather more recently, and we therefore know less about it at this stage than we do about ELFA. The findings of the research to date are nevertheless sufficient to provide some clear indications of the nature of BELF. For example, as in ELF more widely – and possibly even more so in the highly content-oriented context of business communication – correctness according to NES norms is generally considered secondary to pragmatic skills such as accommodation (see, e.g., Kankaanranta and Planken 2010). There is also some evidence that NNESs are more skilled accom-modators than NESs in BELF interactions (e.g. Charles and Marschan-Piekkari 2002, Sweeney and Zhu 2010). On the other hand, as Ehrenreich (2011) points out, native English norms are still widely regarded as important in written BELF communication, where they are seen as transmitting a prestigious image. This is not in the least surprising given that written norms are usually more conservative and resistant to change than are spoken norms. And given the prevailing negative attitudes in some quarters even towards spoken ELF, it is not likely that orientations to the written medium will change much in the very near future.

The nature of ELF

Although much still remains to be discovered about ELF, research over the past couple of decades or so, and particularly since the start of the new millennium, has already yielded extensive information at a range of linguistic levels. And while most ELF research up to now has focused on speech, an interest in written ELF has recently emerged, although at present there are insufficient findings from which to draw any major conclusions about its nature. Having said that, many of the implications of spoken ELF research, and the concepts in which it is grounded, apply to ELF use in general, and therefore have useful things to say about writing too. This is especially so in the case of ELFA research and academic writing (see Horner 2011), which will be discussed in Chapter Three along with research into spoken academic ELF.

ELF research to date demonstrates that ELF seems to be primarily the result of two types of natural language change. In the first case, ELF speakers are exploiting the potential of English to develop in particular ways, that is, to develop in ways to which it is in some sense predisposed. By this, I do not mean to imply that English has underlying 'rules' in a Chomskyan sense. Rather, that ELF forms are sometimes typologically similar to those that have already developed in post-colonial Englishes and even (though more slowly) in native Englishes. This is especially true of certain regularization processes such as the turning of nouns that are uncountable in ENL (e.g. *information*) into countable ones (e.g. *two informations*). The speed with which ELF is developing in this respect seems to be a function of its situation of accelerated language contact, which means that regularizations which in some cases may eventually occur in ENL are happening sooner in ELF, and are conventionally considered to be errors until/unless they are sanctioned by NES use in the same way that items such as *coffees*, *accommodations*, and the like already have been.

In the second case, the bi- and multilingual majority of ELF speakers (i.e. mainly NNESs) also draw in innovative ways on their multilingual resources (their first languages and often other languages they also know) to create forms of expression that they prefer (forms that, by definition, are not available to monolingual English speakers). ELF is thus marked by a degree of hybridity not found in other kinds of language use, as speakers from diverse languages introduce a range of non-English forms into their ELF use. They may do this, for example, to project their cultural identity (e.g. by code-switching), or to signal solidarity with their interlocutors (e.g. by switching into an interlocutor's first language), or to prioritize communicative effectiveness over narrow orientations to 'correctness' (e.g. by accommodating to an interlocutor's use of English regardless of whether or not it is correct according to ENL). And in all such cases, it seems that both the speed and extent of developments relates to the fact that NNESs have weaker attachment than NESs to the norms of ENL, and as Hülmbauer (2007: 9) argues, are thus "not influenced by standardizing forces [of ENL] to the same extent".

Turning to the forms themselves, as regards spoken ELF, the linguistic levels that have been most extensively investigated so far are phonology, lexicogrammar, morphology, pragmatics, and idiomaticity. Two of the earliest studies, Firth (1996) and House (1999), focused on pragmatics. However, as mentioned earlier, they are not considered ELF studies 'proper' because they did not consider ELF communication as a potentially legitimate kind of English in its own right (Firth), or used a classroom simulation methodology (House). In the first case, then, the speakers' English was measured against ENL, while in the second case, the simulation participants did not employ the kinds of communication strategies such as accommodation that were found in subsequent ELF research based on naturally occurring interactions.

The first empirical ELF research 'proper' was thus Jenkins (e.g. 1996a, 1998, 2000). While the data for this project was collected mainly in classroom and examination practice settings, it was naturally occurring in the sense that the participants were going about their normal daily business in those settings. No data was collected from role-play or other simulated activities, and the database also included social interactions. And although NESs were excluded from the research, they did have a presence of sorts in that the researcher herself, an NES, was almost always present as a participant observer and as an active participant in the social exchanges.

The phonology research, a five-year project, explored two interrelated phenomena: accommodation and intelligibility. The aims were to identify the ways in which, and the extent to which, pronunciation is both a cause of problems and subject to accommodative processes[5] in communication among NNESs from different first language backgrounds. The accommodation findings demonstrated that when speakers were engaged in interactions where mutual understanding was crucial, they replaced (consciously or otherwise) some but not other non-native features of their pronunciation with something closer to the native 'target', provided the replacement items were within their pronunciation repertoires.

Meanwhile, the intelligibility findings cast light on the accommodation findings by demonstrating which features of NES pronunciation did and did not contribute to intelligibility in ELF communication. These, according to my data, were essentially: most consonant sounds apart from the dental fricatives /θ/ and /ð/ (respectively voiceless *th* as in 'thin', and voiced *th* as in 'this'); consonant deletion in word-initial and word-medial clusters (as in the words 'script' and 'country'); vowel length distinctions (as in 'rich' and 'reach'); and nuclear (tonic) stress (as in the meaning difference between 'You deserve to be SACKED' and 'You deSERVE to be sacked').[6] On the other hand, some NES pronunciation features such as weak forms, elision, and assimilation, were regularly eschewed without causing miscommunication, whereas their presence was even found to detract from intelligibility. And when the intelligibility and accommodation findings were compared, it turned out that the accommodative adjustments towards more native-like pronunciation occurred, in the main, in respect of those features whose absence had led to miscommunication in the intelligibility side of the research.

On the basis of all my findings, I argued that for NNES learners of English who needed to be able to communicate internationally with speakers from diverse L1s (this includes the majority of students in HE), it would make more sense, subject to replication of my findings, to focus pronunciation teaching on the items shown to enhance such communication, rather than on the entire NES pronunciation inventory. At the same time, I noted, it was critical to develop learners' accommodation skills so that they were able to produce these items as and when appropriate (depending, in turn, on who their interlocutors were). This would then mean that for the purposes of ELF communication, the L1-influenced ways in which NNESs habitually pronounce the unnecessary items could be considered as legitimate aspects of their regional English accents rather than as pronunciation errors (see Jenkins 2000, 2002 for full details of the original phonology research, and Walker 2010 for ways of developing the theory into practice). While there have so far been very few investigations of the original research (primarily Deterding and Kirkpatrick 2006, Osimk 2009, Pickering 2009, Pickering and Litzenberg 2012, Rajadurai 2007), these have tended to be broadly in agreement with its findings, and in the main only to identify areas where fine-tuning may be needed.

Turning to lexicogrammar and morphology, empirical ELF research demonstrates how speakers engaged in ELF interactions habitually manipulate the linguistic resources at their disposal. In the case of the bi- and multilingual majority, this means their own multilingual resources as well as previously unexploited potential inherent in the English language. Examples of unexploited potential include the extension of countable nouns to nouns that are currently uncountable in ENL (e.g. *evidence*, *feedback*), and the use of one or other of *who* and *which*. As Cogo and Dewey (2012) point out, NESs use *that* in defining relative clauses for both persons and things without problems, so there is clearly no need for two terms to disambiguate people and things. These examples demonstrate how NNES ELF speakers are speeding up the regularization of English that is already in progress and always has been (note how the six inflected endings of the Old English present tense have been replaced over the centuries by zero marking, leaving only the third person singular -*s* still intact – for now!). This is not to suggest that ELF is likely to develop into anything as regularized as the native and Outer Circle Englishes, let alone into a variety (or varieties). There is far too great a potential for diversity for this to be feasible. Rather, as has become clear in more recent research and conceptualizing, it seems to be more a case of the emergence and ad hoc use of certain features that tend to be (but are not always) preferred by ELF users from a wide range of L1s (see also pp. 35–38).

Earlier ELF research was nevertheless concerned principally with identifying typical features of spoken ELF. These features have been found to occur frequently among speakers from a wide range of linguacultural backgrounds, and have been shown, by means of close analysis including the use of concordancing software, to be used systematically. They have also been shown, by means of careful qualitative analysis, to be communicatively effective, and as Cogo and Dewey (2012) point out, arguably more so than the equivalent forms of ENL. In effect, they tend to replace ENL forms that ELF speakers do not find communicatively important (ibid.). In an early article discussing preliminary lexicogrammatical findings, Seidlhofer (2004: 220) presented the following ELF features, which she described at the time as a set of hypotheses:

- 'dropping' the third person present tense -*s*
- 'confusing' the relative pronouns *who* and *which*
- 'omitting' definite and indefinite articles where they are obligatory in ENL and inserting them where they do not occur in ENL
- 'failing' to use correct forms in tag questions (e.g., *isn't it?* or *no?* instead of *shouldn't they?*)
- inserting 'redundant' prepositions as in *We have to study about* ...
- 'overusing' certain verbs of high semantic generality, such as *do, have, make, put, take*
- 'replacing' infinitive constructions with *that*-clauses, as in *I want that*
- 'overdoing' explicitness (e.g., *black colour* rather than just *black*)

This represents a major ideological departure from traditional descriptions of non-native English, with the scare quotes indicating Seidlhofer's own scepticism towards the pejorative terms used (although they were mistakenly removed by the 2004 publisher and have been replaced here). As with the phonological findings,

Seidlhofer offers these items as ELF uses in their own right rather than as automatic errors according to an ENL yardstick. Although Seidlhofer was tentative at the time and made no strong claims, much subsequent empirical research into ELF lexicogrammar has supported her findings by providing evidence of a substantial degree of typicality in ELF lexicogrammar (see, e.g., Breiteneder 2005, 2009, Cogo and Dewey 2012, Hülmbauer 2009, Klimpfinger 2007). And despite counter-claims from some quarters that forms such as *informations* are not found at a statistically significant level in ELF corpora, and therefore not worthy of serious consideration (see, e.g., Crystal's comments on VOICE in Stotesbury 2009), they miss the point that the occurrence of even a relatively small number of forms may be indicative of change in progress. They also ignore the functional use and semantic properties of the forms, which is the focus of more recent ELF research (see Dewey 2009, Seidlhofer 2009b), which demonstrates that these exponents are not random learner errors or idiosyncracies, but widely used innovations (see Cogo and Dewey 2012).

Research into other linguistic levels has yielded similar findings. In morphology, for example, Björkman (2008, 2009) identifies novel morphological formations that would be considered errors by comparison with ENL (e.g. *forsify, levelize*), but which occur frequently in her ELF corpus. As she puts it, ELF speakers using morphemes in such ways "adopt and adapt the language to get the job done" (2009: 225), and quite possibly get it done better than they would if they stuck rigidly to ENL morphology. ELF speakers are also found to use idiomatic language in innovative ways, resulting in the creation of idioms that do not exist in ENL, often as a result of what Pitzl calls the "metaphorization" of existing ENL idioms (2009: 306). These idioms involve both the influence of the speaker's first language and the desire to accommodate towards an interlocutor to enhance understanding (the communicative efficiency motivation for convergence; see this chapter, note 5). They are thus used very differently in ELF from the way they are used in ENL where, as in any native community, they serve as territorial markers and/or indicators of the native identity (Seidlhofer and Widdowson 2009). The copious available examples include *we should not wake up any dogs* in place of ENL's *let sleeping dogs lie* (Pitzl 2009), *in my observation* replacing ENL's *in my experience*, and various uses of the word *head* instead of ENL *mind* (Seidlhofer and Widdowson 2009: 33).

As mentioned above, some of the earliest research in NNES–NNES communication focused on pragmatics, albeit that unlike later ELF research, it either took a more conventional deficit view of the speakers' English or did not use naturally occurring data. Nevertheless, the early pragmatics research identified that establishing mutual understanding took precedence over approximating to ENL norms, and that mutual cooperation was a main feature of this kind of communication. Subsequent research into ELF pragmatics has continued in this direction focusing, in particular, on the ways in which ELF speakers pre-empt and negotiate non-understanding by means of a range of accommodation strategies such as repetition (e.g. Cogo 2009, Lichtkoppler 2007), clarification and self repairs (Mauranen 2006a), paraphrasing (Kaur 2009), and accommodative dovetailing[7] (Hülmbauer 2009). The research has found that overall, misunderstanding is less frequent in ELF than in EFL (NES–NNES) communication, perhaps because the responsibility for a successful outcome in the latter is widely seen as that of the NNES participant. Moreover, on occasions when misunderstanding does occur in ELF, participants have been shown to resolve it in a discreet manner that does not interrupt the flow of conversation (see, e.g., Pitzl 2005). A general finding of this branch of ELF pragmatics is thus that speakers make strenuous efforts to avoid potential communication problems, seem to be skilled in doing so, and perhaps, for this reason, miscommunication is reported as being relatively rare in ELF.

Other research into ELF pragmatics has focused on speakers' use of their multilingual resources that I mentioned above, and particularly on code-switching. As noted earlier in the chapter, when an EFL speaker switches into another language while in conversation with a NES, this is typically interpreted as a sign that the EFL speaker is ignorant of the English for what he or she wants to say. In post-colonial contexts, by contrast, code-switching is habitually used among speakers who share the same variety of nativized English, such as Indian English, and who code-switch in order to express a shared local identity (see Kachru and Nelson 2006 for examples).

Code-switching in ELF is very different from both these scenarios. On the one hand, supplying gaps in knowledge is merely one of several functions that it performs. On the other hand, because the linguacultural backgrounds of ELF users are substantially more diverse than those of speakers within the post-colonial nations, ELF code-switchers cannot rely on familiarity with each other's norms, let alone on the existence of shared norms. Instead, they may code-switch precisely to introduce their own cultural norms to ELF speakers from other backgrounds. For example, Cogo (in Cogo and Dewey 2012) demonstrates the way in which a French speaker introduces the French expression *fleur bleue* to gloss the English word *cheesy* (which he had just used to describe the honeymoon photographs his friends were posting on the internet), even though his German and Italian interlocutors already know the meaning of 'cheesy'. This cultural-norm-signalling function has been identified frequently in empirical ELF data. Another regularly documented function of ELF code-switching is expressing solidarity with interlocutors. This can involve speakers switching into a language other than their own which, in turn, can be the interlocutor's first language or even a language that is neither interlocutors' first language. Meanwhile, Klimpfinger (2007: 352) notes two further functions: "specifying an addressee" and "introducing another idea". Code-switching in ELF is thus a valuable multilingual resource that serves multiple functions and enriches rather than reduces communication as speakers "engage in code-sharing with regard to cultural reference and expression of metaphor", and in the process "shape, and transform their cultural expressions ... making them available to the other speakers in a creative meaning making enterprise" (Cogo and Dewey 2012: 78).

From what has been said so far, it should be clear that while ELF is a natural development arising out of language contact and involving normal linguistic processes such as regularization, in certain other respects it is a rather different phenomenon from what is traditionally considered to be a 'language' or 'regional dialect'. This is primarily on account of its flexibility relative to other known languages, a flexibility that arises essentially from the vast linguacultural diversity among ELF speakers, unprecedented in the history of language. In this respect, Mauranen's (2012) distinction between L2 lects and regional dialects is a useful one. As she points out, "unlike dialects, which arise in communities of speakers talking to each other, L2 lects result from parallel L1 influence on their speakers" (p. 29). She suggests we think of these L2 lects as 'similects' "because they arise in parallel" among speakers of the same L1 rather than in communication between them, and thus "there is no community of similect speakers" (ibid.). In other words, the ELF spoken by, say, Japanese speakers, shares similar Japanese influences, but because it is used in intercultural interaction, is also subject to the influence of the other similects with which its speakers come into contact within (but not necessarily beyond) the context of any specific interaction. In this sense, we could perhaps talk of 'Japanese ELF' and the like (see Wang 2012 on Chinese ELF).

It follows that another difference between ELF and traditional languages or regional dialects relates to stability. As is well known in the field of sociolinguistics, language contact is the driver of language change. What distinguishes ELF is that because of its contingent nature, the change resulting from contact does not display the kind of stability we are used to: a stability that enables languages to be documented in dictionaries and grammar reference books at any one point in time (albeit with a fair degree of idealization). Some linguists take this to mean that it will not be possible to codify ELF at all. This is not necessarily so. But if there is some kind of codification, it will have to be a new and more dynamic kind, one that is able to represent a new and more dynamic kind of language use and therefore, as Cogo and Dewey note, is "concerned more with communicative practices and interactive processes" (2012: 167) than with stable language forms. They explain (ibid.) as follows:

> Linguistic resources are deployed so dynamically in ELF settings that nativization as such does not have time to take hold: there is simply not the longer-term stability required for sedimentation to take place, with the effect that language forms remain more or less continually in a state of suspension. We feel there is much to be gained in ELF therefore from orienting to our research findings in much the same way language is conceived in complexity theory, as a dynamic, process-like, contingent and non-linear phenomenon (see Larsen-Freeman and Cameron, 2008).

In other words, while ELF exhibits a number of observed regularities in its use of forms across speakers from a wide range of linguacultural backgrounds, the point is that accommodation and other communication strategies take precedence over a desire for conformity to these (or any other) forms. It is by means of employing such strategies that ELF speakers render their English, and therefore the specific forms they select, appropriate to the specific interaction in hand. Codification of ELF, then, would need to be more about "[documenting] emerging trends in the ways in which speakers in ELF select from the … linguistic choices available to them, even though they may do so during more fleeting moments of language contact than is the case in Inner Circle or Outer Circle varieties" (Cogo and Dewey 2012). Pennycook (2009: 195) refers to this as ELF being "always under negotiation", while Canagarajah (2007: 926) likewise describes it as being "intersubjectively constructed in each specific context of interaction. … negotiated by each set of speakers for their purposes".

What we are looking at in ELF, then, is an entirely new, communication-focused way of approaching the notion of 'language' that is far more relevant to twenty-first century uses of English (and probably other global languages) than traditional bounded-variety approaches, and one that has far more in common with post-modern approaches to language than with the more modernist positivistic SLA approaches (Will Baker, personal communication). To put it another way, the phenomenon of ELF calls for new definitions of some of the most taken-for-granted terms, not only 'language' itself, but also 'variety' and 'speech community'. For as Seidlhofer points out, these terms "are, by and large, still used in the same way as they were long before the days of mass international travel, let alone electronic communication" (2009a: 238). She argues that "at a time of pervasive and widespread global communication, the old notion of community, based purely on frequent face-to-face contact among people living in close proximity to each other, clearly does not hold" (ibid.). ELF researchers have therefore moved away from the notion of bounded speech communities, each with its own discrete language variety, to that of communities of practice (henceforth CoP), "characterized by 'mutual engagement' in shared practices, taking part in some jointly negotiated 'enterprise' and making use of members' 'shared repertoire'" (Wenger 1998: 73). And given the diversity of speakers involved in a typical ELF "enterprise", it is not surprising that the "shared repertoire" appropriate to the specific interaction has to be "negotiated" afresh each time.

At the same time, ELF also resonates with the concept of 'imagined communities' (Anderson 2006). These are not the defined physical communities of the CoP, but psychological spaces. In ELF's case the imagined community involves a sense of 'shared non-nativeness of English use' among ELF speakers, and particularly among its NNES majority (though not forgetting that ELF is an additional language use for NESs too, and that NESs may see themselves as part of this imagined ELF community). Hence, there may be a feeling of virtual bonds among ELF speakers around the world, or among a particular sub-section of them, for example fellow East Asian ELF speakers (see Nogami 2011). Thus, it seems plausible that the psychological link of the imagined ELF community may predispose ELF speakers in some way to establish CoPs and communicate effectively within them as and when the opportunity arises. In terms of HE, this would translate into students' (primarily, but not exclusively, NNESs) sense of themselves as part of an imagined international academic community that predisposes them to forge physical links and devise appropriate ways of communicating when they come together to study on the same English medium course in the same university (see Montgomery 2008: 21–23, and Erling 2007: 128). This dual notion of ELF speakers as both members of wider imagined communities and potential members of smaller-scale CoPs also fits well with Pennycook's idea of a 'translocal language', which he describes as "a language of fluidity and fixity that moves across, while becoming embedded in, the materiality of localities and social relations" (2007: 6).

In view of the variability and hybridity of ELF use as speakers from different linguacultural backgrounds contribute to and draw on "a situational resource pool" (Hülmbauer 2009: 325) that, itself, changes according to the composition of the specific CoP, there is also a question mark over what would constitute an error in ELF. Given both that variability is one of ELF's defining characteristics (Firth 2009), and that ELF represents a more inclusive communication-focused approach to language than traditional exclusive bounded-variety approaches, errors can no longer be defined in terms of departures from one particular set of norms. Cogo and Dewey argue that determining what is an error in ELF is "possibly not a particularly ELF-compatible way of thinking about language" (2012: 78). They go on to observe that "it is also probably the wrong kind of question to ask in the context of ELF" (ibid.). This is because ELF is premised on such a different notion of language use from traditional EFL, whose goal is to enable learners to approximate the English of NESs (i.e. ENL), and whose teaching is directed towards eradicating forms that fail to do so, which are automatically perceived as errors. But this approach to errors is incompatible with the nature of ELF communication, which involves, instead, the ability to use the (often multilingual) resources at speakers' disposal in a flexible and contingent way: not conforming to some or other predetermined norms, but converging appropriately within the confines of the specific interaction in progress. Thus it is the skill of converging appropriately that constitutes 'correctness' in ELF. And this has implications for assessing English use in HE, for the teaching of EAP, and for the kinds of guidelines given to learners in EAP textbooks, all of which will be explored in Chapter Three.

The native/non-native English speaker dichotomy

The notion of ELF speakers as members of an imagined ELF community and their physical role as participants in shared CoPs together raise important questions about the traditional native/non-native dichotomy, a dichotomy that has already been opposed by World Englishes scholars (see, e.g., Kachru 1992, 2005). If, on the one hand, nobody is a native speaker of ELF (since ELF is additionally acquired by all its users), and on the other hand, ELF is not about how closely someone approximates ENL, but about how skilfully users communicate in intercultural settings, then nativeness loses both its relevance and its traditional positive connotations. So while there may be some point in retaining the distinction for the purposes of EFL, where it is self evident that those learning English as a second or subsequent language are not native speakers of the language they are learning,[8] there seems to be no point at all in retaining it for ELF. And this is also true of academic ELF, including academic writing where, as Ferguson points out, "the native speaker and the non-native speaker both start out as novices, a position of parity that the native/non-native dichotomy obscures" (2007: 28; and see Chapter Three below).

A little over ten years ago, I suggested the alternatives of Monolingual English Speaker (MES), Bilingual English Speaker (BES), and Non-Bilingual Speaker (NBES). Although I would now argue that these categories are too tight and do not in themselves incorporate the crucial element of intercultural communication skills, I believe that for ELF they are still, nevertheless, an improvement on the old dichotomy. This is because a BES, whether English is his or her first or subsequent language, is likely to have developed more enhanced communication skills than someone who speaks only English (an MES). On the other hand, I would probably not retain the NBES category at least for now. My reasoning is, as discussed above, that research has demonstrated over the past few years that ELF is extremely fluid. Thus, it would be difficult, if not impossible, to determine who is a BES and who an NBES, and on what criteria to base the decision given the lack of the criterion 'error' (against a set of target forms). It may well be that in future a means will be devised to measure intercultural ELF communication skills and the use of accommodation strategies and the like in situ (and examination boards above all need to work on achieving this). But until that happens, there is not much to be gained by trying to separate ELF speakers into these two sub-categories.

The connotations of the terms 'native' and 'non-native' have, in any case been shifting over the past ten years or so. And, as Seidlhofer (2011: 6) observes:

> The phenomenon of English as the first truly global language, and globalization with its consequences for how we now live and communicate, is bound to lead to such a shake-up of our traditional ideas of what constitutes 'a language' and 'legitimate speakers' that the terms themselves will simply become obsolete. So my own feeling is that, after so much agonizing about the terms 'native' and 'non-native', the problem will actually resolve itself in that new and appropriate words will emerge. It may well be that in the not too distant future we will be wondering why we ever thought that we needed these terms at all.

But it is not simply that the terms 'native' and 'non-native' are beginning to be seen as obsolete in relation to global uses of English. Another possibility is that their connotations will reverse, with 'native' becoming the pejorative term and 'non-native' the positive one. As I hypothesized some years ago:

> It will be interesting in years to come to see whether the term 'native' undergoes another change in connotation. In the days of empire, the natives were the indigenous populations and the term itself implied uncivilized, primitive, barbaric, even cannibalistic ... With the spread of English around the globe, 'native' – in relation to English – has acquired newer, positive connotations. 'Native speakers' of English are assumed to be advanced (technologically), civilized, and educated. But as 'NSs' lose their linguistic advantage, with

> English being spoken as an International Language [= ELF] no less – and
> often a good deal more – effectively by 'NNSs' … and as bilingualism and
> multilingualism become the accepted world norm, and monolingualism the
> exception … perhaps the word 'native' will return to its pejorative usage.
> Only this time, the opposite group will be on the receiving end.
>
> *(Jenkins 2000: 229)*

And in my experience, there are signs that this is already happening in ELF communication contexts including in academic settings. However, there is still a very
long way to go. The sociolinguist Trudgill has argued that "[t]he true repository of
the English language is its native speakers, and there are so many of them that they
can afford to let non-natives do what they like with it so long as what they do is
confined to a few words here and there" (2002: 151). Although he has developed a
slightly more nuanced approach since he wrote this (see Trudgill and Hannah
2008), his position still remains broadly that NESs are at the top of the English-
speaking hierarchy and that ELF is deficit by nature. And Trudgill is by no means
alone in holding such attitudes towards ELF and the English of NNESs in general,
but is typical of a substantial number of people including many academics and EAP
teachers, an issue to which we will return in Chapter Six.

To sum up …

ELF, then, is the primary lingua franca of globalization, and it is no coincidence
that when globalization is discussed, English is very often mentioned in the same
breath, even though usually only in a passing comment, with little thought given
to its significance. However, the implications of the globalization of English are
immense, not least for HE. Indeed, as mentioned earlier in the chapter, the rapid
growth of English medium instruction is seen by some as a – and possibly *the* –
main driving force behind ELF (Bolton 2011). And given the vast numbers of
international students communicating in lingua franca groups in universities around
the world, the idea of such a strong link between ELF and global HE is not at all
surprising. For good or bad, English is undoubtedly the global academic lingua
franca. And yet the linguistic implications of ELF are poorly understood in HE and
in the academic world more widely, while the sociolinguistic rights of ELF's
NNES majority and the responsibilities of NESs remain to be acknowledged, as
the next chapter will demonstrate.

Notes

1 This is not to suggest that the Outer Circle Englishes even in their earlier colonial
manifestations necessarily demonstrated the stability and lack of variation typical of the
other kinds of earlier lingua francas referred to here. And it is certainly not intended to
imply that such stability is characteristic of the post-colonial Englishes. The point is
simply that these Englishes have never had the massive geographical spread of ELF, and
thus the amount of diversity among their users that results from such spread.

2 The Expanding Circle is Kachru's (1985) term for those countries in which English is learned and used but which, unlike the Outer Circle, were never colonized by native English speakers. The Inner Circle refers to the mother tongue English countries, primarily the US, Canada, the UK, Australia, and New Zealand. While Kachru's three-circle model is nowadays criticized by some scholars for being out of date (see Jenkins 2009 for some of the criticisms that have been made), it still serves, in my view, as a useful shorthand to describe the global spread of English.

3 The Association of South East Asian Nations comprises ten member states (Brunei, Myanmar, Cambodia, Indonesia, Laos, Malaysia, Philippines, Singapore, Thailand, and Vietnam) plus three others (China, Japan, Korea). Together they are known as ASEAN + 3 and comprise approximately 450 million English-knowing multilinguals (Kirkpatrick 2010: 67).

4 This is not to suggest that ELF is supplanting other lingua francas such as Arabic, Portuguese, and Spanish.

5 The main accommodation processes are convergence and divergence. These involve, respectively, making one's speech either more or less like that of the interlocutor, and derive from either affective or communicative efficiency motivations in the case of convergence (respectively, the desire to be liked by, and to be more intelligible to, the interlocutor), and in order to signal different group membership and to disassociate from an addressee in the case of divergence (see Beebe and Giles 1984).

6 This example is taken from Ian McEwan's novel *Amsterdam*.

7 Accommodative dovetailing occurs when one speech partner repeats the 'incorrect' (against ENL) form that another has used, and the first repeats it again.

8 However, this wrongly implies that things are more clear-cut than they are in reality. Many have argued that the 'native speaker (of English)' construct is a myth (e.g. Davies 2003), that it is socially rather than linguistically constructed (e.g. Brutt-Griffler and Samimy 2001), that it is linked to racism (e.g. Kubota and Lin 2006), and that it is too heterogeneous and loose to be meaningful (e.g. Ferguson 2007), among several other arguments against use of the term. Despite all this, as Bright and Phan Le Ha point out, "the native/nonnative dichotomy continues to have real-world effects, with nonnative-speaking teachers facing discrimination, pay inequity issues, skepticism from students and self-doubt about their status as both users and teachers of English" (2011: 127).

3

ELFA AND OTHER APPROACHES TO ACADEMIC ENGLISH

The status quo in academic English/EAP

Academic English, as Mauranen, Pérez-Llantada, and Swales (2010: 636) observe, has become an "immense phenomenon" with vast numbers of research papers being published, lectures delivered, and PhD theses completed in the medium of English year on year. Whether this is, in general, a good or bad thing, and whether it advantages and disadvantages particular groups of students and scholars,[1] is part of a separate debate, and one to which I will return in my final chapter. The fact nevertheless remains that in a very large number of cases, the writers and speakers involved are NNESs who are using English in lingua franca settings. That is, they are speaking to and writing for a wide international audience, the majority of whom are, like themselves, NNESs. To put it another way, this "immense phenomenon" is, above all, an ELFA (English as a Lingua Franca in Academic Settings)[2] phenomenon. And as I pointed out in previous chapters, this can be as true in mother tongue English countries, most notably at postgraduate level in HE, as it is in many other parts of the world.

However, as Mauranen et al. (ibid.) go on to point out, whereas the historical trajectory of academic English, particularly in its written channel, has been well documented in the mainstream academic English literature (see, e.g., Gross, Harmon, and Reidy 2002 among many others), more recent developments have not been accorded similar attention. This means that the many NNES authors and presenters who use English as an academic lingua franca, along with the increasing variation, nuance, richness, and complexity that they bring to the language, both written and spoken, are largely ignored in the literature except in so far as their English is seen as a 'problem to be addressed'. Research into ELFA is likewise marginalised or, more usually, completely ignored in the mainstream literature. Thus, "[a]lthough English is the global lingua franca of academic discourse, most research in academic English is oriented towards … native speakers of English and the normative tenets of Standard [native] English as used in academia" (Mauranen et al. op.cit.: 638). And as Chapters Four and Five below demonstrate, this research bias in turn seems to exert a strong (native English) normative influence on academic English policies and pedagogies.

This kind of marginalization of research into non-native English is, of course, not restricted to ELFA (or ELF in general), but extends potentially to any paradigm shift involving language. We saw in the previous chapter how negatively ELF research is perceived in some quarters. In the field of EAP, the same kind of problem appears to beset the relatively recent approach known as 'Academic Literacies' (see, e.g., Lea and Street 1998, 2006, Lillis 2001, Lillis and Scott 2007, and this chapter below). Like ELFA, Academic Literacies is criticized on both conceptual and pedagogic grounds. And in both cases, as was pointed out in Chapter Two, such criticisms seem to arise at least in part from a desire to remain with traditional conceptualizations of 'language variety', and a concern over new ways of thinking that seem less clear-cut (or, perhaps, are less simplistic) in terms of what the English language actually *is* on the one hand, and what, specifically, can be *taught and learned* on the other hand. In other words, people, and perhaps English teachers especially (in this case, teachers of EAP), tend to feel uneasy about the relatively more open, flexible, variable, hybrid, accommodative, diverse, and thus less constrained, or 'standard', kinds of English that typify ELFA use. They therefore orient negatively to the research that describes this use and the theory that underpins it. And while Academic Literacies comes from a rather different starting point (although having shared ground with ELFA in its resistance to traditional notions of 'the standard'), and comes to some different (but also some similar) conclusions, its relatively fuzzy, non-conventional orientation to English use seems to elicit some of the same kinds of criticism (see, e.g., Tribble 2009, Wingate and Tribble 2012).

Another link between ELFA and Academic Literacies, and also with Genre approaches, is their de-trivializing of academic language within the Academy. As I pointed out in Chapter One (p. 12), NNES university students, unlike the majority of content staff, do not regard language as a trivial issue. Rather, they see it as critical to their academic experiences and outcomes. Thus, Hyland, from a Genre perspective, refers to the need to "[unpack] the black box of academic discourse", not least because of "its traditional role as a carrier of what counts as legitimate knowledge and as authorized ways of talking about this knowledge" which, in HE, "is constructed and transmitted through relatively uniform practices of literacy and pedagogy" (2009: 5). Hyland goes on to observe that in HE, "literacy is presented as a set of discrete rules and technical skills" and that this perception "contributes to an ideology which transforms literacy from a key area of academic practice … into a kind of add-on to the more serious activities of university life … on the margins of academic work" (p. 9). Likewise, but coming from the perspective of Academic Literacies, Lillis argues that "[t]he kinds of writing that are demanded, and the ways in which these are taught, cannot be thought of as an adjunct to the 'mainstream' curriculum or pedagogy, but rather are integral to our aims in, and for, higher education" (2001: 167).

However, while many scholars working in the field of academic English recognize the centrality of English language to academic life in general, and HE in particular, they have so far made little progress in convincing those outside the field, particularly content staff in universities. Hence, there has been little change in practice (and practices), and certainly nothing of a more radical nature in university content teaching and assessing. Instead, HE continues to operate as it has done for several decades, with non-native (and, less often, native) English still being treated merely as a subject for remedial action until it more closely resembles some kind of idealized, illusory standard. Meanwhile, within the field of EAP itself, while at the theoretical level there has been substantial debate over recent years as to how academic English should be conceptualized, again little has changed in practice (and practices). Thus, the majority of EAP courses in the second decade of the second millennium continue to reflect the traditional EAP theory that was current well before the end of the first.[3]

The framing of academic English/EAP in the literature

We turn now to consider some of the current theoretical approaches to EAP, and then to explore ELFA in detail. However, structuring a discussion of theoretical approaches to EAP is not a simple matter. On the one hand, different scholars tend to categorize and name the various approaches in diverse ways depending on their particular orientation to academic English, for example, traditional, critical, and so on (just as my own take on the subject is through an ELFA lens). Moreover, as Tribble (2009: 400) points out in his survey of approaches to academic writing and published resource materials, "accounts of what is meant by EAP" are "fragmented and sometimes contradictory". And on the other hand, as already mentioned, there is a fair degree of overlap across aspects of some of the different theoretical positions. I will therefore begin by reviewing how the different approaches have been categorized and presented by a number of key scholars in the field of academic English/EAP,[4] before going on to explain how my own discussion of the approaches is structured.

The earliest categorization to be presented here is of a rather different order from the others in that it comprises a set of influences from outside the field of academic English rather than a framing of approaches towards it. I am referring here to Swales, whose (1990) interest is in the genre analysis of academic English, and who focuses on "the substantial debt to previous work in both applied and non-applied fields" of the genre-based approach (p. 13). Swales identifies the following areas of influence: variety studies, skill and strategy studies, notional/functional approaches, discourse analysis, sociolinguistics, writing context studies, and cultural anthropology (pp. 13–20). He goes on to discuss how each of these fields feeds into a genre-based approach, and hence to the eclecticism of an approach whose originality "probably lies as much in integrating the work of several different traditions as in new thinking per se" (p. 13).

The other categorizations described here focus, in the main, on the different approaches that are taken to academic English/EAP and most, if not all, primarily or exclusively on written English. This is not surprising, given that apart from some of the corpus research projects of the past decade such as MICASE (the Michigan Corpus of Academic Spoken English), BASE (the British Academic Spoken English Project) and ELFA (the Corpus of English as a Lingua Franca in Academic Settings), that all prioritize speech, the written channel has received by far the most attention in the literature, with a few rare exceptions such as Hyland (e.g. 2009). Tribble (2009), for example, focuses entirely on academic writing. He begins his survey of EAP resources with an account of what he considers the major EAP writing traditions, which he frames as "varieties" or "strands" of EAP. The first strand that he identifies is labelled "Social/Genre" (p. 402). This approach originates from earlier research into ESP (English for Special Purposes), register analysis, and genre, and "typically requires thorough accounts of both the communicative context *and* the linguistic behaviour arising from this context as the starting points for any pedagogic solutions that are developed to meet learners' needs" (p. 401; his italics), and in particular, the recognition of the linguistic requirements of the different academic disciplines. The 'Social/Genre strand' of EAP has also resulted in large-scale corpus projects such as MICASE, BASE, and BAWE (the British Academic Written English project)[5] that provide descriptions for both analysis and the development of EAP resources.

While Tribble's first 'strand' represents a mainstream/traditional UK orientation to EAP, his second one, which he terms "Intellectual/Rhetorical" (p. 402), represents a mainstream/traditional North American orientation. And whereas the direction taken in the UK was driven by the massive increase in students coming from outside, that is international students, in North America it was primarily a response to widening participation from within, and the need to improve the literacy skills of non-traditional students who, hitherto, had been excluded from HE. This approach to EAP, generally known as Composition Studies, is generic, that is, it is not discipline-oriented, but involves the teaching of composition skills to first year university students in free-standing programmes, and is often influenced by a 'process writing' method of instruction (see White and Arndt 1991). While this is, in the main, a North American rather than UK approach, it nevertheless has something in common with the kinds of 'study skills' approaches that many UK universities make available to home students, based on the somewhat dubious assumption that unlike NNES students, home students already know the literacy requirements of academic writing in general, as well as of their discipline in particular.

The third tradition that Tribble discusses is the one known in the UK as 'Academic Literacies' and in the US as 'Writing in the Disciplines' (Lea and Street 1998, 2006). While this tradition has connections with both Composition Studies and Genre approaches, it is more disciplinary than the former and more critical than either in its stance towards the requirements of the Academy. Academic Literacies has links with work in Critical Discourse Analysis, systemic linguistics, and cultural anthropology which, as Street (2004: 15) observes, "see student writing as constitutive and contested rather than as skills or deficits" (ibid.). According to the Academic Literacies approach, problems in students' academic writing "might be seen in terms of the gaps between faculty expectations and student interpretations of what is involved in student writing and in terms of an institutional rather than an individual approach" (ibid.; see also Lea and Street 1998, 2006).

While the primary interest of Academic Literacies is in the widening of participation in HE to non-traditional home students, and that of ELFA is in EMI instruction for international students, as mentioned above, the two share a non-deficit orientation to students' output (both written and spoken in the case of ELFA), a concern for identity, and a belief that the status quo should be opened up to examination rather than accepted unquestioningly. Tribble (2009), however, says nothing about ELFA, and appears to be ambivalent about Academic Literacies. He argues, on the one hand, that its proponents are unaware of the contribution of Social/Genre approaches and that it does not "constitute such a radical new direction" (p. 403). On the other hand, he concludes that "[w]here Academic Literacies does make a unique contribution is in the way it *contests* currently held views of what constitutes academic discourse and challenges teachers in higher education to question their own practices and the demands that it makes of their students" (p. 404; his italics). This strikes me as an immensely "radical new direction", and one that has much in common with ELFA approaches.

Hyland, as mentioned above, works within a Genre approach, and his 2009 book on academic discourse therefore takes this as its starting point. He nevertheless devotes an early chapter to considering a range of orientations, which he divides into textual, contextual, and critical. The textual category, approaching academic discourse as "a spoken or written instance of *system*" within which "individuals employ language to structure and express their ideas, identities and communities" (p. 25; his italics), is further broken down into genre analysis, corpus analysis, and multimodality. The contextual category has something in common with the approach of Swales (1990; see above, p. 44) in that Hyland explores the ways in which analyses of academic discourse are informed by the sociology of science, socio-historical approaches, and ethnographic approaches. His third and final category is critical approaches, which he argues are "better characterized as an attitude to discourse" rather than "a particular theory or set of methods for analysing data" (p. 38). For Hyland, this category comprises two different critical orientations, those of critical discourse analysis and Academic Literacies.

Hyland's perspective on academic discourse reveals an awareness of three broader issues that tend to be overlooked in the mainstream academic English/EAP literature: the role of gatekeeping processes in academic writing and in the assessment of academic English skills; the fact that there is no single academic English relevant to the entire academic community (at the lingua-cultural as well as discipline level); and, as the subtitle of his book, "English in a Global Context" anticipates, the need for a more 'global' view of the subject as a whole. Having said that, as Xiao (2011) points out, and as the discussion of ELFA below demonstrates, Hyland's treatment of the globalization of academic English could have gone considerably further.

Coming from a critical perspective (Critical EAP and Critical Pedagogy), the scholar Benesch (2001) provides yet another way of categorizing approaches to EAP. She frames the categories that she discusses as a series of historical trends that had taken place over the 30 years prior to the writing of her book, rather than as a number of concurrent approaches (or even influences). She begins with 'register analysis' in the 1960s, with its move towards EST (English for Science and Technology) and away from English taught as a means to access literary texts. This corresponds roughly to the ESP research that Tribble describes as being the precursor to his 'social/genre strand' (see p. 45 above). Benesch then turns to 'rhetorical analysis' in what she calls "the second stage of EAP during the 1970s" (ibid.: 6). This seems to have begun as merely a more 'rhetorical' approach to EST, but in its later phase in the 1980s to have something in common with the earlier Genre approaches of those such as Swales. Her third trend is that of 'study skills and needs analysis', in part a reaction against cross-discipline process approaches (see p. 45 above on process writing). This was a somewhat narrow mechanical approach, whose aim was primarily to identify the kinds of tasks students were likely to be asked to carry out and to supply them with the necessary skills to do so in very explicit ways.

Benesch's next category comprises an extension of the study skills approach, the 'linked courses' that gained ground in the mid-1980s, have been used in some institutions ever since, and which involve collaborations between language and content staff, and the use of team teaching. Finally, Benesch considers genre analysis, pointing out that while it involves attending to the linguistic features of texts, "genres go beyond the text to take social purposes into account, including ways members of discourse communities are guided by shared rhetorical purposes when they speak and write" (p. 18). Benesch then summarizes the five trends she has explored, arguing that "the strength of EAP has been its sensitivity to context" (p. 23). On the other hand, she points out that "the definition of context has been revised continually" over the 30 years of her survey. More crucially, she argues, EAP research and teaching have focused on preparing students "unquestioningly for institutional and faculty expectations" (ibid.), and thus promoting a situation that has not necessarily been in students' interests. This is a concern that is very much shared by those who work within an ELFA framework.

Although they take a different approach, that is, Academic Literacies, the authors of the final categorization, like ELFA researchers, share the concern of critical EAP scholars such as Benesch with the need to problematize the existing situation. In a series of papers, Lea and Street (e.g. 1998, 2006, and Street 2004), frame academic English/EAP in terms of three distinct approaches, or models. The first of these is the 'study skills' approach, which, they argue, is based on an assumption that literacy is merely a set of discrete skills that students will be able to learn and then transfer to any context. Their second category is 'academic socialization'. This, they explain, is based on the notion that students need to be inculcated into the culture of the academy, and premised on the assumption that there is but one monolithic academic culture. Like the critical EAP scholars, those working in Academic Literacies criticize this approach for ignoring issues of power and for not empowering students to question and challenge current practices. Lea and Street's third approach is the one they themselves have played a key role in developing, an approach that views literacy as social practice and that encourages students to project their own identities and preferred social meanings in their academic writing, rather than feeling that they have to conform to pre-existing academic/disciplinary norms of English. While Academic Literacies shares some common ground with Genre approaches, a major difference, then, is that the latter are more concerned with texts and the former with practices.

Another Academic Literacies scholar, Lillis (2001), while sharing Lea and Street's perspective on EAP, categorizes the various approaches rather differently. In her "framework for exploring pedagogical approaches to student academic writing" (pp. 163–64), she presents five approaches to student writing in UK HE. These are: "Skills – teaching discrete elements of language", "Creative self-expression – teaching as facilitating individual expression", "Socialization (1) – teaching an implicit induction into established discourse practices", "Socialization (2) – explicit teaching of features of academic genres", and "Academic literacies/critical language awareness". Lillis describes the first four of these approaches as being, to varying degrees, "dominant" in UK HE, with the first, the skills approach, being the pre-dominant one, while she characterizes the fifth as "oppositional". According to Lillis's framework, for those practitioners engaged in the more "dominant" approaches, the HE community is "viewed as homogeneous" with "[p]ractices oriented to the reproduction of official discourses" (ibid.). By contrast, for those at the "oppositional" end of the framework, the HE community is "viewed as heterogeneous" with practices being "oriented to making visible/challenging/playing with official and unofficial discourse practices" (ibid.).

Although Lillis does not mention ELFA approaches in her 2001 framework (this is not surprising, given that ELFA research was then in its infancy), she takes it up in a later publication (Lillis and Curry 2010), pointing out, for example, that ELFA's position "questions the privileged status of the English spoken/used by 'native speakers' above the varieties of many other users of English around the world" (p. 22). However, outside the publications of ELF(A) scholars themselves, it is rare to find any references to ELFA, let alone observations of this kind in writings on academic English/EAP, even in texts such as Hyland (2009; and see above) which argue against a monolithic approach and consider their own to be 'global'.

And so to the structuring of my own discussion of the various approaches to academic English/EAP. As both mentioned earlier in the chapter and demonstrated in the presentation of the categorizations of scholars coming from different 'persuasions', this is not a straightforward process. For the labels given to the various approaches can be confusing, accounts of the approaches are, as Tribble points out, sometimes contradictory, and overlaps among approaches may complicate things still further. Meanwhile, ELFA, the approach that may yet prove to be the most relevant and influential in the current century, is not even mentioned in the above categorizations.

Taking all this into account, I have divided the various approaches towards and perspectives/positions on academic English/EAP, spoken as well as written, into three groupings. The first of these is made up of *conforming approaches*. Coming from my ELF(A) perspective, I see the approaches in this group as 'conforming' in that they conform by default to native academic English. The group comprises stronger and weaker versions. At the stronger end is what is sometimes called 'General EAP', but which I prefer to call 'Traditional EAP'. Research and publications at this end of the conforming scale (particularly EAP materials for students) tend to be concerned with standards, to assume and/or focus on idealized native English academic norms, and not to question whether these norms are the most appropriate globally or why they should still be considered in some way better than other possibilities. At the weaker end are EAP/Genre approaches and Corpus studies. These are more nuanced and exploratory, and less concerned with norms and standards, but are still premised on native academic English as internationally appropriate (Hyland 2009 is an exception in that he at least considers global issues, although he does not follow them through; see Xiao 2011). In fact what I find surprising about Genre approaches in general is that while, on the one hand, scholars talk about NNESs' developing their *own* individual identities in their academic English (e.g. Flowerdew 2011), on the other hand, they do not seem to see any contradiction in expecting NNESs to develop these identities through the medium of *native* English norms and forms (see, e.g., Hyland 2008a on NNESs' 'need' to acquire native-like formulaic phrases, or chunks, as contrasted with Mauranen's (2009) ELFA approach to the same issue).[6] Those who favour genre approaches also, to my knowledge, fail to consider the implications of the strong current shift towards a favouring of interdisciplinary research, although this is beyond the scope of my current discussion.

My second group consists of *challenging approaches*. These are 'challenging' in the sense of questioning in various ways what lies behind the linguistic conformity involved in the previous category. The challenging category comprises Critical EAP, Contrastive Rhetoric, and Academic Literacies, all of which share, to an extent, some of ELFA's socio-ideological concerns. Finally, my third group consists of a single *paradigm shifting* approach, ELFA itself. I see this approach as constituting an entirely new paradigm in academic English research (as general ELF does in respect of research into English Language Teaching), as it starts from an entirely new premise and involves new (and, for some people, disturbing) ways of looking at some of our most cherished linguistic constructs such as language, variety, and speech community (see Chapter Two).

Inevitably, just as the categorizations and commentaries above are presented from the particular perspective of each individual author, so mine come from my own (ELFA) perspective. In other words, my interest in the discussion that follows is in how far research into academic English/EAP and EAP teaching texts reflects and promotes particular assumptions about the nature of academic English in relation to its largely lingua franca, or 'international', contexts of use in today's academic world.

Approaches to academic English/EAP seen through an ELF(A) lens

Because the main approaches to academic English/EAP have already been covered in detail above, I focus in my own categorization on aspects of them that I see as especially relevant to the discussion of ELFA and/or that inform the research presented in Chapters Five, Six, and Seven.

Conforming approaches: Traditional (General) EAP, Corpus Studies, EAP/Genre

The 'stronger' end of the conforming approaches represents what actually goes on in the majority of universities around the world: in the teaching of academic English (typically in dedicated EAP centres or units), in the requirements of the examinations that NNESs have to pass in order to be admitted onto university degree courses, and in the monolithic expectations (however vaguely articulated) of subject staff within the disciplines vis-à-vis their students' use of English. While this tends to be more so in universities in the mother tongue regions as well as in their off-shore campuses, it is by no means absent from those in other parts of the world, as can be seen below and in Chapters Five and Six. These traditional orientations, as well as being the most widespread, are also the most distant from ELF(A), and thus from the most extensive source of global influence on English, that is, that of its majority NNESs. Instead, the traditional orientations are premised, whether consciously or not, on the out-dated notion, coming from an earlier phase of Second Language Acquisition theory, that non-native English is either 'learner English' (or 'interlanguage') in need of remediation, or English that has 'fossilized' while still retaining 'imperfections' (where it differs from ENL) after learning has ceased (Selinker 1972).

Thus, Klitgård (2011), a Danish scholar based in Denmark, a typical proponent of this orientation, apparently, argues as follows:

> I want to stress that I am not advocating the teaching and acceptance of a more or less creative English language use in university writing, such as the **radical proposals for a new ELF** (English as a lingua franca) where, for instance, certain grammatical and phonological deviations from *standard English* ... are also accepted ... So far I find it impossible to distinguish between **systematic traits of a virtually recognisable ELF** and **systematic traits of foreign language learners' various interlanguages**. Besides, an authorisation of ELF will **endanger international standards** for language testing and examining.
>
> *(p. 186; her italics, my bold)*

It is something of an irony that this is said in an article within an edited volume whose theme is 'the international university' and whose subtitle is 'From English Uniformity to Diversity and Hybridity'. The passage from Klitgård's article presents almost verbatim the traditional SLA orientation to ELF: that is, that it is a single kind of English ("a new ELF"), that it is interlanguage, or at least "impossible to distinguish from foreign language learners' various interlanguages", and that it is a threat to "international standards". Note, too, that there is no attempt to define what "international standards" actually are (though I infer that she means educated varieties of British and American English), and that there is no acknowledgement that 'international' could, let alone should, involve the "[d]iversity and [h]ybridity" of the volume's title. In this, Klitgård's approach echoes the new(ish) Pearson Test of English (Academic). Speaking to the *EL Gazette*, a Pearson representative described the process of designing the exam as follows:

> To create an international exam we started by hiring item writers from *the UK, the US and Australia* ... Because we are not using a single standard model of English we can grade all non-native students on a single scale. The first thing we look for is comprehensibility – are they *understandable to the native speaker?*
>
> *(September 2008, p. 10; my italics)*

Again, we find an equation of 'international' with 'native', an assumption that the spread of English around the world is – and should be – the spread of native English, and a corresponding lack of awareness of the sociolinguistic reality of contemporary English use.

Klitgård leaves little doubt that this is indeed her position, as she makes a similar point on pp. 180–81 of the same article:

> As Diane Schmitt tells us: 'Language acquisition is not about creatively developing one's own idiosyncratic method of speaking or writing; rather, *it is about learning to use the conventionalised language of the community one finds oneself in and learning to appropriate others' language to establish group membership*' (Schmitt, 2006: 68). Hence, EAP instructions in using the many conventional and forumulaic academic phrases as can be found in for example, the *celebrated* Academic Phrasebank from The University of Manchester. And here they thoughtfully emphasise that, 'The phrases are content neutral and generic in nature ... '.
>
> *(http://www.phrasebank.manchester.ac.uk/ (accessed 4.4.11); my italics)*

Various objections might justifiably be made by those working within Critical EAP, Academic Literacies, and ELFA to Schmitt's and the University of Manchester's assumptions about NNESs' (lack of) rights to develop their *own* voice in their academic speaking and writing rather than "learning to appropriate others'", and about the assumed internationalness of "formulaic phrases". And again we observe Klitgård's underlying conviction that the global academic "community" to which NNES academics belong is essentially an NES-led one, and that "group membership" therefore means acquiring the academic English norms (e.g. formulaic phrases) specific to NES academic varieties of English, in other words, to particular *local* varieties. The overall focus of the article is in fact on plagiarism, but the author's presentation of native English as the only acceptable model does little, to my mind, to help reduce the plagiarism problem for NNES students and scholars.

I have discussed this article in some detail as it is a recent example of the traditional orientation to EAP/academic English. But it is by no means an isolated case, or even restricted to the stronger version of the conforming group. For the weaker 'conformers' who subscribe to more nuanced EAP/Genre approaches[7] nevertheless share to a great extent the same ENL-oriented premise, even if norms and standards are not their focus. For example, another edited volume, Charles, Pecorari, and Hunston (2009) explores corpus and discourse approaches to academic writing. The articles in two sections of the book focus more on Genre approaches, with varying degrees of orientation towards native English norms and assumptions of 'native as expert'. And while some authors at least regard both NES and NNES students, rather than NNESs only, as novice writers of academic English, there is little explicit support to be found anywhere in the volume for the notion that NNES writing might differ from that of expert NESs and still be considered expert.

The third part of Charles et al. (2009), 'Focus on learner discourses', as its title implies, is concerned with non-expert writers. Again, the assumptions seem to be that the process of acquiring expertise equates at least in part with the process of acquiring native academic English and, therefore, that non-native academic writing is still lacking in certain ways. This is perhaps most explicit in the article by John, who argues that "[l]earning to write for *the* academy ... involves taking on a new identity" and "is particularly problematic for second-language students" because "they have to undergo an *identity transformation* when writing in the L2" (p. 274; my italics). This is reminiscent of Schmitt's (2006) point in Klitgård (2011) that NNESs need to learn to "appropriate others' language to establish group membership" (see above, p. 51).

On the other hand, the native-normative orientation is least explicit in the contribution of Gardezi and Nesi, who compare the writing of British and Pakistani students in universities in their own countries, that is Britain and Pakistan. While the authors find differences between the two groups, they do not draw inferences about their relative quality, and argue instead that both "are still undergoing apprenticeship into the discourse of their field" (p. 248). However, they end by cautioning, in line with Duszak (1997), that while "[c]onformity to the local [i.e. own cultural group's] style may be the safest choice during undergraduate studies in the home country", NNES academics may meet with problems if they try to publish in these norms. In this respect, though, the authors seem unaware of changes that are underway, with an increasing number of edited collections (e.g. Archibald, Cogo, and Jenkins 2011, Mauranen and Ranta 2008, Murata and Jenkins 2009), and journal special issues (e.g. Carli and Ammon 2007, Mauranen and Metsä-Ketelä 2006), as well as the new *Journal of English as a Lingua Franca*, new book series, *Developments in English as a Lingua Franca* (both DeGruyter Mouton), and the online journal, *Asian EFL Journal* (http://www.asian-efl-journal.com), all accepting any English, regardless of whether it is native or non-native, provided that it is intelligible to a wide international audience. Indeed, it is not altogether impossible to imagine a time when NES academics' submissions are sometimes rejected for not satisfying new international intelligibility requirements.

Even when authors appear to believe that their approach is less traditional and more global in orientation (as may be the case with the authors of some, if not all, the articles and chapters that have just been discussed), this is not necessarily so. For example, in an article whose title specifically refers to writing "in an English as a Lingua Franca context", Anderson, Hargreaves, and Owtram (2009), present what is in essence a traditional orientation to academic English. For while the focus of their study of student writing at the European University Institute in Florence, Italy is on the manifestation of identity, their participants are all "highly competent language users, post–C1 level and above" (p. 118). In other words, the authors are judging competence in English according to the Common European Framework of Reference (CEFR) which, itself, assesses according to native norms for all the European languages it covers, including English. While its assessment framework may (or may not) be suitable for assessing proficiency in languages that are learnt principally for communication with their native speakers, it is entirely *un*suitable for assessing proficiency in a lingua franca (see, e.g., Jenkins and Leung 2013, McNamara 2011). This somewhat invalidates from the start Anderson et al.'s claim to be exploring "an English as a Lingua Franca context". If their doctoral partici-pants are "post–C1 level and above", their English is already near-native, while any improvements in their academic writing over the course of the 15-month study seem to be in the direction of developing skills considered typical of competent NES academic writers (in this case, the ability to demonstrate authorial stance effectively).

Nowhere in Anderson et al. (2009) is there a sense that the "lingua franca con-text" of the title has any relevance to the study described beneath it, beyond the basic facts that the ten doctoral student participants themselves come from eight different language groups, and that six of them had previously studied and/or worked in EMI universities in continental Europe (and two in the US and the UK). There is no suggestion that the participants' ELF past and/or present has (or should have) some kind of role to play in the development of their doctoral writing skills (e.g. do they work and/or socialize in ELF groupings?), or that there is anything about their use of English that reflects 'ELFness'. This is even so in the case of one participant, Mario, who apparently "looked up to a particular senior bilingual-bicultural scholar in his field as a model to be emulated" (p. 128). The implications of this are not discussed, which leaves this reader, at least, wondering whether the senior scholar in fact wrote in 'native-like' academic English and was esteemed precisely for that reason. This would not be surprising given that Anderson et al.'s unqualified use of the term 'academic English' seems to assume some kind of monolithic (and therefore, very likely, native) academic English (e.g. one participant, Eldin, has "considerable exposure to *academic English*", pp. 133–34; my italics).

Overall, then, an article supposedly about academic writing in an ELF context turns out to be about "the way junior academics respond to institutional forces as they engage in shaping and reshaping their identities as writers" (p. 136). The fact that these particular junior academics are NNESs working in an ELF context is not made relevant to the study even if it does actually have relevance to their lived experiences. Though we have no way of knowing.

As mentioned earlier, traditional approaches to academic English/EAP predominate around the globe. Hence, the unspoken native-normativeness of the previous article underpins, and is often made far more explicit in, much that is published on EAP practice. This ranges from weighty research articles at one extreme to teaching materials for EAP practitioners and their students at the other. Of the weightier kind is a recent article on international students' understanding of lecturers' use of metaphor (Littlemore, Trautman Chen, Koester, and Barnden 2011). University lecturers, we are told, "use metaphors for important functions, such as explaining and evaluating", and because of lack of familiarity with these metaphors, "international students may thus be missing valuable learning opportunities" (p. 408). The authors frame the problem as one of "*misunderstanding* and *non-understanding*" (ibid.; their italics) by international students, and present the "error categorization scheme" (ibid.) that they have devised to 'help' international students overcome their 'comprehension problem'.

On the other hand, from an ELF(A) perspective, this would be seen as a problematic solution. Native English metaphors and idioms are local forms that do not have international currency, while ELF users are creating their own metaphorical (and idiomatic) usages (see Pitzl 2009, 2011, 2012). Arguably, then, the onus should be on the lecturers to adjust their use of metaphor (and idiom) to suit their international audience. In fact the only recommendation for lecturers is that "[i]t would also be useful for [them] to be aware of the range of potential difficulties that metaphor presents to such international students, and to take measures to ensure that key metaphors used in their lectures have in fact been understood by all" (p. 427). This is the assimilation model that I discussed in Chapter One, and is echoed the following year by Martinez and Schmitt, who argue for the principled incorporation of non-transparent formulaic sequences in the teaching of EAP and general English for learners' receptive use, because "formulaic sequences form an important part of the lexicon" (2012: 299). Again, it is evident that the lexicon in mind is an ENL one. And again, an ELF(A) approach would encourage NES academics to acquire the skill of avoiding such non-transparent formulaic language when communicating with an international reader- or listenership, rather than advocating that NNESs should acquire this kind of language.

Turning to EAP materials, I have picked just three standard published EAP texts out of the hundreds of potential choices. The first (Moore 2007, already on its third printing when I bought my copy in 2008) is a text that prepares prospective university students for IELTS. This is a high-stakes exam, as many students need to pass it in order to gain university admission around the world. The book's title, *Common Mistakes at IELTS Advanced … and how to avoid them*, reflects the fact that NNES students (and non-native users in general) at high proficiency levels are, nevertheless, found to make what, from a traditional perspective, are regarded as "common mistakes". As the blurb on the back cover points out, the mistakes presented and tested in this book are "real" mistakes: the book "looks at real errors made by learners in the test". The contents page clarifies what these kinds of 'errors' involve: articles, prepositions, countable and uncountable nouns, singular and plural verb forms, to name but a few categories.

Exploring the countable and uncountable section (p. 35), we find that the items presented and/or tested include, for example, *equipment(s), furniture(s), information(s),* and *software(s)* among several other similar items. The use of 'furnitures' as a countable noun, is of course well known among World Englishes scholars, as an established form that occurs in many Outer Circle Englishes (see, e.g., Lowenberg 2000). The other items on p. 35 all appear in ELF corpora with reasonable and increasing frequency. In terms of the way these uncountable-to-countable nouns have evolved, they reflect the same kinds of regularization processes that have been affecting uncountable nouns in native Englishes down the centuries (see Seidlhofer 2011). The only justification for regarding them as "common mistakes" rather than acceptable new forms thus seems to be that in these NNES cases, the items have not, at least so far, been 'sanctioned' by NES use (see Chapter Two for further discussion of this point).

The orientation to academic English just described is typical of all the well-known EAP exams and, in turn, of all published EAP materials that prepare students for them. This insistence on the learning of ENL norms at a time when these represent a small minority of English use around the world thus constitutes a gatekeeping practice being carried out by the large examination boards which, though international in their reach, are ENL-run, mainly from the US, the UK and, to a lesser extent, Australia. Students desperate to gain university places, will do all they can to achieve success in ENL-based exams such as IELTS and those of its competitors (e.g. TOEFL and TOEIC). Many therefore attend expensive exam courses, buy the books that they believe will help them in their attempt, and endeavour to acquire the forms used by the NES minority that are presented in these books.

The process, however, does not stop with gaining an acceptable IELTS (or other) score. For, once at university, many international students are required (or at least made to feel they need) to attend 'remedial' EAP courses that involve more of the same kinds of published materials. I will mention just two typical examples of the materials available: McCarthy and O'Dell (2008) and Bailey (2006). My reason for selecting the first is that these authors are particularly well known and well sold around the world. I chose the latter, on the other hand, because it is among the texts used by EAP staff and students in my own university, which runs traditional pre- and insessional EAP courses. I could equally have chosen one of the other similarly ENL-oriented texts used on University of Southampton EAP courses, such as Gillett, Hammond, and Martala (2009), Jordan (1999), Oshima and Hogue (2006), and Swales and Feak (2004) (Mary Page, personal communication). But I wanted to make a point of choosing a Routledge publication (Bailey's) in order to demonstrate that I am neither targeting CUP in my choice of both Moore, and

McCarthy and O'Dell, nor reluctant to critique outputs from my own current publisher where I see this as relevant.[8]

McCarthy and O'Dell's (2008) book focuses specifically on academic English vocabulary. This is how it is described on its CUP web page:

> Academic Vocabulary in Use is the perfect study aid for *anyone* using English for their academic work. Ideal for students of any discipline, from engineers or social scientists to business students or lawyers, it covers *all the key vocabulary* they will come across in academic textbooks, articles, lectures and seminars, allowing them to function confidently in an English-speaking academic environment. The book is designed for students at good intermediate level and above as well as those preparing for IELTS and other university entrance examinations.
>
> *(http://www.cambridge.org/gb/elt/catalogue/subject/project/pricing/isbn/
> item1163598/?site_locale=en_GB; my italics)*

Note the assumption that the book contains "*all* the key vocabulary" that anyone engaged in academic work could need. This vocabulary is presumably drawn entirely from native academic English, although this is not specifically stated, while the authors also make use of examples of learner English to show the kinds of "errors" students make (p. 7).[9] There is, too, an assumption that the vocabulary presented is appropriate across the academic disciplines. In the latter respect, the authors expand as follows in their introduction 'To the student and teacher':

> [The book] does not deal with the specialist vocabulary of any particular subject such as medicine or physics. *Such specialist terms are often relatively easy to master* – they will be explained and taught as you study the subject and these words may indeed sometimes be similar in English and your own language. However, it is *the more general words* used for discussing ideas and research and for talking and writing about academic work that *you need to be fully familiar with* in order to feel comfortable in *an academic environment*.
>
> *(p. 6; my italics)*

Their comments about the greater importance of "the more general words", and the *ease* of learning discipline-specific norms may come as news to those researchers who take a disciplinary-based Genre approach to EAP. One is left wondering whether some all-purpose approaches to EAP (and to English Language Teaching in general) are to an extent, at least, more a reflection of publishers' concerns to sell large numbers of books globally than concern for what is best for the students who use them. Having said that, I would not want to imply that this is always the case. For example, another text that takes a monodisciplinary approach, Swales and Feak 2004, does so because the authors believe a multidisciplinary approach "turns attention away from whether the information or content in a text is 'correct' toward questions of rhetoric and language" and that "[i]n this way it encourages rhetorical consciousness-raising" and "leads to interesting group discussion among members who come from very different parts of the university" (p. 4). In its focus on "rhetorical consciousness-raising" rather than the offering of 'right answers', this represents a different orientation to academic English from that of many others who opt for 'one-size-fits-all', notwithstanding that both are grounded in the notion that "[a]cademic English tends to be a truly international language" (McCarthy and O'Dell 2008: 6) predicated on native-English-normativeness.

And so to Bailey (2006). Like the majority of other publications discussed above, this text focuses on writing. Unlike Moore (2007), it is not specifically directed towards exam preparation, though like McCarthy and O'Dell (2008), it is descri-bed as being useful for this purpose as well as for study while at university. The book is divided into four generic sections, described as "The writing process", "Elements of writing", "Accuracy in writing", and "Writing models". By far the largest of these is the third, dealing with accuracy, which has 23 units as contrasted with 16 for each for the first and second sections, and six for the fourth. The 23 accuracy units cover ground very similar to that of Moore's IELTS preparation book, including articles, prepositions, and countable/uncountable nouns. And taking the latter as a point of comparision, much the same can be said about Bailey's approach as was said above about Moore's (see pp. 54–55) in that the 'uncountable' list includes items that are established as countable in many varieties of World Englishes (e.g. 'furnitures', 'equipments', 'staffs') and/or found in ELF corpora to be used by speakers from many different first languages (e.g. 'advices', 'informations', 'vocabularies'). Bailey does at least seem to accept that 'data' has now superseded 'datum' as the singular form in ENL, though not that NNESs are already regularizing 'datas' as its plural – presumably because, like Moore and the other authors discussed above, his notion of acceptable usage is premised on correctness according to NES norms.

Kachru (2005) takes the argument against native-normative approaches to EAP a political stage further by describing the notion of a global academic English as a "myth ... essentially promoted by the ELT 'empire' and nurtured by English as a Second Language programmes in the USA and the UK. ... further supported by multinational corporations in collaboration with the British Council", and "a major export commodity to Anglophone Asia and Africa" (p. 216). Whether or not this is an exaggeration, it is undoubtedly the case that the international student market provides huge financial gains for the Anglophone nations.

Challenging approaches: Critical EAP, Contrastive Rhetoric, Academic Literacies

I turn now to the group of approaches that in their various ways challenge tradi-tional assumptions about academic English and EAP. Two of them, Critical EAP and Academic Literacies, were considered earlier in the chapter, so I have restricted further comment to pointing out aspects of them that resonate with ELFA. The third, Contrastive Rhetoric, was not included in any of the categorizations discussed in the previous section. Much has been written at the theoretical level on all three 'challenging' approaches. However, to date, unlike Traditional (or General) EAP and EAP/Genre, none of them has had widespread impact on official EAP policies and teaching practices, although some working within Critical EAP have reported their own use of 'challenging' practices in the classroom. For example, Canagarajah (2011) discusses his use of the approach he calls 'codemeshing',[10] or "the realization of translanguaging in texts" (p. 403), in a second language writing classroom in the US (see, too, Canagarajah 1999 and 2002 for earlier descriptions and discussions of his critical writing teaching practices, and Canagarajah 2013 for his most recent approach, published too late for me to take account of it in my own discussion).

Starting with Contrastive Rhetoric, as Mauranen et al. (2010) observe, there seem to be "notable differences in cultural preferences in academic rhetoric" with the field of Contrastive Rhetoric providing "compelling evidence of how non-native scholars adopt the standard rules of academic English, yet transfer some L1 [first language] text organization and rhetorical preferences to their texts when published internationally" (p. 643). The authors conceptualize this co-existence of conventional native English academic forms and local non-native forms as a "tension" between the two that leads to "hybridization" (p. 644), a kind of mixing of standard (and supposedly global) native English written norms and local non-native preferences (see, e.g., Y. Kachru 1997, 2009, Y. Kachru and Smith 2008 chapter 9, for local preferences in Outer Circle contexts). Mauranen et al. (op.cit.: 644) argue, citing Robertson (1995), that "this may call for a redefinition of contemporary academic prose in terms of 'interdiscursive hybridity', which could perhaps be seen as a manifestation of the glocalization process".

Scholars working within a more critical Contrastive Rhetoric (such as Kubota 2010, Kubota and Lehner 2004) object to what they see as the essentialist, static binaries of traditional Contrastive Rhetoric. Baker (2013), from an Intercultural Communication perspective, agrees, but points out that there have been recent attempts to address this issue, and "[i]n particular, the move from contrastive rhetoric to intercultural rhetoric suggests a greater awareness of the intercultural nature of much of the communication studied in the field". The work of Connor (e.g. 2004, 2008, 2011) and Flower (e.g. 2003) are cases in point. Baker concludes, however, that the process has not gone far enough because "[t]his intercultural dimension entails a paradigm shift with recognition of the dynamism, complexity and fluidity of cultures and communicative practices", and that the kind of research being done in ELF would be productive in this respect.

While an ELFA approach, like that of critical Contrastive Rhetoric, does not see non-native English forms in the 'neat' locally bounded way in which they tend to be conceptualized within the field of (traditional) Contrastive Rhetoric, the notion of hybridity is one that is particularly relevant to ELF(A). The extent to which such hybridity is well received in HE or by journal reviewers and publishers, is of course another matter (see Belcher 2007, Flowerdew 2001), and one which remains as much a problem for Contrastive Rhetoric as for the newer phenomenon of ELFA (see also note 6, p. 69).

We turn next to Critical EAP. This approach, itself influenced by Freire, Foucault, and feminist pedagogy, has been largely US-led by scholars such as Benesch (e.g. 2001), Canagarajah (e.g. 2002, 2007), and Phan Le Ha (e.g. 2009). But as will be seen in the next two chapters, it has relevance, at the language level at least, for English-medium institutions, programmes, and courses in many other parts of the world. Scholars working within this approach criticize mainstream EAP "for adopting an unquestioning stance toward the departments and disciplinary practices that students encounter" (Benesch 2001: x), and thus for their accommodationist and hierarchical assumptions "that students should accommodate themselves to the demands of academic assignments, behaviors expected in academic classes, and hierarchical arrangements within academic institutions" (ibid.: 41). The resulting conflation of learners' 'needs' and institutional requirements, as Benesch points out, "naturalizes what is socially constructed, making externally imposed rules seem not just normal but also immutable" (p. 61). Like those working in ELFA, then, Critical EAP scholars attach importance to NNES students' identities and to sociopolitical context. Thus, they problematize taken-for-granted terms such as 'English for Academic Purposes', asking "which English is being referred to? If English is not monolithic, whose gets taught? In EAP what is 'academic'? And what are the purposes?" (Benesch op cit.: xvii).

However, the focus of Critical EAP, unlike that of ELFA, has in general been less on language-related questions and more on issues of structure, content, and culture in terms of their effects on academic life. Benesch (2001), for example, focuses, in a discussion of how Critical EAP ideas might be put into practice, on areas such as the negotiation of assignments, and issues of access to courses and what is covered on them, rather than on linguistic matters (and see, e.g., Brunner 2006, Hyland, Trahar, Anderson, and Dickens 2008, Singh and Doherty 2004, Summers and Volet 2008 for a range of other non-linguistic critical orientations). Nevertheless, in the way it distinguishes between learner's needs (the needs that require addressing in order for learners to be able to fit in with institutional expectations and targets) and learners' rights (their right to challenge those expectations and targets), and in raising students' awareness, in the first place, of how institutional power is structured and maintained in HE, Critical EAP resonates loudly with ELFA's linguistic interests.

Academic Literacies, the final of the three approaches I categorize as challenging, has already been discussed at various points in the chapter. Lillis and Curry (2010) describe it as referring to "a social practice approach to the study of the range of academic literacy practices associated with academic study and scholarship, with the writing of students at university level attracting the largest part of research inquiry to date" (p. 21). And as Street (2009) notes, "[t]he model recognises academic writing as social practice within the given institutional and disciplinary context and … highlights the influence of factors such as power and authority on student writing" (p. 3).

Lillis (2001) argues that "any decisions about student writing pedagogy involve questions about the project of higher education itself: What is it for? Who is it for? Which practices are to be valued, and why?" (p. 167). Her questions are very similar to the kinds of questions asked by scholars working within a critical paradigm (see above for Benesch's questions about EAP). Indeed, Lillis herself points out that Academic Literacies and critical language awareness (e.g. Ivanič 1998, Ivanič and Camps 2001) "start from the same notion of language as socially situated discourse practices" (p. 166). However, as she goes on to note, there are significant differences between the two in that Academic Literacies is a model (one of three originally developed by Lea and Street, see above, p. 47) with no pedagogical application (though see below, this section), whereas critical language awareness is presented as a "pedagogic-research tool" (Lillis op. cit.: 172). Ivanič and Camps (2001), for example, explain how they raised L2 writers' awareness of issues of identity, and argue that "an L2 writing pedagogy that raises critical awareness about voice in the sense of self-representation can help learners maintain control over the personal and cultural identity they are projecting in their writing" (p. 31).[11]

Academic Literacies researchers seem to be even more critical and, at the linguistic level, more specific, in their stance towards the requirements of the Academy than those working within Critical EAP. For example, as Street (2004), in a discussion of Genre approaches and their concern with texts, points out:

> The emphasis [of Academic Literacies] on identities and social meanings draws attention to deep affective and ideological conflicts, for instance in the ways [in genre approaches] that students are called upon to switch between different discourses and to use features of the linguistic repertoire which sometimes appear alien to them. A student's personal identity – who am 'I' – may be challenged by the forms of writing required in different disciplines, notably prescriptions about the use of impersonal and passive forms as opposed to first-person and active forms, and students may feel threatened and resistant – 'this isn't me'.
>
> *(p. 15)*

In a subsequent article, Street (2009) discusses the "hidden features that are called upon in judgments of academic writing that often remain implicit" (p. 1), and looks specifically at framing, setting out one's contribution, expressing voice and stance, and structuring. He describes a writing project that he conducted during a literacy course at the University of Pennsylvania Graduate School of Education to raise students' awareness of the 'hidden' features in these areas, and ends with a quotation from one of the student participants, who notes: "this process made us confront our own assumptions or norms of 'correct' academic writing in terms of these different features and to make explicit to our peers why we were adapting them in certain ways" (p. 15).

Street's (2009) study, although small-scale, suggests a way forward for Academic Literacies in order to address its "lack of pedagogical application" (Wingate and

Tribble 2012: 483). In this respect, as Lillis and Scott (2007) point out, "in a field which is constituted by teacher-researchers" it is crucial to "sustain current support and critical discussion systems that exist for the development of researchers in academic literacies, acknowledging the marginal position of many in this field … through participation in professional groups … institutionally organized pedagogical projects … and informal organisations and events organized by teacher-researchers" (p. 22). The same can be said, to quite an extent, about my final approach, ELFA, in terms of both marginalization (in that its researchers' work is widely ignored in mainstream EAP research), and (lack of) pedagogic application, as well as "the fluidity and even confusion surrounding the use of the term 'academic literacies'" (p. 5), a problem which, as was discussed in Chapter Two, also besets ELF(A).

A paradigm-shifting approach: English as an Academic Lingua Franca

Last, but in the context of this book, most rather than least, we come to ELFA. In Chapter Two I defined the phenomenon of ELF and explored it at length, so I will give no introduction to ELF in general at this point and, instead, turn immediately to academic contexts of ELF use.

As has been observed at various points in the chapter so far, ELFA's underpinnings have a substantial amount in common with those of both Critical approaches to academic English and Academic Literacies. For like them, ELFA challenges dominant assumptions about academic English (that it should defer to native versions with NESs acting as gatekeepers), and instead regards it as a social phenomenon that is dependent on context, and in which voice and identity are key concerns. On the other hand, there are some important differences. In particular, ELFA is interested above all in language issues, whereas Critical EAP focuses more on other areas of academic life (see the previous section). Again, Academic Literacies is mainly concerned with non-traditional mother-tongue English home students in UK HE, whereas ELFA's prime concern is with non–mother-tongue international academics (at any level in their career) who use English in intercultural communication in academic contexts anywhere in the world. A further difference between ELFA and both Academic Literacies and Critical EAP is that ELFA has to date been primarily interested in speech, whereas the principal focus of Academic Literacies and Critical EAP is on writing.[12]

Turning to ELFA's beginnings, in 2003, a short article with the title 'The Corpus of English as a Lingua Franca in Academic Settings' appeared in the 'Brief reports and summaries' section of *TESOL Quarterly* (Mauranen 2003). This much cited article was, to my knowledge, the first publication devoted to considering ELF from a specifically academic perspective,[13] while the corpus it described, the ELFA Corpus (started in 2001; see Mauranen and Ranta 2008, Mauranen, Hynninen and Ranta 2010, Mauranen 2012, for details), was also the first corpus of academic ELF to be compiled. Fast-forwarding a few years, Mauranen's monograph on ELFA, *Exploring ELF in Academia: Academic English shaped by non-native speakers* (2012) has recently been published. And in the relatively few years between her original article on ELFA and the publication of her ELFA monograph, the field of academic ELF has become a major area of research and publication, with two other monographs already published (Björkman 2013, Smit 2010), others in the pipeline, and a vast number of journal articles, book chapters, and PhD theses on the subject.

As mentioned earlier, however, those working within mainstream EAP/academic English have so far paid little or no attention to ELFA, by whatever name, with just a few mentioning it in passing (e.g. Hyland 2006, Lillis and Curry 2010). Even Hyland in his 2009 book, which is subtitled 'English in a Global Context', has little to say on the subject. This is somewhat surprising given that as Mauranen (2012) points out, a vast amount of academic discourse (in HE, at conferences, in research collaborations, and so on) takes place in English, and that most of those involved are NNESs. Instead, as Mauranen (op.cit.) notes, "the unquestioned assumption has been that 'good English' equals that of the educated native speaker", and as a result, "[i]nnumerable native speakers have been recruited to help non-native scientists and scholars in their struggle with the language", while it is still "standard practice in publishers' style sheets to require non-native writers to have their text checked by a native speaker of English prior to publication" (p. 68).

Although a small minority within academia is starting to question the current linguistic state of affairs, this is not so for the vast majority, be they engaged in content teaching and assessing, providing EAP support, selecting and editing for publication, choosing conference plenary speakers, or the like. Yet academia is nowadays, above all, international in character (note how many universities proclaim their 'international'/'global' credentials on their websites), and we "must expect English to accept new usages along with new user groups" (Mauranen 2008: 258). And for international communication in which the greatest number involved are NNESs from a range of different first languages communicating in lingua franca groups, or CoPs (see Chapter Two), it is "accuracy and effectiveness in reporting findings and constructing arguments", not "the 'native-likeness' of a text, accent, or turn of phrase" that is crucial (ibid.). Hence, international academia "is not a realm where nationality or national standards and practices take first priority" (ibid.). Rather, we need to know much more about how those engaged in international HE around the world (teachers, students, publishers, and so on) employ spoken and written English successfully, regardless of whether their discourse features, accents, and the like differ from those of NESs, Thus, "we must complement our existing databases with English in international use" (Mauranen 2006b: 155), in other words, with information from ELFA corpora. Mauranen is not suggesting that descriptions of native English have no value. On the contrary, she goes on to argue that such descriptions are "of fundamental significance to any description of the language as a whole, but at the same time, we must respond to change" (ibid.).

The largest corpus of academic ELF, the Corpus of English as a Lingua Franca in Academic Settings (ELFA),[14] now numbering over one million words of spoken academic English, is by some way the most extensive and long-standing corpus of academic ELF. As stated on the project's home page (www.helsinki.fi/englanti/ elfa/project.html), it consists of two main parts, the ELFA Corpus project and the SELF (Studying in English as a Lingua Franca) project. In addition, more recently the team have started compiling a database of written academic ELF, WrELFA (see also Mauranen and Ranta 2008, Mauranen, Hynninen, and Ranta 2010). The recordings for the ELFA Corpus project were all made in authentic academic situations where English was the contact language but not the subject of study, such as lectures, seminars, and workshops, in a range of disciplinary domains (technology, humanities, natural sciences, behavioural sciences, and economics and administration). The speakers on the recordings come from a wide range of first language backgrounds, including African languages (e.g. Akan, Dagbani, Igbo, Kikuyu, Kihaya, Somali, Swahili), Asian (e.g. Arabic, Bengali, Chinese, Hindi, Japanese, Persian, Turkish, Uzbek), and European languages (e.g. Czech, Danish, Dutch, French, German, Italian, Lithuanian, Polish, Portuguese, Russian, Romanian, Swedish). While NESs are not excluded, they represent only 5 per cent of the total number of speakers.

This is not the place for a detailed description of the kinds of features that are emerging in ELFA research as occurring non-randomly and non-idiosyncratically in lingua franca communication in academic settings, but that (notwithstanding the points made previously about ELF(A)'s contingent variability) are demonstrating certain patterns of ELF(A) use; or, as Mauranen puts it, "unique features which constitute an important part of the pool of global English" (2009: 231). For fuller, more detailed analyses of (spoken) ELFA use and the processes underlying it than is possible here, readers are referred to the accounts in book-length treatments by Björkman (2010, 2013), Mauranen (2012), and Smit (2010), as well as in Volume 6 of *Helsinki English Studies*, which is dedicated to academic English (available at http://blogs.helsinki.fi/hes-eng/volumes/volume-6/), and numerous recent journal articles and book chapters by these and many other scholars of academic ELF.

It will nevertheless be helpful to provide a few examples of the kinds of features that have been identified as typically occurring in spoken ELFA, though it should be noted that many of the kinds of features regularly found in most other ELF settings are also found in ELFA settings. Erling and Bartlett (2006), for example, discuss the use of nouns that are (at least for now) uncountable in ENL but often countable in ELFA communication, such as *an advice, a proof, a research*, and *vocabularies*. On the other hand, some features seem to be particularly prominent in ELFA settings. The following three features, extended use of the progressive aspect, innovative use of the 'vague' expression *more or less*, and use of chunking to manage discourse, all draw on the ELFA Corpus.

Firstly, extended use of the progressive aspect. Non-native use of the progressive is typically associated with lack of proficiency (caused, for example, by transfer of first language use or by lack of a progressive aspect in the speaker's first language). As Ranta (2006) points out, however, this ignores the attractiveness of the progressive form: it seems to attract NNESs (though its use is also extending slowly in

ENL – note, for example, the informal use of *be* + *loving it* to describe a habitual action for which the simple form would be 'correct'). Ranta divides the many examples of extended use of the progressive in the ELFA Corpus into three categories: stative verbs, habitual activity, and points in past time, which she illustrates with the following examples (among many others):

> Stative verbs:
>> properties and relation *are belonging* to the same ontological general area or category
>> (mother tongue speaker of Danish at a Philosophy seminar)
> Habitual activity:
>> communication is so all embracive a concept, like air that we *are breathing*
>> (mother tongue speaker of Finnish at an Information Society seminar)
> Points in past time:
>> this comes to the point I've *been* just *mentioning* before, it can lead to a clash of civilisation
>> (mother tongue speaker of Somali at a Social Dimension of Globalization Lecture).

Ranta concludes that the participants in these interactions are assigning the progressive with an extra function as contrasted with its functions in ENL. This, she argues, arises out of their realization of its communicative value, that is, that the longer *-ing* ending gives verbs more prominence and expressiveness in speakers' utterances, thus drawing the attention of their interlocutors, and ensuring greater clarity. According to this argument, ELFA speakers are making innovative use of a resource provided by the (virtual) English language for their own purposes for what Ranta calls an 'attention-catching' function.

The second feature, use of the vague expression *more or less*, has been found to be one of the most frequent markers of vagueness in spoken ELFA, and in her analysis, Metsä-Ketelä (2006) finds that it is used substantially more than it is in NES academic discourse. She identifies three main functions of the exponent in ELFA: minimizing, comparing similarities, and approximating quantities. Most intriguingly, she finds that one of these functions, minimizing, is restricted to ELFA use, where it can be found particularly in question and answer situations (e.g. research seminars and doctoral defences), in which a researcher presents his or her study and then engages in critical discussion of it. The following is a typical example:

> Do you think this *more or less* bureaucratic difference makes the situation so different that Lithuania doesn't have the problem with the minority, while the other countries they do have?

Metsä-Ketelä notes that this ELFA minimizing function is unproblematic in the sense that it causes no confusion, and provides an illustration of how ELF(A) speakers negotiate new meanings for old words.

Finally, Mauranen (2009) demonstrates how ELFA speakers from a range of first languages use multi-word wholes, or 'chunking', as a means of managing their interactions and co-constructing successful discourse. This involves the use of both shorter, fixed expressions and longer variable units, with the latter being more amenable to online innovation that departs from conventional ENL use. She demonstrates this point with the exponents *in my point of view / on my point of view*. Although, notes Mauranen, speakers in the ELFA Corpus are also found to use the shorter ENL versions *in my view / in my opinion*, they exhibit a preference for the longer forms. She relates this to Ranta's point about the longer *-ing* form having greater visibility and expressivity (see above). She also observes that the longer ELFA methods of opinion flagging are blends of two forms close in meaning, a phenomenon that, as she points out, commonly occurs in language internal changes in monolingual contexts. In the case of ELFA speakers, she argues, "this could be seen as an instance of 'approximation,' the tendency of ELF speakers to latch on to salient features of a phraseological unit, which they use in its established sense, but without exactly reproducing the standard form" (p. 230). She concludes that in view of the repeated use of these blended forms in the corpus, it would not make sense to attribute them to the speakers' inability to master the ENL form (see Mauranen 2012, Chapter 5, for a more detailed discussion of these and other exponents).

Turning to written ELFA, as noted earlier, most research into academic ELFA has so far focused on speech rather than writing. Meanwhile, most non-ELFA research into academic English, with the exception of the relatively small amount coming from the fields of Contrastive Rhetoric and Critical EAP (see above), as well as ELFA itself, has focused on standard (i.e. native) academic English. Where the English of NNES academics is considered at all, it is typically framed as 'learner English' and studied primarily as a first stage in planning remedial steps to bring it in line with the required 'standard'. On the other hand, as Mauranen et al. (2010: 638) observe, while good academic English writing has always been (and still is) equated with that of NES academics, scholars working in Contrastive Rhetoric have demonstrated that "textual practices and preferences develop in our socialization into a particular culture of writing, and since writing cultures vary, there is no universal standard of 'good writing'". Thus, they contend, because educated NESs have their own entrenched notion of standard English norms, this does not mean that their preferred ways of writing are internationally superior to those of NNES academics. Rather:

> [w]hen English is written for a world-wide audience, criteria for good rhetoric or effective text organization may be quite different from those required in writing for a British or American audience. In particular, it is important to see that Anglo-American rhetoric is not necessarily the most effective, comprehensible, or 'natural' choice for structuring academic texts even if we use English. It goes without saying that it is not more 'scientific'.
>
> *(p. 639)*

The co-existence of standard native academic English and local culture-specific uses, they go on to argue, is leading to a tension and, in turn, to a process of hybridization which may require the redefinition of academic writing in terms of the notion of 'interdiscursive hybridity' (Fairclough 2006: 25).

Although he does not use the name ELF(A), Ammon was probably the first scholar to argue for the acceptance of written academic English that both departs from native academic English and implies the kind of hybridization for which Mauranen et al. (2010) argue. In the earliest of a succession of publications on the subject, a 2000 chapter, Ammon talks of NNES academics' "right to linguistic peculiarities" and calls on NNESs to "demand more linguistic tolerance from the language's native speakers" using "their growing number as the argument" (p. 116). This was followed, in a 2003 article, with the claim that "the greater attention non-native speakers pay to the language in their endeavour to acquire it caus[es] them to shape it into a form more apt for a lingua franca" than NESs are able to do (p. 34). He goes on to suggest that if "Dutch English is easier to understand for non-native speakers than British English, the British, and perhaps the Americans, might learn from the Dutch how to change English into a practicable lingua franca" (ibid.).

In 2006, Ammon took his argument further, questioning both the justification and need for ENL to be required in academic texts. In order to highlight the differences between ENL and (what amounts to) ELFA, he goes on to say the following:

> I have suggested calling such new language norms for international, especially scientific communication, neither English nor by any compound of English, but instead *Globalish*. This new name would raise awareness of a status and function fundamentally different from the [native] English language, namely a lingua franca, whose norms are no longer under the control of native speakers of English.
>
> *(p. 25)*

Finally, a year later, Ammon returns to his 2000 point, this time referring directly to ELF(A) and referring explicitly to the implications for publishers:

> it is obvious that there are numerous non-native features that do not seriously hinder communication. The comprehensive studies of English as a Lingua Franca ... provide ample proof of that. They should be used for encouraging the acceptance of non-native forms to a much greater extent than today and to motivate editors and publishers to consider them accordingly.
>
> *(2007: 131)*

Ammon's position contrasts dramatically with the perceptions of the many who favour ENL norms in HE and regard "non-native features", by definition, as problems to be addressed regardless of whether or not they "seriously hinder communication". For example, in the same year as Ammon's final quotation above, the following was published in response to an article that had argued in favour of accepting NNES forms in international universities, provided that the forms were internationally intelligible:

> It seems clear that if you are teaching English to a foreign student and fail to point out that there is a rather important difference in form and meaning between singulars and plurals then you are not doing your job properly and deserve to be sacked – all the more so if you actively or passively encourage them just to ignore that difference.
>
> *(Harris,* Times Higher Education Supplement, *14 September 2007)*

While research into written ELFA has been slow to get going, in very recent years the process has at least begun and there has been a small but increasing number of important studies in this area. These include Anderson (2010) on peer reviewing of academic ELF; Baker (2013) on the advantages of an ELFA approach to writing (over an Intercultural Rhetoric approach) as it is "more complex and less certain but also more empowering, with learners having greater agency"; Ferguson (2007), and Ferguson, Pérez-Llantada, and Pló (2011) on questions of equity and disadvantage for NNESs writing in English for international publication; and Hüttner (2008) on "writing models that are achievable for [NNES] students, appropriate in reflecting their communicative purposes, and acceptable to the gatekeepers of the discourse community involved" (p. 161).

Horner (2011) takes Hüttner's position further. While he would no doubt agree with her point about the need for students' writing to reflect their own communicative purposes, he does not subscribe to the notion that NNESs' writing should have to be acceptable to the gatekeepers of "the discourse community involved", that is, the gatekeepers of some version of standard native English. Or, rather, given the multilingual nature of global HE, he would more likely contend that the "discourse community" involved is primarily an ELF one. At least, I understand him to mean something like this when he argues against the traditional transmission model of writing pedagogy in favour of an ELF(A) writing pedagogy "in which students have as much to contribute, and as much say, in determining acceptability", and that in ELF, "the traditional concept of fluent mastery is inapplicable when applied to language understood as re-invented in each situation" (p. 307). Instead of seeing NNESs as the only ones who need to raise their standards, he notes that "[f]rom a perspective informed by ELF, we are all simultaneously both always 'competent' and always 'language learners'" and that "[i]n this double role, both we and our students are always rewriting English" (ibid.).

For Horner, then, the key considerations are to introduce student writers to texts written in a range of Englishes, and to "help students develop strategies to encourage their readers to tolerate and accommodate differences in their writing" rather than to help them appease the gatekeepers of standard English. Baker (2013) makes a similar point, but also cautions that "the extent to which the rhetorical construction of texts are negotiable may be controversial and careful research is needed to establish how pedagogic practice can best help learners of writing". This is likely to remain a dilemma for some time yet, as is demonstrated by the findings of a focus group study (Maringe and Jenkins in preparation, Jenkins and Maringe in preparation), where the PhD student participants discuss the risks involved in writing their theses in *their* English.[15] For as Belcher (2009) points out, despite the increasing multilingual diversity of academic writers, and their different (from NESs') preferred approaches to their academic writing, there is a reluctance to break with tradition. In other words, as several of the focus group participants put it, they still feel the need to 'play safe'.

Despite the fact that things are slowly moving in a more ELFA-amenable direction, with a handful of publishers (for some of their publications), and in terms of the growing global interest in ELF and ELFA, there is still a very long way to go. In this respect, there are two problems that ELFA research will need to address (and to some extent the same applies to Academic Literacies). The first is a conceptual question: what is 'academic English' according to an ELFA perspective? Given ELF(A)'s attested variability, can we (try to) describe academic ELF in any meaningful and useful way? If so, how is it different from traditional descriptions of academic English? If not, what can we propose to take the place of existing (albeit highly idealized) descriptions? The second problem concerns EAP pedagogy. If ELFA is conceptually different from traditional academic English, can it be taught and learnt? ELFA scholars would say yes and argue that it is a question of skills and awareness rather than one of forms per se. But the issue remains: how can these skills be taught and developed? What ultimately happens to ELFA will depend, above all, on the perceptions of users of academic English, both NNES and NES across all areas of academic life. It is to such users that we turn in the research-based chapters that follow.

Notes

1 Swales (1997), for example, questions whether academic English is becoming too successful, too triumphalist, and even a "*Tyrannosaurus Rex* ... a powerful carnivore gobbling up the other denizens of the academic linguistic grazing grounds" (p. 374).

2 English as a Lingua Franca in Academic Settings (ELFA) is also the name of the largest corpus of academic English drawn from lingua franca settings (see Mauranen and Ranta 2008, Mauranen, Hynninen and Ranta 2010, and pp. 62 ff.). Alternative acronyms used occasionally in the literature to refer to academic ELF are AELF (Academic English as a Lingua Franca) and EALF (English as an Academic Lingua Franca).

3 There are of course exceptions to my claim that nothing has changed in orientations to EAP pedagogy (see, especially Hyland 2006, a comprehensive and challenging resource book for EAP teachers). In addition, in the UK context, BALEAP has at last begun to show an interest in debating the implications for EAP of the processes of internationalization. Thus, by the time this book is published, it is not inconceivable that change may be almost within sight, if not yet in progress.

4 In theory, 'academic English' refers to the language itself (however defined) and therefore in research terms to its description and analysis, while 'EAP' refers to the teaching of this language (however defined) "with the aim of assisting learners' study or research"

if they work in English medium (Hyland 2006: 1). However, in practice, the two terms are often used interchangeably in both research publications and instructional materials.

5 This corpus, which is available at http://ota.ahds.ac/headers/2539.xml, includes assignments written by both NES and NNES university students. However, the lack of any 'non-native English flavour' in any of the samples that I have studied suggests that only the texts of those NNES students whose writing was considered 'nativelike' were selected for inclusion. Although they were apparently selected on the basis of the quality of their content (Sheena Gardner, personal communication), this raises the question of whether the content was (perhaps unwittingly) being evaluated in relation to the English in which it was articulated (on this phenomenon see, e.g., Flowerdew 2001, Lillis and Curry 2010).

6 However, as Hyland (2008a) points out, academic writing needs "acceptance by expert readers" (p. 42), and in the current climate, this still means readers who are likely to favour ENL norms, including "native-speaker (and monolingual) readers" who "could also be reading their essays, adopting their own norms one-sidedly for interpretation" (Canagarajah 2011: 408). The dilemma for many NNES academics and students, then, is whether they should defer to these norms or challenge them, given the loss of identity and voice involved in the former and the potential risks in the latter.

7 I categorize EAP/Genre approaches as 'conforming' because they are still grounded in assumptions that native academic English is globally relevant. This point is made emphatically by those who take a critical approach to academic writing such as Canagarajah (e.g. 2002) and Zamel (e.g. 1997), whose interest is in the different discourses that a global *multilingual* approach involves. Such scholars contest assumptions that genres, for example research articles, student essays, seminars, and the like, are – or should be – globally uniform (i.e. uniform according to native academic English). Multi-disciplinary Genre approaches (see, e.g., Hyland 2008b) at least move away from a one-size-fits-all approach to the disciplines. Yet Genre approaches of any kind rarely discuss, let alone research or promote, a 'multi' approach in terms of the multilingual nature of academic English use, Hyland (2006, 2009) being a rare example in terms of raising awareness of some of the global issues.

8 As a general comment on the 'big' publishers, there is an astonishing gap between the theoretical and practical orientations of many of their English language related publications. To take some typical examples, Routledge publishes some of the most political texts in the fields of applied- and socio-linguistics (e.g. Bex and Watts 1999, Pennycook 2007, 2010), but also EAP materials whose orientations are diametrically opposite, such as Bailey (2006). Similarly, Oxford University Press, on the one hand, has been a pioneer of ELF for more than a decade (e.g. Jenkins 2000, 2007, Seidlhofer 2011, Walker 2010), while on the other hand, it publishes EFL texts such as the *Headway* series, thus participating in what Gray describes as "the hegemony of the global coursebook" (2010: 189). And CUP is the publisher of Mauranen's (2012) monograph on ELFA.

9 The book draws on the Cambridge International Corpus (CIC), which, the authors tell us (p. 5) "is a computerised database of contemporary spoken and written English which currently stands at over one billion words. It includes British English, American English and other varieties of English. It also includes the Cambridge Learner Corpus, developed in collaboration with the University of Cambridge ESOL Examinations".

10 Codemeshing appears to have a lot in common with ELF(A), to the extent that new forms are "given fresh meaning by those who are prepared to negotiate for meaning in context", that "[e]ven what might seem like errors from a native speaker's perspective will be renegotiated by multilinguals to coconstruct new meaning", and that "[m]eaningful communication is an interactional achievement" (Canagarajah 2011: 408). Canagarajah makes the link himself by adding "[i]t is for this reason that, surprisingly, 'misunderstandings are not frequent in ELF interactions,' according to Seidlhofer (2004, p. 218)" (Canagarajah: ibid.).

11 However, Critical approaches, whether Ivanič's critical (language) awareness, Benesch's (2001) suggestions for the Critical EAP classroom, or Canagarajah's 'resisting (linguistic imperialism)' (e.g. 1999) and codemeshing (2011) practices, tend to be individual and ad hoc, rather than structured into curricula on the basis of widely used published materials, as is the case with Traditional EAP and Genre/EAP approaches.

12 I do not intend to imply that ELFA researchers are not interested in written academic English, only that research into spoken ELF has predominated up to now. Publications on written ELFA have nevertheless started to appear more recently (see the discussion of written ELFA below (pp. 61 ff.), and the Written Academic ELF project at www.helsinki.fi/englanti/elfa/wrelfa.html, which is part of the larger ELFA project at the University of Helsinki).

13 This is not to suggest that previous publications on ELF did not report findings drawn from academic contexts (e.g. Lesznyák 2002 reports a study of topic management in ELF communication, and draws on data collected from interactions among NNESs at an international students' conference). My point is that it was only with Mauranen (2003) that ELFA became identified as a bona fide domain of research within the broader field of ELF studies. Or, to put it another way, the fact that ELFA is central rather than peripheral or incidental to studies of ELF in academic contexts can probably be dated from Mauranen's (2003) article.

14 It may be helpful to remind readers that I am using the acronym ELFA to refer both to the *Corpus of English as a Lingua Franca in Academic Settings* and to *academic ELF in general*. Although this has the potential for confusion, on the one hand, ELFA is, to my mind, preferable to other possible acronyms for academic ELF such as EALF and AELF, and on the other hand, it would be unacceptable to adapt the acronym of Mauranen's corpus project for the purposes of this book. However, it should always be clear from the context which of the two ELFAs I am referring to, and where there is any risk of confusing readers, I refer to ELFA in general as 'academic ELF'.

15 As an external examiner of PhD candidates, I have started checking the respective university's website, and (regardless of their geographical setting) if they proclaim themselves to be 'international' or 'global', ignore all intelligible non-native English in the thesis, and add the following to my examiner's report: "Note that my policy in assessing work in universities that present themselves as international is to request revisions only where an item is potentially unintelligible to an international readership, not merely where something differs from native English". I hope it will not be long before many others follow suit.

4

RESEARCHING ENGLISH LANGUAGE POLICIES AND PRACTICES IN INTERNATIONAL UNIVERSITIES

Chapter Four introduces three research-based chapters. Chapters Five and Six range across universities in four macro regions, East/South-East Asia,[1] Latin America, Mainland Europe, and three Anglophone countries, as well as Anglophone branch (or 'offshore') campuses in two countries. They explore, by means of a study of university websites in Chapter Five, and an open-ended questionnaire administered to academic staff in Chapter Six, notions of what it means to HE institutions and their staff, English-language-wise, to be an 'international' university and what they do English-language-wise in respect of their proclaimed international status. Chapter Seven, by contrast, focuses on a single institution in an Anglophone region, the UK, in order to investigate in depth, through unstructured interviews, how international students themselves experience and orient to their institution's English language policies and practices.

My overall aims in conducting the research reported in the next three chapters were threefold. Firstly, I wished to examine current academic English language policies in HE around the world in relation to the extent of their stated and implicit attachment to native English norms, and the ways in which their policies are actualized in their language practices. The research I had conducted for my 2007 book demonstrated a high degree of similarity in the negative perceptions of non-native English by users of English from a range of nationalities and first languages (including English), and I wanted to find out how far the same applied specifically within international HE. Secondly, I aimed to explore in a more nuanced way than has generally been done hitherto how NNES (international and EU) and NES students and staff orient to their institution's English language policies and practices. In this respect, I also wanted, on the one hand, to tease out evidence of any influence of these orientations on NNES students' academic identities and self-esteem, and on the other hand, to explore student and staff perceptions of the effect of policies and practices on students' and staff's intercultural communication skills. Finally, on the basis of all the findings in relation to these aims, I hoped to be in a position to make some recommendations as to what kinds of steps universities could take, should it prove necessary, in order to bring themselves more in line linguistically with their avowed international status.

These aims generated three specific research questions and sub-questions as follows:

1 What are the prevailing academic English language policies and practices of universities around the world that teach partly or entirely in English medium, in respect of native academic English norms?

- To what extent do universities require native academic English norms of their NNES students officially or unofficially, overtly or covertly?
- Are links made explicitly or implicitly between English and/or native English norms and internationalization?
- Are there any signs of differences across macro regions/countries and/or disciplines and/or branch and locally run universities?
- Is there any evidence of a shift in the direction of acceptance of non-native and/or hybrid forms of English to reflect the sociolinguistic reality of the contemporary use of English around the world?

2 What are academic staff's dominant beliefs about non-native (academic) English?

- Do they broadly perceive non-native (academic) English as unacceptable, needing to be tolerated (up to a point?), or legitimate?
- If there are any substantial differences in dominant beliefs, are there signs that these differences relate to region, and/or L1 (first language), and/or discipline?

3 What are the perceived effects of current English language policies and practices on international (including EU) and home students?

- How are the linguistic expectations of and requirements made of NNES students by their institution and teachers perceived by the students themselves, and by staff?
- What effects, if any, are the institution's policies/practices, and staff and NES students' orientations to English, perceived to have on international students' academic identities and self-esteem?
- What effects, if any, are the institution's policies and practices considered to have on NES students' intercultural communication skills?
- Is there any evidence that staff and students at English-medium universities in Anglophone contexts have less positive orientations towards non-native English than their counterparts in non-Anglophone contexts (including branch universities) or vice versa?

The primary research carried out to answer each question is shown in Table 4.1 below.

The project as a whole used entirely qualitative methods of data collection and analysis, and as is already clear, even in its slimmed down version, was multi-method in approach. For while mixed methods research entails the integration of

TABLE 4.1 Research questions and datasets

Research question	Principal dataset[1]
1 What are the prevailing academic English language policies and practices of universities around the world that teach partly or entirely in English medium, in respect of any stated or implicit attachment to native academic English norms?	Study of a selection of university websites in East/South-East Asia, Latin America, Mainland Europe, Anglophone countries, and Anglophone branch universities that teach content courses entirely or partly in English medium.
2 What are academic staff's dominant beliefs about non-native (academic) English?	Open-ended questionnaire study administered to university staff.
3 What are the perceived effects of current English language policies and practices on international, EU, and home students?	Unstructured interviews with international (including EU) students.

Note
1 Other datasets also informed the answers to the questions 1, 2, and 3. In particular, responses to parts of the questionnaire contributed to research questions 1 and 3, while points made in the interviews informed research question 2.

qualitative and quantitative methods within a single study (e.g. Cresswell 2011, Dörnyei 2007, Hashemi 2012), multi-method research involves the use of different methods within qualitative or quantitative research. Indeed, as Denzin and Lincoln point out, "qualitative research is inherently multimethod in focus", using multiple methods "in an attempt to secure an in-depth understanding of the phenomenon in question" (2011: 5). On the basis that "[o]bjective reality can never be captured", they see multi-method research, or 'triangulation', as "an alternative to validation … a strategy that adds rigor, breadth, complexity, richness, and depth to any inquiry" (ibid.). In line with Ellingson (2009), however, they prefer to conceive of qualitative inquiry as a crystal with its multiple lenses, rather than a triangle with its three sides: "in the crystallization process, the writer tells the same tale from different points of view" (ibid.).[2] And as Ricento (2006b) points out, such an approach is particularly important in language policy research, which "requires an understanding and use of multiple methods in exploring important questions about language status, language identity, language use, and other topics that fall within the purview of research" (p. 129). Presenting the same story from different points of view is precisely what the research in this book endeavours to do in telling the 'university English tale' from the perspectives of international and home students, staff, and management.

Chapters Five and Six, which primarily address the first two research questions, are concerned with the extent to which internationalization as a concept has been linked to and had an impact on (academic) English language policies and practices across the international university sector[3] around the world: what these universities actually do top-down in their written and unwritten rules and practices in respect of English language, the extent to which this does or does not give them some kind of international flavour, and how far and in what ways their policies and practices are perceived, engaged with, and/or contested by their staff. The website study enabled me to discover what kinds of things universities are saying (and not saying) publicly about their English language policies and practices and how they are saying them. This includes what is implicit rather than stated, or what Shohamy describes as 'mechanisms' (2006: 52 ff., and see the next section below). Meanwhile, the open-ended questionnaire study elicited much further information, supplementing the website data by filling gaps and indicating disparities between stated policy and real-life practice, as well as providing staff orientations to what is and is not happening language-wise in English-medium education internationally.

Overall, then, the research reported in Chapters Five and Six provides a global overview of international universities' English language policies and practices, and of how these are perceived by the academic staff involved. This is not to suggest that the findings presented in these chapters provide a full picture, let alone to claim that they are generalizable. Even if it had been feasible for me to study a still larger number of university websites and explore the thoughts of more academic staff, there would still have been a degree of variation among them that no website study or questionnaire, however open-ended, could hope to capture. Rather, the findings of these two chapters identify a number of key regularities in English language policies and practices and orientations to them across the sampling, as well as differences, some of which will require investigating in further research. At a time when the number of international students around the world is rising dramatically (see Hughes 2008, OECD 2010, Ryan 2013, and Chapter One above), and hand-in-hand with this, the teaching of university courses in English medium is becoming increasingly commonplace, it is crucial that all of us involved in HE, whoever we are and wherever we are, develop a greater capacity to understand what is (and is not) involved English language-wise in our own and the wider context. It is my hope that the findings of the next three chapters will make a small but meaningful contribution to the process.

We move on now to consider the way in which language policy is conceptualized in this research in relation to previous work on language policy.

The English language policy–ideology interface

Language policy has traditionally been seen as relating to top-down language planning, and more specifically to the development and maintenance of standard language, that is, the particular language (in a multilingual society) or particular version of a language (in a monolingual society) that is to be considered as having the highest status. Haugen (1966) suggested that the process involved four stages: the selection of the language or variety that is to serve the high-status function, that is, the 'norm' (also known as 'status planning', Kloss 1969), its codification in reference works such as grammars and dictionaries (or 'corpus planning', ibid.), its elaboration to render it capable of serving the full range of uses in the society in question (e.g. in science, literature, government, law, and the like), and its acceptance by the target population.

Language, of course, is not as simple and straightforward as the conceptualization of language-policy-as-language-planning suggests, as it omits both the covert ideological processes involved and the choices that language users make in practice. And while Haugen's 'elaboration' stage entails continued modification in line with societal developments, all four stages tend to be interpreted as discrete and complete. This leads, in turn, to the impression that language norms are fixed, rather than dynamic and changing over time through contact among users of a language. This is undoubtedly how many traditionalists see it in respect of English, leading in turn to their antipathy towards ELF, as was discussed in Chapter Two. And it is not only the general English-speaking population that tends to think like this. As Milroy (2001) argues, "(t)his is a view held by people in many walks of life, including plumbers, politicians and professors of literature. It is believed that if the canonical variety is not universally supported and protected, the language will inevitably decline and decay" (p. 537). Blommaert (2006: 245) likewise points out that many linguists and sociolinguists even today "assume the existence of bounded, rule-governed, and reified 'languages' as their units of study" (as an example, see Chapter Two for comments on ELF by Trudgill, himself a professor of sociolinguistics rather than a plumber or politician).

Turning to my own study, while I was interested in finding out about university English language policies from a language planning perspective, I was still more interested in exploring the ideologies[4] that underpin these policies, as well as what the various 'players' think of the policies, what in their view "counts as *legitimate* knowledge in the domain of language" in respect of university English (Milani and Johnson 2010: 5; their italics), and what people (both students and staff) actually do. Thus, for my purposes Spolsky's (2004) conceptualization of language policy as comprising three interrelated components – practice, beliefs, and management – provided a particularly helpful framework (and see Cots 2013, who also uses Spolsky's framework in his study of EMI at the University of Lleida in Catalonia). Spolsky describes his three components as follows:

> Language *practices* are the observable behaviors and choices – what people actually do. They are the linguistic features chosen, the variety of language used. They constitute policy to the extent that they are regular and predictable ... in one sense, this is the 'real' policy although participants may be reluctant to admit it ... The second important component of language policy is made up of *beliefs* about language, sometimes called an ideology. The beliefs that are most significant to language policy and management are the values or statuses assigned to named languages, varieties, and features ... The status of a variant or variety derives from how many people use it and the importance of the users, and the social and economic benefits a speaker can expect by using it ... The third component of policy is language *management*, the explicit and observable effort by someone or some group that has or claims authority over the participants in the domain to modify their practices or beliefs.
>
> *(2009: 4, his italics; see also Spolsky 2004, 2012)*

As Spolsky points out, his 'management' component is traditionally known as 'language planning'. However, he favours the term 'management' to describe the "efforts by some members of a speech community who have or believe they have authority over other members to modify their language practice, such as by forcing or encouraging them to use a different variety or even a different variant" (2012: 5). But as Spolsky adds, "just as speed limits do not guarantee that all cars abide by them, so a language law does not guarantee observance" (ibid.). Hence, it is crucial to explore not only the policy statements themselves (along with covert unstated policies), but also their underlying ideologies, and actual language practices.

Two of Spolsky's original three components, language management and beliefs about language, have recently been linked to the work of Ball (1993), who explores "two very different conceptualisations of policy ... **policy as text and policy as discourse**" (Ball 1993: 10; his emphasis). In discussing policy as text, Ball describes policies as "textual interventions put into practice", which "pose problems to their subjects" and "create circumstances in which the range of options available in deciding what to do are narrowed or changed" (p. 12). Policy as discourse, on the other hand, involves "what can be said, and thought, but also ... who can speak, when, where and with what authority" (p. 14).

Looking at language policy specifically, Bonacina-Pugh links the conceptualization of policy as text to Spolsky's component 'language management', pointing out that according to the notion of policy as text, language choice is influenced by "an authoritative statement (either verbal or written) of what should be done" (2012: 215). She goes on to note, "this conceptualisation of language policy was widely used in the 'traditional approach' to language policy research, when scholars were primarily concerned with language planning issues arising in post-colonial countries". Their assumption was that "language diversity was a problem and that it could be solved through language policy and planning" (ibid.).

The assumption of 'diversity-as-problem' haunts orientations towards non-native English to this day, particularly in respect of non-native uses of English, and "[p]urist doctrines of linguistic correctness [still] close off non-native sources of innovation" (Woolard and Schieffelin 1994: 64). And yet, writing about post-modernism in language policy, Pennycook (2006: 67) observes, quoting Hopper, if we view systematicity as "an illusion produced by the partial settling or sedimentation of frequently used forms into temporary subsystems", then the notion of English as a fixed code becomes simplistic. Instead, as Ricento argues, it is "more appropriate (and accurate) to discuss 'Englishes' as hybrids reflecting complex processes of borrowing, mixing, and styling with other language varieties (or discourses)" (2006a: 4). One therefore needs to ask who is being served by the continued insistence on seeing English as a fixed code ('standard' English), and what kinds of unequal power relations are resulting from this insistence in high-stakes settings, in this case, universities.

Bonacina-Pugh's second link is between what Ball (1993: 10) calls "policy as discourse" and Spolsky's component 'beliefs about language'. She points out that according to the notion of policy as discourse, language choice is influenced by people's beliefs and ideologies (Bonacina-Pugh 2012: 215) or, "put simply ... what speakers think should be done" (Spolsky 2004: 14). Bonacina-Pugh adds that this conceptualization underpins the critical approach to language policy (cf. Tollefson 2006). This approach sees language policy and planning as "ideological processes which contribute to maintaining unequal power relationships between majority and minority language groups", and that aim "to identify the ideologies and discourses that influence policy texts and language practices" (Bonacina-Pugh 2012: 215, citing Tollefson 2002 as an example of the approach).

Oddly, despite their relationship of unequal power English-language-wise with native speakers of English, NNESs are not in reality a 'minority' group at all, but form the vast majority of the world's English users (on a global ratio of four or five NNESs to one NES). This is even the case when international and EU students attend universities in Anglophone countries, where they constitute anything from a sizeable minority to a very large majority on any given programme of study. And yet the prevailing beliefs and ideologies about NNESs' use of English position them in the same unequal way vis-à-vis NESs as genuine minority language groups are positioned in relation to genuine majorities (which is not to suggest that I support the existence of unequal power relations in *any* language situation). In the university context this generally means that NNESs' use of English, where it differs from native English, is seen as a problem in need of remediation (see Chapter Three), and at best tolerated but not condoned (see, e.g., the discussion of my questionnaire findings in Chapter Six for staff views; McKenzie under submission, for NES student views; and Chapter Seven for NNES students' comments on this state of affairs). Henderson (2011) therefore argues in respect of UK universities that while NNES students "are the agonistic 'foreign element' that legitimise an institutional claim to be international in a local context ... the validity of their different Englishes" is not "formally acknowledged within curricular practices such as assessment criteria". Thus, "we are dealing with ... an ideological positioning of Anglo-English as a dominant form" (p. 282; and see Chapter Seven for further discussion of language ideology in UK HE).

Shohamy (2006) likewise draws on Spolsky's (2004) framework for her expanded view of language policy that links to language ideology. She describes the framework as "the foundation for the introduction of the concept of mechanisms, or policy devices, as means through which policies are introduced and incorporate the hidden agendas of language policy" (p. 52). Mechanisms, Shohamy notes, are "overt and covert devices that are used as the means for affecting, creating, and perpetuating de facto language policies" (p. 54), and within Spolsky's three-component framework they "lie at the heart of the battle between ideology and practice" (ibid.). Real language policy, she argues, "is executed through a variety of mechanisms that determine de facto practices" (ibid.), and hence these mechanisms need to be examined. Her full "List of mechanisms between ideology and practice" consists of: Rules and regulations, Language education, Language tests, Language in public space, and Ideology, myths, and propaganda coercion" (p. 58). Of these, the first three are particularly relevant to the present focus on English language policy in HE, and are therefore discussed further in relation to my website study findings in the next chapter.

Woolard (2005) identifies two ideologies that also have particular relevance for the study of English language policy in HE: 'authenticity' and 'anonymity'. The ideology of 'authenticity', she explains, "locates the value of a language in its relationship to a particular community" such that "a speech variety must be perceived as deeply rooted in social and geographic territory to have value … must be very much 'from somewhere' in speakers' consciousness, and thus its meaning is profoundly local" (p. 2). The result is that "[t]o profit, one must *sound* like that kind of person who is valued as natural and authentic, must capture the tones and nuances". Thus, "within this logic, the acquisition of a second language can seem to necessitate the loss of a first. A speaker can't risk that the traces of a first language will spoil the claim to a new and valued identity, and so eschews that language" (p. 3). This is, of course what is behind the notion – and practice – of 'accent reduction' in the US (see, e.g., Lippi-Green 2011). At a more covert level, I would argue, it is also behind the notion – and practice – where it exists of NNESs in HE being required to conform to the academic English norms of one or other of two local academic communities, British or North American English.

Woolard's ideology of anonymity, by contrast, concerns the way in which "hegemonic languages in modern society often rest their authority on a conception of anonymity" (op.cit.: 5). According to this notion, a dominant language gains authority from "sounding like it is from 'nowhere'" (ibid.). Speakers are "supposed to *sound* like an Everyman, using a common, unmarked standard public language", such public languages being "open and available to all in a society if only, as Michael Silverstein (1996) reminds us, we are good enough and smart enough to avail ourselves of them" (ibid.; Woolard's italics). Hence arises the frequent misconception that native (and 'proficient' non-native) English has 'no accent'. Hence, also, the derogatory way in which NNESs' English is at risk of being described where it diverges from 'native-like' use. This is at least in part because, as Woolard points out, citing Bourdieu (e.g. 1991), "[t]he concept of misrecognition tells us that the standard isn't *really* everybody's language and that it really does belong to specific "someones" more than to others" (2005: 8). Thus, NESs with certain ('standard') ways of using English (primarily the 'standard' Englishes of North America and the UK) can safely diverge from each others' varieties without arousing negative views of their English. NNESs, on the other hand, often cannot.

The ideologies of authenticity and anonymity, despite their apparently opposite orientations, come together in a way that has a doubly pernicious effect on non-native English users. For while the ideology of authenticity identifies certain local (native) varieties of English as the only genuine and valued ones, the ideology of anonymity presents these same local (native) varieties as unmarked and universal. Thus, although English is often said to be an international language, *the* global lingua franca, it is only internationally acceptable if it is used in accordance with the marked, but supposedly unmarked, preferences of selected members of two national NES groups. A major question for my research, then, was how far this is the case in universities that teach in English medium.

The ideology of authenticity shares similarities with what has been called a 'monoglot' ideology (Silverstein 1996, in Blommaert 2006). As Blommaert explains, this ideology "rests on an ideologically configured belief that a society is *in effect* monolingual – that monolingualism is a fact and not an ideological perception – coupled with a denial of practices that point towards factual multilingualism and linguistic diversity" (2006: 244–45; his italics). Thus, the fiction of 'one nation one language', itself deriving from the eighteenth century notion of the nation-state, is preserved and, along with it, in respect of English, the fiction of two 'authentic' monoglot varieties. This leads to a failure "to see the fine shades of identity often articulated not by one monoglot 'language', but by delicate and moment-to-moment evolving variation between *varieties* of language" (ibid.; his italics). And as Ricento (2006a, 2006c) points out, the idea of the nation-state, and with it that of monolingualism (and mono-varietalism) is not adequate – if it ever was – in a world characterized by globalization, transnationalism, and mobility (see also Wright 2012 for further discussion of these issues).

The problem for the vast majority of English users (i.e. Expanding Circle users of ELF) is that despite centuries of colonialism and post-colonialism, and the emergence of established 'new' Englishes in parts of the Outer Circle, the monoglot ideology, along with the other language ideologies discussed above, still persists in respect of their English use. There is thus a mismatch between the kinds of English that are actually practised by these ELF speakers, including in international HE, that is, L1-influenced ELF, and the policies that stipulate how they should be practised, that is, native-like English, typically North American or British.

From the above discussion, it will be clear how intricately language policy is bound up with language ideology, and how both are enacted (as well as resisted) in language practices, or what Spolsky calls the 'real' language policy (see above, p. 75). For as Ricento (2006a) notes, language ideologies "have real effects on language policies and practices, and delimit to a large extent what is and is not possible in the realm of language planning [or, in Spolsky's framework, 'language management'] and policy-making" (p. 9).

I referred earlier in the chapter to *the* critical approach to language policy. In fact, as Tollefson (2006: 42) points out, in language policy research, "the term 'critical' has three interrelated meanings: (1) it refers to work that is critical of traditional, mainstream approaches to language policy research; (2) it includes research that is aimed at social change; and (3) it refers to research that is influenced by critical theory". In respect of his third meaning, Tollefson goes on to discuss the work of thinkers such as Bourdieu, Foucault, Gramsci, and Habermas, and the practical aim of their work "to uncover systems of exploitation, particularly those hidden by ideology and to find ways to overcome that exploitation" (pp. 43–44). The research presented in the next three chapters is critical in all three of Tollefson's senses: firstly, all ELF research is, by definition, premised on the inadequacy of "traditional mainstream approaches"; secondly, one of my aims is to stimulate change, in so far as it is needed, in the ways English and its users are regarded and treated in HE; and thirdly, I hope the book will uncover both the ideology underlying current English language policies and practices in HE, and, more specifically, the exploitation (unwitting perhaps) of international students in many, if not all, Anglophone institutions.

Notes

1 Three East/South-East Asian postcolonial countries, Hong Kong, Malaysia, and Singapore, were included in the research for Chapters Four and Five. However, the other countries explored in these two chapters do not have a history of Anglophone colonization. This is because a number of factors beyond the scope of this book are involved in the Asian and African postcolonial settings, such as their lengthy history of L2 English language use, their much longer practice of teaching in English medium, and the existence in several cases of established local English norms. This is not to suggest that the use (or not) of EMI in these regions is uncomplicated. See, in particular, Tollefson and Tsui's (2004) edited volume for a range of discussions about EMI in postcolonial states. These discussions, though, pre-date the recent rapid acceleration of EMI, including the setting up of (Anglophone) branch universities, across the non-postcolonial East/South-East Asian states over the past ten years, and even more recently, across some parts of the Middle East.
2 See also Richards (2003: 251), who argues "[t]he problem with triangulation is that it suggests a rather mechanical approach".
3 The term 'international university sector' refers to all those universities that present themselves as 'international' regardless of either the ideological underpinnings of their internationalism, or of how and to what extent they translate it into policy and practice. My only other criteria were that they take international students and teach at least some of their content courses in English medium. This was not because it is my view that 'international' equates with 'English', but because my research purpose was to explore English policies and practices in HE, and it would therefore have been pointless to look at universities that conducted no teaching in English.
4 I understand language ideology, in line with Woolard and Schieffelin (1994), as "a mediating link between social structures and forms of talk" (p. 56). Woolard and Schieffelin also note "a basic division in studies of ideology ... between neutral and critical values of the term" (p. 57). They point out that a "critical stance often characterizes studies of language politics and of language and social class" (ibid.) and go on themselves to discuss language policy from a critical ideological perspective.

5

HOW INTERNATIONAL UNIVERSITIES ORIENT TO ENGLISH ON THEIR WEBSITES

The study of university websites was carried out in order to investigate the first of my three research questions, that is, 'what are the prevailing academic English language policies and practices of universities around the world that teach partly or entirely in English medium, in respect of any stated or implicit attachment to native academic English norms?' (see Chapter Four, p. 72 for the sub-questions). I wanted to find out the extent to which a sample of EMI and partially EMI universities around the world require native-like norms of academic English of their NNES students (whether stated explicitly on their websites or implied in the kinds of discourses used), and to explore the ideology underlying any such requirements, particularly in terms of conceptual links between 'international' and 'English'.

Despite the role of marketing/branding staff and webmasters in designing their institution's website, because of each website's crucial place as the institution's 'global face', I assumed that most of the substantive content, especially anything relating to policy found in mission statements, 'about university X' texts, messages from the president/vice chancellor/head of faculty, and so on, as well as anything relating specifically to language requirements, would be under the ultimate control of senior management and faculty. Thus, any findings relating to English language policies and practices were likely to reflect thinking (or lack of it) about English language issues at senior university level. This would then constitute 'language management' in Spolsky's sense (see Chapter Four), with its potential for those in authority to "influence speakers to modify their practice or belief" (2009: 6), in the HE case by, for example, influencing prospective students to learn the kind of English that will enable them to pass an institution's English language entry examination.

Collecting the website data

The websites were selected by my research assistant, Sonia Moran Panero and me from various sources, in particular, the '4 International Colleges & Universities' search engine.[1] This covers North America, Latin America, Europe, Africa, Asia, and Oceana, and provides links to all major HE institutions in the countries within each macro region. Its use of the term 'international', however, merely indicates that the search engine covers HE institutions around the world. It was therefore necessary for us take an initial look at each website we had selected on the basis that the institution is likely to offer EMI, regardless of whether or not the institution describes itself as 'international' (or 'global'), in order to find out whether it does indeed take international students and conduct some or all of its teaching in English medium. Only then could a decision be made as to whether to include the university in the study or eliminate it.[2] In other cases, it was possible to 'short-circuit' the process with the help of websites that provide information specifically on universities offering EMI courses. In the case of Japan, the Global 30 project website[3] provides a list of universities which, by definition, offer degree programmes in English medium. And in the case of Malaysia, South Korea, Sweden, Thailand, and Turkey, personal contacts were able to narrow our search still further by providing lists of EMI institutions in their own countries, while Moran Panero's knowledge of Mexican HE enabled her to make an informed selection there.

As a result, data was collected from 60 university websites in all, across various countries within East/South-East Asia, Latin America, and Mainland Europe, as well as three Anglophone countries (the US, the UK, and Australia), and five US and UK branch universities.[4] While this was a rather large sample to analyse, it was necessary given my interest in finding out whether particular discourses are dominant across the (global) board. The countries and numbers of institutions accessed (in parentheses) were as follows:

There is obviously quite a disparity in the numbers of institutions in the various macro regions. This relates to EMI potential rather than to the current situation. For while there is undoubtedly more EMI currently taking place in university programmes and courses across Mainland Europe than East Asia,[5] the sheer number of HE institutions in China and Japan, and the drive towards internationalization in these and other East Asian countries such as South Korea, mean that the EMI landscape is changing fast. China is of particular interest in this respect. According to the Chinese Ministry of Education, Chinese universities are increasingly using English as a medium of instruction: in 2011 there were 290,000 international students studying in Chinese universities (around two-thirds of them from elsewhere in Asia, although some were studying Mandarin rather than for degrees). The aim is to attract 500,000 international students by 2020 (see: http://www.moe.gov.cn/publicfiles/business/htmlfiles/moe/s5987/201202/13117.htm).

Interestingly, more Chinese university staff were willing to respond to my questionnaire (see Chapter Six) than those at universities in any other country, which could be indicative of their greater interest in the issues involved in EMI. At any rate, it seemed to me that China could, before long, be in a position – and maybe have the desire – to exert a substantial influence on English in HE around the world.

TABLE 5.1 Countries in the university website study

Macro regions	Countries
East Asia[1] (total 26)	Cambodia (2)
	China (9)
	Japan (6)
	Malaysia (2)
	South Korea (5)
	Thailand (2)
Mainland Europe (total 16)	Belgium (1)
	Croatia (1)
	Finland (1)
	Germany (2)
	Hungary (1)
	Netherlands (1)
	Poland (2)
	Spain (3)
	Sweden (2)
	Turkey[2] (2)
Latin America (total 6)	Argentina (2)
	Brazil (2)
	Chile (1)
	Mexico (1)
Anglophone (total 7)	Australia (2)
	UK (2)
	US (3)
Anglophone branch (total 5)	UK (2)
	US (3)

Notes
1 From now on I use the term 'East Asia' more broadly to include the countries of South-East Asia.
2 I have included Turkey in Europe. Some might have chosen to put it into a separate Middle East, West Asian, or Eurasian category.

On the other hand, while the Anglophone countries currently have, by default, the largest number of English medium universities and highest recruitment of international students, their share of the international student market is likely to drop over the next few years on account of factors such as visa problems (particularly in the UK, where, as I write, an irresponsible government is using international students to reduce overall immigration figures for political ends) and high fees, as well as the increasing availability of EMI universities at, or nearer, home. And against this backdrop, the kinds of issues raised in the interviews reported in Chapter Seven by international students in the UK may, if not urgently addressed, soon start to act as a further deterrent.

Once it was evident that a given university had sufficient EMI for it to qualify for the purposes of this study, data collection from its website began. We aimed to spend approximately two hours exploring each website. In practice, however, the material was sometimes too dense and layered to be covered effectively in this relatively short time, and it had to be extended to enable us to access all the relevant linked material, such as programme documents, entry forms, videos of classes, and the like. Specifically, we collected the following kinds of content information, where available, from each of the institutions:

- the institution's stated/implied conceptualization of 'international' HE
- the institution's stated/implied approach to 'EMI'
- range of courses/subjects/levels offered in EMI
- language requirements (entrance/exit examinations, mandatory language courses, differentiation between groups in terms of requirements)
- type of EAP support offered, if any
- teaching staff on EMI courses (local/non-local, NES/NNES)
- resources used on EMI courses (based on Anglophone or own)
- visuals (videos, photos, logos, images, graphs, hyperlinks, typography, etc.)
- testimonials, discussion boards, interactive features
- other (anything of interest and relevance not covered by the above).

The information, once collected, was analysed as described below in order to identify each university's orientation to English and any areas of commonality across institutions, as well as any intriguing differences relating to macro region and/or country (including differences between institutions that are locally run and those that are branches of Anglophone universities). A systematic examination of similarities and differences across disciplines was beyond the scope of the website study, although where interesting points relating to individual disciplines emerged, these are mentioned.

Analysing the website data

The primary analytic tool that I used was discourse analysis. For this, I drew on social constructionist approaches: critical discourse analysis's orientation to discourse as ideological, political, and power-related (e.g. Fairclough 2010), discursive (social) psychology's focus on how reality is constructed in talk and texts in the execution of tasks (e.g. Potter and Edwards 2001), and the "key assumptions" of all such approaches: "A critical stance to taken-for-granted knowledge", "Historical and cultural specificity", "Knowledge is sustained by social processes", and "Knowledge and social action go together" (Burr 2003: 2–5, from Gergen 1985; and see Jørgensen and Phillips 2002 on multiperspectivalism).

Discourse analysis is a tool that Saarinen and Nikula (2013) also found effective in their analysis of EMI policy on four Finnish HE institutions' websites in helping them "to come to an understanding of how the policy setting for English-medium instruction is constructed in Finnish higher education" (p. 146). In their study, discourse analysis revealed, for example, an implicit link between 'globalization' and 'English', and the extent to which the phrase 'foreign language' is merely a euphemism for 'English'. I was interested in finding out the degree to which such phenomena are prevalent among EMI-practising institutions more widely around the world. I was equally interested in carrying out what Pauwels (2012) describes as a "negative analysis", by attending to items that seem to be "meaningfully absent" (p. 253), and which "exactly by their absence seem to become significant" (p. 256). As Saarinen and Nikula (op.cit.), citing Blommaert (2010), argue in this respect, it is important to "to be observant to absence of references to language use and learning because it may also be indexical of ideologies".

Pauwels (op.cit.) presents a "multimodal framework for analysing websites from both a medium-specific and socio-cultural perspective" (p. 247). His six-phased framework comprises "a structured repository of potential cultural signifiers" and "a plan of attack, a methodology for moving from the general/salient/quantitative to the specific/implicit/qualitative and from monomodal to multimodal analysis" (p. 251). Thus, Pauwels observes, it has the potential to help those researching websites "make more and better use of the many layers of potential meaning that reside in the rich multimodal nature of websites" (p. 247). The breadth and level of detail involved in Pauwels's framework meant that it was way beyond the scope of my own website analysis. However, I took certain aspects of it into account, particularly in respect of his phase 2 (present and absent features and topics), phase 3 (potential meanings inherent in verbal, typographic, and layout/design signifiers and in absent features identified in phase 2), and phase 4 ("embedded goals and purposes, only some of which are explicitly stated", p. 257).

Another factor I took into account was the importance of exploring both the local and the global, and the interplay between them. For, as Pauwels (ibid.) notes, the internet is "not simply a data repository' but "a highly hybrid multi-authored cultural meeting place" that "can be considered a cultural agent in its own right, exemplifying processes of globalization and glocalization in an unparalleled manner" (p. 260). To this, Androutsopoulos (2010) adds the process of "localization", which he describes as "a discourse process by which globally available media content is modified in a (more or less salient) local manner, involving some linguistic transformation to a local code and an orientation to a specific audience, defined by means of language choice" (p. 205).

Pauwels's and Androutsopoulos's observations highlight the need to consider the extent to which universities retain some kind of local flavour when their primary aim is to demonstrate their 'global' credentials, so as to attract students from around the world. Greenall (2012) did precisely this in exploring the bilingual website of the Norwegian University of Science and Technology (NTNU). The English version of NTNU's website is directed at recruiting international students, while its Norwegian version is aimed at the local students. Greenall comes to the conclusion that the international version, although likely to be perceived by prospective international students as a direct translation of the Norwegian, deliberately avoids providing "a faithful portrayal of the University and the cultural context it is situated in" (p. 75). Rather, it prefers to present the University as "internationalized, Englishized, globalized" (p. 84) and to demonstrate its success "in mastering the new, 'universal' culture and language" (ibid.). In my own website analysis below,

I likewise consider the extent to which this phenomenon appears (or not) to be repeated across EMI universities in other countries as I explore the ways in which English language policy is constructed, and the stated/unstated ideologies that appear to inform it.[6]

Finally, I bore in mind that an analysis of websites needs to consider their multimodal nature. While a full analysis of presentational aspects was beyond the scope of this study, these visual (and auditory) aspects could not be ignored altogether, in particular, their interface with the textual information, such as the extent to which they support or contradict it, and their positioning in relation to it. For as Johnson, Milani, and Upton (2010) point out, websites are designed to draw attention to particular material, with positioning decisions being especially crucial for home pages, since these are normally the first to be accessed.

In this respect, I found Knox (2007) useful. This is a revised version of Kress and van Leeuwen's (2006) proposal of three main dimensions according to which websites can be analysed. In Knox's (2007) version, the categories are as follows. Firstly, 'MacroTheme-Rheme' on account of the "particular significance [afforded] to the top-left corner of the screen immediately below the browser window" which "constitutes *the* guaranteed viewing area on any computer screen and is therefore a strategic location which is most often employed for foregrounding of, say, the corporate identity" (Johnson et al. 2010: 231; their italics). Secondly, a 'head-tail' dimension. This relates to the need to scroll downwards or sideways so as to view an entire text, and thus, "the key distinction becomes that of 'first screen' versus 'remainder' of a webpage" and "the hierarchy of information is typically indexed according to a continuum of 'diminishing salience'. That is, the longer it takes to reach the information in question, the lesser its overall importance" (p. 230; their italics). The final category is 'primary-secondary' because "unlike in other visual media, particular significance tends to be accorded to the *central* column ... whilst less important information ... is generally located in the left- or right-hand columns" (ibid.; their italics).

Knox's (2007) proposals seemed to me to make good practical common sense for the purposes of my website study. I therefore made use of them to analyse the positioning of visual and textual items on the 60 university websites where it seemed to have the potential to provide a further layer of evidence for my interpretation. In practice, this primarily involved factors such as ease of access from the L1 home page to the English language version and from there to material for prospective international students, as well as the positioning and content of visual and textual items on the home page.

While I began the website study with an open mind, in line with the case studies reported in Doiz, Lasagabaster, and Sierra (2013a), I expected my analysis to identify both common ground and local distinctiveness in orientations to EMI policy and practice across the institutions in the study. For on the one hand, Doiz et al. found that "many commonalities" emerged among institutions across four continents (2013b: 213). But on the other hand, the authors also observe that "[e]very context has its own characteristics" (p. 219), an observation that for website analysis has potential connections with Androutsopoulos's point about "localiza-tion", and indicates the need for "studies rooted in each context", with each institution conducting its own research (Doiz et al.: ibid.).

On a more practical level, while I explored each of the 60 websites system-atically in respect of the various factors described above, space constraints inevitably meant being selective in reporting my analysis. Even so, I took account of Jørgensen and Phillips's suggestion that to be valid, the analysis should be "solid", "comprehensive", and "transparent" (2002: 173), and a substantial amount of data is therefore provided to support the analysis. Because of their heavier representation in the study, the analysis of the East Asian websites is presented at greater length than that of websites of the other regions. In addition, the nine Chinese websites are analysed separately from the other 17, partly to demonstrate how I approached the analysis in the first instance (including, where relevant, at the national level), and partly to provide a convenient basis for comparison and contrast with the content of the other websites.

I began by examining the selected websites within each macro region[7] starting with East Asia, then Mainland Europe and Latin America. Finally, I moved on to the Anglophone and Anglophone branch university websites. The analysis and discussion therefore follows this pattern, while the final part of the chapter draws together the findings across the macro regions and explores their main areas of commonality and difference in relation to Shohamy's 'mechanisms' (see p. 77) and the research questions.

East Asian websites

This section begins with an analysis of the nine Chinese websites,[8] followed by those from the other five East Asian countries.[9]

As with all the websites produced in languages other than English, the first thing I investigated on the Chinese websites was how obvious the link to the English language version was on the original-language home page (henceforth HP). And in all but one case, there is a conspicuous 'English' link along the top of the HP, usually on the far right hand side, but twice on the far left hand side (Fudan Uni-versity and Beijing Normal University), and once in a band across the middle of the photograph occupying the entire first window (Shanghai International Studies University). When foreign (i.e. non-Chinese) languages other than English are also available, English is first-named. Only in one instance (Shantou University) is the link not immediately obvious as a result of being positioned lower down the HP beneath a large photograph, although still in the first screen. But even this link took me only a few extra seconds to locate. In other words, it seems that easy access to an English version is seen as a priority by all the institutions studied, and most of all by Fudan and Beijing Normal according to Knox's MacroTheme-Rheme dimension (see p. 86).

All nine sites also have a substantial visual element, in particular making copious use of photographs. Each has a large photograph or series of alternating photographs, most occupying the left-hand half (or more) of the English HP immediately below the browser. In most cases, these photographs contain a strong Chinese flavour showing for example, scenes from campus life, Chinese landscapes, and Chinese culture. Where people appear, most or all are ethnic Chinese and other East Asians. In one instance only (Shanghai International Studies University, or SISU) do the HP photographs in the English version feature Caucasians, with one photograph foregrounding a Caucasian student and another a Caucasian lecturer. Though in both cases there are Asian students in the background, and views of the campus buildings appear in other photographs in the set.

The strong focus on Chinese/Asian visual material in conjunction with the prioritizing of the English language version of the websites constitutes an interesting juxtaposition of localization and globalization, one that occurs again at the content and textual levels, as well as in the embedded points of view. On the other hand, it is obvious, even to someone who cannot read Chinese, that the Chinese versions contain an even greater visual element promoting Chinese culture. For example, SISU's Chinese HP features a link to photographs and a text about the launch of its Confucius Institute at the University of Szeged in Hungary, whereas this material does not appear in the English version.

Next we turn to the main content categories and topics, which corresponds to Pauwels's (2012) phase 2 present and absent features and topics (see p. 85). There is a remarkable degree of similarity across all nine in terms of what is present and absent. What is present above all is an emphasis on 'internationalization'. All nine focus on this in various easily accessible places, from their 'About us' pages and Presidents' statements to their programme and course descriptions. There is a particularly strong emphasis on international teaching/research partnerships, cooperation, and exchange programmes with 'foreign' or 'international' institutions (of which the majority are Anglophone and mainland European), and on the presence on campus of 'international experts' and/or the 'international experience' of their local staff.

As far as entry to these institutions is concerned, the recurrent theme is the need for international students for whom English is not the native language to have achieved certain TOEFL or IELTS scores and in some cases to pass an English language examination on arrival, such as Beihang's English Level Test. Meanwhile, Chinese students, too, have to pass an English language test (as part of the Gao Kao) not only for entry to most of these universities, but also in order to graduate from them (e.g. TEM, the Test for English Majors and CET, the College English Test for non-English majors).

Many of the websites also recommend that international students should take classes in basic Mandarin Chinese, and in a number of cases this is a programme requirement. For example, Shanghai University requires students on its EMI masters programmes in International Trade and Business Administration to master Mandarin and produce a 1500 word abstract of their dissertation in the language. Some also require international students to demonstrate their competence in Mandarin by passing the HSK test (Hanyu Shuiping Kaoshi), a Chinese proficiency test. But language-wise, the primary emphasis on these websites is on proof of English language competence, even in institutions where Chinese, too, is required.

On the other hand, as with the visual material, there is again a strong Chinese cultural element recorded in the textual material even though this appears not to equal that on the Chinese language version. For example, several of the websites refer, if briefly, to their establishment of Confucius Institutes in other countries, and/or to their desire to spread knowledge of China around the world. For example, SISU's mission includes the wish to "introduce the world to China and present China globally". Several also refer to the availability for international students of introductions to Chinese cultural events, such as visits to historical and cultural sites, and to classes in Chinese music, calligraphy, painting, Tai Chi, and the like. And as well as promoting Chinese culture, the majority refer to their wish, as Guangdong University put it, to nurture on-campus culture "diversity" and "flexibility" or, in SISU's words, to "embrace the diversity of cultures". Again, then, we see the juxtaposition of the Chinese local with the English (mainly Anglophone) global, as well as a general sense of cultural openness.

By contrast, there is not much reference to any kind of English language support (e.g. EAP classes) for international students. The School of English for Specific Purposes at Beijing Foreign Studies University (BFSU) provides compulsory English courses to foreign language non-English majors. Shantou offers English classes in its English Language Center, and Shanghai includes a course on communication skills in its (English taught) Chinese Business Programme, including a focus on the skills of listening, reading, writing, and the use of "language appropriate for tutorial situations". But these apart, I could not locate any other information on offers of EAP or general English support, only of classes in Chinese. This is not to say that such support does not exist, but if it does, then it is not easily accessible. Likewise, there is a general lack of information clarifying whether EMI programmes/courses are taught entirely in English, or partly in Chinese.

Turning to the discourses in which this content is expressed (corresponding to Pauwels's phase 3), one of the most noticeable aspects of all the Chinese websites is their repetition of the word 'international'. To take just one institution, Beijing International Studies University (BISU), to illustrate this point, there are references to "international exchanges", the aim to turn students into "internationally-minded professionals", the importance of "international cooperation", links to "international institutions", BISU's holding of "first-class international academic conferences", and the description of BISU as "a truly international university", to give but a few examples from the website. The other eight Chinese websites in the study are similar in this respect.

However, when it comes to what they actually mean by 'international', the situation is by no means straightforward. I mentioned earlier that Saarinen and Nikula (2013) found in their Finnish website study an implicit conceptualizing of 'globalization' and 'foreign language' as 'English'. This is not true to the same extent in the Chinese websites on account of the latters' orientation to their own language and culture. In other words, these Chinese institutions seem to see internationalization or globalization (they use 'international' and 'global' inter-changeably) as more of a two-way process. Their juxtaposition of discourses of both Anglicization and Sinicization indicate a view of it as involving not only the introduction of Anglophone academic mores into China, but also the reverse; or, as they put it, for them to become "well known throughout the world" (Beihang), to "enter the global spotlight" (Shantou), and to leave "their footprints all over the world" (SISU). From the fact that these institutions promote Chinese on their websites (not only in their visuals relating to Chinese culture, but also in terms of their Chinese language offerings), and from their establishment of Confucius Insti-tutes in universities around the world (including Anglophone settings), it seems that they do not conceive globalization to be as exclusively bound up with English as the Finnish institutions in Saarinen and Nikula's study do. And it also seems from their many references to international cooperation with mainland European universities, that they may see 'foreign' language as bound up to an extent with 'western' language rather than exclusively with English (although whether their communications with mainland Europe take place primarily in Chinese, German, French, and so on, or via interpreters, or, indeed, in English, is an empirical question).

Despite this, English nevertheless has a strong presence on the websites, and is clearly, for now at least, these institutions' main language of international activity on campus. The question, then, is what *kind* of English do they mean? This brings us to the embedded points of view (Pauwels's phase 4) and especially what seems to be taken for granted by the institutions. The crucial point here is that nowhere is there any overt reference to the kind of English that is appropriate (even when the term 'appropriate' is actually used, as in the blurb quoted earlier about Shanghai's course in communication skills). Instead, readers of these websites are left to infer what is meant by descriptors such as "good command of English" and the like.

Regardless of references to "diversity", "flexibility" (SISU), an emphasis on "successful communication" rather than "high exam results" (BFSU), and so on, there are nevertheless various signs that good English is perceived as native English. It is implicit, for instance, in the English language entry tests that international students are required to pass, predominant among which are the American–English oriented TOEFL, and the British English–oriented IELTS. It is again implicit in the fact that prospective students for whom English is the mother tongue are not required to pass an English language entry test, the assumption being that they already speak and write the kind of academic English that is acceptable. Another sign is the use of native English speakers on auditory material. For example, BFSU has a promotional video on its English HP. And although the video's visuals focus primarily on Chinese content, the accompanying voiceover is delivered by a native speaker of American English rather than by an L1 Chinese speaker (another instance of the juxtaposition I mentioned above). The movie on Fudan's Interna-tional Summer School webpage is also heavily oriented to Chinese visual content alongside mostly American English speech, although this time there are also examples of other kinds of Englishes, including Chinese, among the student speakers who provide the voiceover.

Further evidence that native English is taken for granted as the acceptable norm is the native English-normative focus of any English language teaching on offer, such as in Shantou's English Language Center, on Shanghai's communication skills course, and in the content of BFSU's BA in English and Intercultural Studies, which includes English phonetics, listening, reading, writing, and public speaking as well as courses on America and Europe. BFSU is also the founder (in 1979) of FLTRP (Foreign Language Teaching and Research Press), which publishes ELT course books such as *Speak Up*, *English Conversation*, *Practical Presentations*, and *One World English*. And from the brief blurbs available on the FLTRP website (e.g *One World English* is described as containing "[a] collection of everyday English conversations", and *Practical Presentations* as containing "[a]bundant everyday English conversation"), it seems that these books interpret authentic English as native English. And since this view of English seems to be taken for granted on all the websites, what is therefore missing is any discussion of the possibility that there are other legitimate kinds of English than American or British.[10]

We turn now to the other East Asian websites. The analysis focuses specifically on the following sub-set of features and issues that were outlined in the first section of the chapter:

- ease of access to the English HP and to material for prospective international students
- positioning of visual material on the English HP, type of content (global/local/global-hybrid), and relationship with textual material
- degree of emphasis on the international nature of the institution (e.g. the importance it attaches to its international student/staff composition and to its exchange/cooperation with universities in other countries)
- amount of focus on 'internationalization' and/or 'globalization' and what they seem to mean to institutions (beyond the practicalities in the previous point)
- overt and covert links between international(ization) and the English language in references to English language tests and English language proficiency in general
- meaningful absences especially in relation to the kind of English seen as appropriate for an international university and to languages other than English.

The 17 websites from these other five East Asian countries have a lot in common both visually and textually with those from China, as well as some interesting differences. As with the Chinese websites, in all cases the other 17 English HPs are easily accessed from the local versions of their websites. And in seven cases (the two Cambodian universities, the two Malaysian universities, the Universities of Tokyo and Osaka in Japan, and Mahidol University in Thailand), the link from the 4icu search engine opens directly onto their English HP rather than, as with all nine Chinese websites, onto the L1 version.

These 17 English language HPs, like the Chinese ones, have one large visual or a series of alternating visuals, mostly photographs, occupying much of their first screen. However, unlike the Chinese websites, many of these are exclusively or mostly academic related rather than focusing on local culture. For example, all the Japanese HPs show university buildings and scenes from academic life. The same is true of all but one of the South Korean HPs, the exception being Seoul National University, which features a photograph of a taekwondo class. Underneath the photograph is the caption "Leading the Way. Seoul National University. The *National* University" (my italics). This is interesting given SNU's otherwise strongly international focus and status (e.g. it was ranked 59 in the 2012 Times Higher Education World Rankings). It also provides an intriguing contrast with the International Islamic University of Malaya's HP, whose photographs feature local students and staff, the women all in Islamic dress, along with the caption "IIUM aspires to become the premier *global* Islamic university" (my italics).

As the IIUM HP, with its combination of local and global features, demonstrates, these other East Asian websites are not entirely devoid of local cultural elements on their English HP first screens. Nevertheless, whereas the Chinese website visuals are strong on local cultural features, the other five countries' websites reveal more hybridity. The University of Malaya, for example, shows photographs of campus life as well as Asian pottery, and an advert for an "Ancient Chinese Padlocks Exhibition ... in conjunction with Cheng Kung University Museum Taiwan". Mahidol includes in its alternating HP photographs a local flower, "Kan phai Mahidol, the symbolic plant of Mahidol University". And Paññāsāstra's HP includes in the first screen a large announcement giving condolences to the royal family on the death of the "King Father of Cambodia". It seems, then, that some of these institutions want to present themselves as local and global at one and the same time, a point that Dankook University's 'About Dankook' section on its website makes explicit at the textual level in stating:

> We are aiming to establish the prestige of Dankook around the world by securing our image as both a *regionally oriented* university through services and cooperation with communities and a *globally oriented* university by setting up a global network through international exchange and cooperation. [My italics.]

However, unlike the Chinese websites, there is rarely any emphasis on the local language, including in its video link, which features a majority of Koreans/East Asians, whose activities are described in an American English voiceover.

Moreover, where there is a local focus, it is more often on academic matters such as high profile speeches by the university's president and the academic achievements of its staff. This is particularly so among the Japanese websites. For example, Kyoto has a large photograph of Shinya Yamanaka, a member of their staff who was awarded the 2012 Nobel prize. And while visual Japanese cultural material is not entirely absent from the English versions of their HPs, it tends to be presented in ways that do not prioritize it. For example, the University of Tokyo's main HP photograph of Koishikawa Botanical Gardens is featured as part of its Graduate School of Science rather than as a focal feature in itself. Alternatively, the cultural material, like the examples above, may have a hybrid nature. For example, an 'about Waseda' video linked to its English HP presents a few examples of Japanese culture among the mainly academic content, but these are described in a native (or native-like) American English voiceover. Chulalongkorn University's introductory video likewise presents (a small amount of) Thai cultural material in an American English voiceover. As we saw earlier, the same is true of the BFSU and Fudan website videos, but in China's case, the local cultural element is stronger overall, and less 'diluted' by Anglophone features and other non-local material. And although the Chinese websites contain textual references to notions such as flexibility and diversity, there is less visual support for these than there is on most of the other East Asian websites.

In general the people appearing on the 17 HPs and their linked visuals are a mix of Asian and Caucasian, although on some HPs (e.g. Dankook, IIUM, Mahidol, and Paññāsāstra) there are only Asians. But it is the Japanese visuals that present their institutions in the most multicultural light of all, with photographs focusing on students, researchers, and alumni from a wide range of different ethnic backgrounds. In fact, much of the Japanese visual (and some auditory) material is multicultural. Kyoto University, for instance, has a linked 'movie' that presents the university's history, research, and exchange student life, and shows students from a range of national backgrounds, although, like the Waseda video, its voiceover is provided by a native (or nativelike) English speaker. Osaka has a similar introductory video that shows local and campus scenes and presents international students from several different countries (only one of which is Anglophone). But this time, the students offer, in their L1-accented English, their views of the university, as also do two Japanese and one British member of staff.

On the other hand, while most of the 17 sites project their institutions as being, or planning to become, multicultural in terms of their personnel, this relates primarily to students. By contrast, where lecturers are featured prominently in visual material, these are more likely to be Caucasian, with local and other non-Caucasian staff tending to appear only as names in programme staff lists or to be shown in photographs, but at several removes from the HP. For example, Korea University's HP has five photographs featuring Asian and Caucasian students, but the only lecturer featured is Caucasian. Meanwhile, the Royal University of Phnom Penh shows an Asian research student among its alternating HP photographs, whereas staff appear in the (less accessible) programme webpages, and then only in staff lists or occasionally in minuscule photographs. And even in these tiny photographs, students are featured more often, while western staff are as likely to be shown as local ones. The Chemistry Department, for example, has just one photograph showing local staff (the Rector and Dean opening a workshop), followed by one of a visiting Swedish academic, "Mr Michael Strandell, analytical chemist from Stockholm University, [who] made one of his frequent visits to the chemistry department".

Japan again provides a noteworthy exception, with the six Japanese websites featuring more Japanese than Anglophone or other western teaching staff. Osaka, for example, provides two linked videos from its international chemistry and physics courses. One of these presents two sample chemistry classes, one given by a NES, the other by a German L1 speaker, while the students again come from various international backgrounds. The other video presents Osaka's International Physics Course (IPC). This features a Japanese professor of physics who in his talk emphasizes the international nature of the course. To demonstrate his point, he introduces four international graduate students and their Italian lecturer, Luca, all of whom are heard speaking in their L1-accented English.

These 17 East Asian websites' visual/video primary focus on features relating to the institutions themselves and their academic profiles rather than to local culture is carried through to their textual contents. Here, despite their visual emphasis on academic multiculturalism and willingness to showcase NNES students, when it comes to the English language, things are rather different. Most notably, these institutions share with the Chinese ones discussed earlier the assumption that English language proficiency means native English (American or British). This is demonstrated by the fact that in all these institutions, NNES students are required to achieve certain scores on international (Anglophone) English language entry tests, especially IELTS and TOEFL. And sometimes, as in China, English language test scores are also required of prospective home students even though they will not be studying in English medium.

The same assumption shows up again in the use of native English in the written and spoken texts on these sites (with Osaka being a rare example of the extensive use of non-native spoken English). I have already mentioned the native English accents on Kyoto's and Waseda's video voiceovers. The same Waseda webpage includes the written testimonials of several students from a range of (mostly non-Anglophone) countries such as the Czech Republic, Indonesia, Poland, South Korea, and Canada. However, each is written in the same kind of English: standard native. And again, the majority of these Cambodian, Japanese, Malaysian, South Korean, and Thai websites include an easily accessed address or 'message' from their institution's president in which internationalization, diversity, multiculturalism, and the like usually figure prominently, but which again is written in native or near-native English.

On the other hand, despite the evident concern over NNES students' English language proficiency, as with the Chinese websites, there is little evidence of academic English language support. This is not to say that such support does not exist, only that if it does, then for some reason, many of these institutions are not concerned to highlight the fact by making it easily accessible. One notable exception is Dankook University in South Korea. The 'International' link on its English HP leads swiftly to its international programmes, among which is an International Summer School which includes an "English Village" described as follows:

> English Village is a community at Dankook University designed to simulate an *English immersion environment.* Invited *native English speaking students*

(interns) will teach and lead small groups of DKU students English conversation sessions daily. [My italics.]

Evidently it is seen by Dankook's senior management as important for the institution's students to learn to emulate native English conversation, regardless of the fact that, both currently and in future, they are more likely to interact in multicultural rather than native English communities (see Chapter One, p. 7 on English villages).

The Royal University of Phnom Penh website is also untypical in terms of having easily accessible information about EAP support, with a link from its English HP to 'Centers' and thence to the comprehensive website of its English Language Support Unit. The other Cambodian university in the study, Paññāsāstra, also offers English language support. However, the route to information is more circuitous as well as less obvious, since it is on the university's 'Institute of Foreign Languages' webpage. This webpage briefly lists a handful of other languages that are taught, then goes on to say "[p]resently, English language training has been the main focus", and to provide extensive details of its English language courses. It also states that the institute "utilizes only the *most appropriate* language tools and teaching materials" (my italics), which turn out to be various Anglophone text books and courses such as CUP's *New Interchange* series. In a similar vein, although Waseda has no obvious English language support, in his 'welcome', the Dean of Waseda's School of International Liberal Studies states that students' English ability will improve by around 40 points on TOEFL iBT over the course of the programme. Similarly, the website of the English for Liberal Arts programme at the International Christian University describes their emphasis on students not only studying in English but also improving their English, and refers to courses on how to give presentations, listen to lectures, build vocabulary, on academic writing, and suchlike. Given their TOEFL entry requirement, this presumably again means native academic English.

The evidence so far, then, is that not only is English prioritized over other foreign languages in these 17 institutions, with even less emphasis on promoting the local language than is the case in the Chinese institutions, but also that for all of them, as for the latter, English means native English. And this seems to be the case regardless of how multicultural an institution is or wishes to become. Thus, while the Chinese institutions appear keen to promote their local culture and language while the Japanese and most others seem keener on projecting their multiculturalism, both approaches lead to a major contradiction in terms of English. That is, neither allows for the possibility that other kinds of English than its native versions may be more appropriate for a multicultural international university, despite the fact that other kinds of (non-native) Englishes are by default the norm on these campuses.

A closer examination of the discourses used on the websites provides deeper insights into these institutions' orientations to English in relation both to the internationalization of HE in general, and to themselves as providers of international HE. As with the Chinese websites, internationalization and/or globalization (the two tend to be used interchangeably) are recurrent themes. The question, then, is what do these themes mean language-wise? As we saw above, the visual and auditory features such as adverts and video presentations, and topics such as the institutions' language requirements, make an explicit link between internationalization and the use of English. The same link is also made in the discourses used, particularly in the Presidents' messages. The University of Tokyo's President, for example, explains in his message that they are in the process of establishing more degrees "taught in *English* ... to respond to the *internationalization* of our campuses and create an *optimal* environment for international students" (my italics), thus presenting English as the "optimal" international language. Paññāsāstra's President states the following in his message:

> In order to integrate our graduates into *international community*, we use *English as our primary vehicle of learning*. Indeed, we are the only university in Cambodia, and one of a select few in Southeast Asia to offer *all instructions in English*. [My italics.]

Now the link is implicit, with the unstated assumption that "international community" equates with an 'English-speaking community', as well as the notion that learning in English gives students an advantage over others, and that the university is better than most others, not only in Cambodia, but in the whole of South-East Asia ("one of a select few"), because it teaches entirely in English.

Such discourses are present throughout the websites on their 'about university X' pages and in their Presidents' messages, speeches, welcomes, and the like, reinforcing the point I made earlier that the orientations found on the websites represent those of senior management and faculty. In these texts as well as in the 'international' sections of the websites, internationalization is often linked explicitly and implicitly to English. Their discourses imply, for example, that EMI programmes have an advantage over those taught in the local language, and that students' resulting proficiency in English will provide them with international skills for their future careers. For instance, the 'About Dongseo' pages of Dongseo's website contains a section with testimonials from international students. One of them, an exchange student from Sakhalin, Russia, says the following:

> *My professor said that I will have a great opportunity to learn about Korea by communicating with students from Korea and from other countries, and this will give me a chance to improve my English*. Another thing that impresses me is that Dongseo University shares some of the same subjects with Sakhalin State University. I think Dongseo University is *a good place to network*. That's because I want to work abroad and have a chance to *make friends from other countries* such as Malaysia and Germany. [My italics.]

Thus, both the student and her professor conflate learning about the local region and networking with people from countries such as South Korea, Malaysia, and

Germany on the one hand, with the English language on the other. They also assume that such communicating in English with people from other L1s will help this Russian student "improve [her] English". From an ELF perspective, this would of course be perfectly true. During her stay in South Korea, she is likely to have improved her ability to understand NNESs from a range of L1 backgrounds, as well as the ability to adjust her own way of speaking so as to accommodate to her largely NNES interlocutors. But judging from Dongseo's English language support programme, tucked away in its 'Global Division' webpages, and called 'Global English Program' it is evident that the student's professor had native (American) English in mind:

> The Global English Program offers *intensive ESL/EFL education* both to specially selected Korean students wishing to improve their *international communication abilities* and to international students wishing to enter a specialized degree but lacking the required level of English proficiency.
>
> Through its one-year curriculum, students take 25 hours of intensive English classes. All four language skills are emphasized: speaking, listening, reading and writing. Each class is *taught by a native English-speaking professor*, with special opportunities for enhancing *international understanding* being offered through the Global Colloquiums. [My italics.]

In other words, "global" and "international" are perceived as equating not only with English, but also with "ESL/EFL", that is, native English. And to make sure this point is clear, we are told that all the teachers are NESs.

These kinds of discourses are common right across the 17 East Asian websites, reinforcing the point I made earlier (p. 96) that when these institutions require students to achieve scores in tests such as TOEFL and IELTS in order to gain university entry, it is not English proficiency as such that they require, but *native-like* English proficiency, and thus that it is native(-like) proficiency per se that they see as international. Dongseo again makes this point explicit: "where applicants are entering departments requiring English proficiency, such as the Department of *International* Studies and those of the *Global* Division" (my italics) they need TOEFL 550, IELTS 5.5, as well as TEPS 550 (Test of English Proficiency, a test based entirely on native English developed at SNU for South Korean students). With few exceptions, the only applicants exempt from English language entry tests are NESs. It seems, then, that when these institutions refer to their current or planned diversity, flexibility, multiculturalism, and the like, this has no implications for the kind of English they condone, let alone for the use of the local and/or other languages on campus. They wish for a diverse multicultural population in respect of their students and, sometimes, their staff. But they do not actively welcome diversity in the use of English, even though, as I pointed out above, this is what they get in practice.

Not surprisingly, in view of the above factors, I could find no reference in any of these websites to the notion that non-native Englishes have (or should have) any validity, let alone any kind of status. In other words, while native English has a strong presence on the websites, non-native English is what Pauwels (2012) calls "meaningfully absent". It is as if it has not occurred to those in charge of their institutions' websites, NNESs themselves, that there is any alternative. Native English is simply taken as a given. Even in Chukyo University, with its Graduate School of World Englishes, there is no perceptible difference, even in the Graduate School itself, whose programme in World Englishes is partnered, with no sense of incongruity, by one in British and American Culture Studies, one of whose aims is "an outstanding command of English" (implicitly American or British).

The ELF researcher, D'Angelo, himself a member of Chukyo's staff, argues (2011) that it is the content of the message rather than the medium in which it is expressed that matters most, and that "the exchange of ideas and viewpoints by intelligent people from different cultures and L1 backgrounds around the world" is the principal benefit of internationalized HE. But judging from the East Asian websites in my study, his own institution's included, this perspective is not widely shared across East Asian HE. For while internationalization (or globalization) appears from these websites to involve the kind of multilingual/multicultural "exchange" to which D'Angelo refers, it also appears to be seen as intrinsically bound up with native English. Hence internationalization seems to be interpreted in essence by these institutions' managements as meaning the recruiting of international students and setting up of collaborations with universities in other countries on the one hand, and improving proficiency in native-like English on the other. For example, in its video (see above, p. 94), Dankook describes four key measures that it is has taken in order to broaden its global vision, of which the first, third, and fourth relate to international recruitment and collaboration, and the second to the expansion of its (native-oriented) English immersion programmes.

Even where there is an occasional willingness to showcase students (and in Osaka's case also teachers) speaking in non-native English accents, when spoken English is the focus (e.g. in references to English speaking/pronunciation courses), the NES is once again the point of reference. Furthermore, as with the Chinese websites the occasional flexibility shown to NNES speech is never carried through to the written medium. Apart from a number of (possibly unintended?) non-native English variants such as countable use of nouns that are uncountable in ENL and different uses of articles, the written texts on these English webpages from Presidents' addresses through to individual programme specifications and student testimonials give the impression of having been either written by or checked by a native/near-native English speaker.

By contrast with their emphasis on English, these websites make scant reference to the local language. Even when international students are required (or at least recommended) to learn the language before or during their studies – which is less often the case than with the Chinese institutions discussed above – little tends to be said about this, and then not in key sections of the websites. Some of the South Korean universities, for instance, recommend that international students should learn some Korean, while the University of Malaya requires all international students to take compulsory Malay and/or English courses for six months if they have not already achieved sufficiently high scores in certain Anglophone examinations. But such references to the local language tend to be neither frequent nor highlighted, and unlike references to English, rarely occur outside lists of programme requirements.

It seems, then, that despite their identical orientation to English, the Chinese institutions have greater confidence in the global value of their own L1 than do the institutions in the other five East Asian countries. This is a point that western, and especially Anglophone, institutions might do well to consider, given China's fast growing profile in international HE and its wish to take Chinese language and culture to the world. A comparable confidence in their own English may not be too far behind, given, especially, the current popularity among Chinese students and academics of researching China (or Chinese) English or, more precisely, 'China (or Chinese) ELF' (Wang 2012). The previous point apart, it seems that all 26 East Asian university websites reveal a strong degree of similarity in their conceptualizations of 'international', seeing it as involving multicultural diversity in terms of the people involved, but uniformity in the kind of (native) English these people need as their lingua franca.

As of yet, the managements of these institutions do not seem to have considered the potential appropriateness let alone legitimacy of their own and other NNESs' Englishes. However, this was once the case in the post-countries of the Outer Circle. And in practice, as with the latter, even in these (mostly) Expanding Circle institutions, the situation on the ground is far more hybrid, or glocal, than the theoretical position suggests. The majority of people involved in international HE are NNESs, and regardless of the desire of the managements of these East Asian institutions for their NNES students and staff to acquire native-like English, this is not going to happen. The question, then, is whether or not the ELF(A) argument will ultimately gain ground in East Asian HE once management become aware of it, and thence be built into official policy, with China perhaps leading the way, or whether their native language ideology is unassailable. For now, though, we turn to the Mainland European institutions.

Mainland European websites

This section covers 16 institutions in ten countries ranging across the extent of Europe.

In order to highlight the key points of similarity to/difference from the East Asian institutions, my analysis and discussion focus on the two interrelated areas that proved the most fruitful (albeit in contradictory ways) in the East Asian website analysis. Firstly, how these institutions orient to English: in particular, what kind(s) of English they prioritize, explicitly or implicitly, and the role of English in relation to that of the local and/or other languages. And secondly, how they perceive/project their international nature: in particular, how far they see it as relating to their use of English (do they make overt/covert links between English and internationalization?), and to their recruitment of overseas students/staff and collaborations with institutions in other countries.

The first thing I noticed was that unlike a substantial minority of the East Asian websites, only two of the 16 Mainland European ones, Groningen in the Netherlands and Jacobs University in Germany, opened directly onto their English HP rather than via a link on the local language HP. Further, in a few cases, the link to the English HP was not obvious (and in one case, trying to access the selected website crashed my computer twice, so I switched to a more computer-friendly institution in the same country). This raised the possibility that the well-documented mainland European antipathy towards English as the lingua franca of the EU, including in HE, rather than a policy of multilingualism (see, e.g., Phillipson 2003, 2009; also House 2003, 2006, and Wright 2009 for counter arguments) would be reflected in these websites. By coincidence, on the same day that I began analysing my mainland European data (18 November 2012), an online article by Hans de Wit of the Università Cattolica del Sacro Cuore in Milan and Amsterdam University of Applied Sciences appeared in *University World News* (no. 248)[11] in which he made the following point:

> When the University of Tokyo announced that, starting this autumn, its first undergraduate degree programmes would be taught entirely in English, this was a major breakthrough for the institution – but did not raise much concern or debate. ... In comparison, when the rector of the Polytechnic University of Milan announced in spring that, as of 2014, all of its graduate programmes would be taught in English, there was widespread protest from politicians, the media and academics. Words such as "illegitimate" and "unconstitutional" were used and the move was seen as "a threat to Italian culture and language". The difference in reaction to the spread of teaching in English in Asia and in Italy is remarkable. In Asia there seems to be a more pragmatic approach to the issue, along the lines of: "English is the current common language of communication in both research and teaching and if we want to stay connected to the rest of the world, we had better make use of that reality".

The question for my analysis of the mainland European websites, then, was whether and if so, how, this European antipathy to EMI is affecting their management's orientation to internationalization in general, and to English in particular.

I began by exploring Groningen and Jacobs Universities' websites, since these are the two that open directly onto their English HPs. Groningen evidently prioritizes prospective international students by placing an icon and link to its international student webpages in the prime top left-hand position under the browser, and alongside it on the right hand side, a blurb emphasizing the University's "international reputation" and the fact that many of their degree programmes are "completely taught in English". I could find no more about EMI, so tried a link provided by Wilkinson (2013: 21) to information on how the university implements its teaching in English, only to be told that access to the page is "forbidden" because I have "insufficient privileges".

Once on the 'prospective international students' webpage the focus shifts away from English and onto Dutch and other languages. Across the width of the top of the page in large red lettering is the heading "University of Groningen offers free Dutch courses to international students". The "more" link from this leads to a webpage explaining the importance they attach to international students being able to communicate in Dutch during their time in the region, adding, though, that "[t]he idea behind this initiative … is to encourage more international students to stay in the Netherlands after graduating and develop their talents here". Lower down the first screen, although far less obvious than the link to information about Dutch courses, is a link to a page on which the website can be read in a range of ten other languages than English or Dutch. At the top of the linked page is the following explanation: "[t]he University of Groningen is a truly international university. This is why we provide a brief introduction about the University in several languages for our (prospective) students, staff, their family and friends."

Language-wise, for Groningen, then, 'international' involves not only English, but also Dutch (most importantly), and to a far lesser extent the non-Dutch NNES students' own L1s. Jakobs University is to some extent similar. In a section 'Why Jacobs?', accessed from the HP, in a section entitled 'We speak your language', information on the University can be accessed in 12 languages via links from 12 national flag icons. A longer blurb in English appears immediately below the flags, and includes various statistics such as that the University hosts 1200 international students from 90 countries, as well as the following about its EMI policy:

> **Full English Language Programs:** Both undergraduate and graduate programs are fully taught in *English*, although Jacobs University is in Germany. The *advantages* are clear. Attending an English-language university right after secondary school provides immediate *opportunities* for students who will enter the increasingly *global* workplace, in any *professional* capacity. [Their bold, my italics.]

An explicit link is thus made between the English language and professional opportunities in the global context. However, this is the only reference to English that I could find on the entire website. There is no mention of it in the 'Welcome from the President', or in the page on 'Jacobs Philosophy' where the emphasis in terms of internationalization is on the University's diversity:

> Jacobs University is one of the most *diverse* universities worldwide. More than 75% of our students come from outside of Germany. This *plurality* allows our community to break down cultural barriers and create a community where no one group constitutes a majority. [My italics.]

We are therefore left to make the assumption that communication across this "diverse" university's community, as with teaching, takes place (largely?) in English.

This is also implicit in their website film, which presents students and staff from a wide range of L1 backgrounds (all but two are NNESs) talking about the University in English. Again, though, the emphasis is on 'diversity', while the prevalence of the English language on campus is not mentioned at all.

Other languages do not feature much either. Unlike Groningen, there is little obvious reference even to German apart from a section on 'Language courses' tucked away in a 'General Requirements' page, which mentions that a variety of free optional German, French, and Spanish courses are offered to non-native speakers. Other than that, I could only find one further reference: on an individual UG programme webpage which states that non-German students have to learn basic German in their first two years, while German students have to learn a foreign language (presumably not English). Language, it seems, is the 'elephant in the room'. It is as if they do not want to draw too much attention to the fact that English, and not German, is their working language and therefore avoid discussion of language as far as possible.

Thus, on the one hand, Jacobs and Groningen Universities both emphasize their international nature on their websites. And on the other hand, both make extensive use of English on campus, and link it, implicitly in Groningen's case, both implicitly and explicitly in Jacobs University's, with internationalization. However, it seems that where English is concerned, they prefer to minimize its presence on their websites whether by highlighting their L1 and other languages (Groningen) or by eschewing high profile references to language altogether (Jacobs).

Many of the other institutions seem to be similar in this respect, although there is something of a dichotomy between the western/northern European universities and those in central and eastern Europe. Continuing with western Europe for the moment, the other German university in the study, Freie Universität Berlin, describes "freedom and internationality" as its "guiding principles". Its linked video emphasizes the university's international profile, drawing attention to its exchange programmes, lecturers from many other countries, and Confucius Institute. The video also features speakers (students and staff) speaking in their own L1s including German, with subtitles in English. Nothing at all is said about English, although an American NES provides the video's narrative throughout, while a second NES translates the words of German speakers (who can sometimes be heard in the background), using idiomatic native English such as "the last straw". The same lack of direct reference to English characterizes the 'International network' page, where there is again an emphasis on international students and collaborations, but nothing about English or, indeed, any other language. Even on the 'Studies and Teaching' page, the focus is on the institution's international nature, but nothing is said about its use of EMI. Again, then, it seems the university seems to want to avoid reference to its lingua franca use of English while implicitly demonstrating that it is present and inextricably bound up with its international identity.

In some cases among these western European institutions, there is more emphasis on the local language(s) than in the German and Dutch institutions that I have just discussed. This is particularly so in the websites of the Belgian and

Spanish universities. In the former case, the University of Ghent, or Universiteit Gent, this is perhaps connected with the political divide between Dutch- and French-speaking Belgians. At any rate, the mission statement makes only one reference to language, which is that "[i]n 1930 Ghent University became the **first Dutch-speaking university** in Belgium" (their emphasis). The remainder of the texts about the University focus on its international nature, for example: "Ghent University is an open, committed and pluralistic university with a broad international perspective", and this sentence occurs verbatim in other parts of the website. Again, on the 'Facts and Figures' page, the focus is on their international credentials, such as the number of non-Belgian students they recruit and their place in various university world rankings. The same is true of the three Spanish institutions. Two of them, Carlos III and Pompeu Fabra, advertise the fact that that they have been granted the title of 'Campus of International Excellence' by the Ministry of Education, and they, as well as Navarra, focus extensively on their international character on their websites, citing the presence of international students and lecturers, partnerships with universities worldwide, and the like as evidence.

When it comes to the medium of instruction, Ghent conducts much of its teaching in the local language, as do the three Spanish institutions. Universidad Carlos III teaches both in Spanish medium and in bilingual[12] Spanish–English programmes, while Universidad de Navarra likewise teaches in both Spanish and English (though is rather vague about what is taught in which). Even though it describes English as its "working language", Pompeu Fabra is most oriented to the region's local languages, as is to be expected of a Catalan university, where additional political factors concerning Catalan/Castilian are likely to be involved just as they may be at the University of Ghent in respect of Dutch/French. In many cases, foreign students at Pompeu Fabra are required to have knowledge of both Catalan and Spanish, and it seems in general, that Catalan is particularly prioritized, with internationalization being seen as an opportunity to internationalize the immediately local language.

On the other hand, Ghent and the three Spanish institutions also all make a point of publicizing the fact that they conduct some of their teaching in English medium. Pompeu Fabra, despite its trilingual policy and concern about Catalan, even includes improving the quality of its EMI in the blurb about its internationalization strategy, while on its 'Education and Study' webpage, Ghent says the following:

> The language of instruction at Ghent University is Dutch. Therefore, all bachelor programmes are taught in Dutch. However, as mentioned below, UGent does offer a whole range of international courses instructed in English. The common language of the doctoral programme is English. *Good language proficiency is absolutely necessary and formally required.* [My italics.]

It is not clear whether the reference to "good language proficiency" means in both Dutch and English, but in terms of its positioning in the text, it seems to refer specifically to the doctoral programme, and therefore to English. The north European websites are again similar in their orientations to internationalization and English. The Swedish (KTH Royal Institute of Technology, and the University of Uppsala) and Finnish (University of Tampere) websites provide plentiful information advertising the institutions' international status and plans, whether in explicit mission statements (e.g. one of Tampere's main aims for 2015 is "to be internationally attractive") and details of their international students and collaborations, or implicitly in films featuring international students and their testimonials. And English always features in some way or other as part of their international credentials and plans. KTH even links 'international' directly with 'English' by having the link from its L1 Swedish HP not to 'English' but to the 'KTH international website', which perhaps reflects a slightly more relaxed attitude to the notion of English as the lingua franca of HE in northern than in western Europe. Uppsala nevertheless makes clear that the local language also plays a key part:

> It is important, in view of the globalised character of the world, that Uppsala University's core identity as a Swedish-language university be fleshed out with significant course and programme offerings in *other languages* ... Researchers and students from other countries are to be provided with opportunities to learn Swedish. [My italics.]

The reference to "other languages" is interesting. As much of the website, especially programme webpages, makes clear, the primary "other" language of the university is English, so it is not clear why there is a reticence to name English at this point. On the one hand it could be because it is taken as a given that 'other' or 'foreign' language equates with English. On the other hand, it could stem from a concern to link the local language, Swedish, to globalization at this point.

When it comes to the *kind* of English they have in mind, there is little ambiguity. The north European universities are no different from any of the others. The two Swedish institutions, for example, refer to the need for students to learn "grammatically correct and idiomatic English" (Uppsala), and for staff to have "a good command of English" (KTH). Terms such as "correct" and "good", however, are rarely defined, and we are left to draw our conclusions as to what is meant by 'good English' by turning to the institutions' formal English language entry requirements. Here, as with the East Asian institutions, the requirements generally involve NNESs' English being assessed in relation to a native English benchmark such as that of TOEFL and IELTS, while now, the CEFR is also often mentioned. The required scores tend to be slightly higher than those in East Asia, with TOEFL 575 being more common than 550, and IELTS 6.5 being the norm, with 7 sometimes specified. Where the CEFR is mentioned, it is often B2 (which equates with IELTS 6.5), although sometimes C1, which is only one stage short of 'native competence' (C2). Other examinations that are frequently mentioned are the Cambridge ESOL and the more recent Pearson Test of English (Academic). In all cases, the optimum level of competence in any one skill is 'nativelike'.

Other clues to the kind of English seen as appropriate in these west and north European institutions are provided by information on their English language teaching materials and approaches. Navarra, for instance, offers general English courses to prepare students for the Cambridge ESOL and TOEFL examinations. Even their EAP courses focus on these, while Pompeu Fabra's EAP courses use CUP and OUP materials, with a focus on being able to "follow and understand extended native speaker speech", on "pronunciation issues", and on familiarizing students with the culture of English-speaking countries. Uppsala's EAP courses, as I have already mentioned, are clearly oriented to native English. This is also demonstrated by the kinds of coursebooks they use, such as Pearson Longman's *Focus on Vocabulary: Mastering the Academic Word List*, and the *Longman Dictionary of Contemporary English*. Ghent by contrast provides little information about its teaching materials and methods. However, it offers courses such as "academic English writing skills", from which I infer that "academic English" means native academic English.

We turn now to central and eastern Europe, and to the six Polish, Hungarian, Croatian, and Turkish institutions. Here, as in all the previous websites examined, there is again an emphasis on internationalization, often given greater prominence than it is in the western and northern European websites, and more likely to be linked to the English language. The slight exception to this is the University of Zagreb in Croatia, though this may be a function of its low-detail website rather than of a lack of interest in promoting its English/EMI credentials. So while it refers to internationalization in respect of its international students and exchanges, and states that programmes are offered in Croatian and English, with a list of EMI programmes, I could find no further mention of English. There did not even seem to be a reference to English language entry requirements, making it unique in this respect among the 60 websites.

The other five central and eastern European websites are more detailed overall, and more informative about the role of English. Poland's University of Łódź website implies a strong link from the start, not only with English, but also with Britain, in that its English version is accessed from the Polish HP by a tab called 'international cooperation' accompanied by a British flag icon. As with the other websites, its emphasis is on factors such as its international students, international atmosphere, cultural diversity, and the association of 'international' with the curriculum. It mentions Polish, English, and French as languages of instruction, though I could find no link to any webpages written in French nor any detailed information about French medium programmes. As is the norm for mainland Europe, it lists TOEFL, IELTS, and Cambridge ESOL examinations in respect of English language entry requirements, demonstrating its orientation towards native, and especially British, English. This is further demonstrated by its offer of an EAP course taught in conjunction with the British Council, and including conversation classes with NESs. There is also a course on "writing an MA thesis in English", which implies that there is only one way to do this.

Warsaw University of Technology (WUT)'s orientation to internationalization is similar. In its linked Studies in English handbook, a section on the 'Internationalisation of WUT' includes the following:

> Having a wide experience in the management of *international exchange pro-grammes* for students, teaching staff and researchers, WUT puts special emphasis on its students' and workers' participation in *international exchange programmes and internships* to make studies at the Warsaw University of Technology *open doors to global labour markets*. [My italics.]

Implicit in this, given that English is the institution's language of international exchange and internships, is that it is English that opens such doors.

The 'Welcome word from the Rector' emphasizes the role of diversity in its internationalization practices:

> We are pleased and proud that many international students from *all parts of the world* come to study at our university … we place great weight on strengthening *international knowledge exchange* and stimulating *understanding, tolerance* and *respect for different ideas and culture*. [My italics.]

Once again, there seems to be an assumption that English is the language in which such knowledge is to be exchanged, given that this Handbook for international students contains over 30 pages on 'Studies in English', just one on 'Studies in Polish', and no reference to teaching in other languages. And in view of the website's strong focus on native English (entry examinations, courses offered, use of NES staff, or, more euphemistically, those with 'international experience'), it seems that the Rector's claim of his institution's "understanding, tolerance and respect for different ideas and culture" does not extend at all to the kind of English preferred on campus.

The Budapest University of Technology website also goes to great lengths to profile its international credentials. Its English language HP begins with a lengthy account of its international role and aims, and its large number of international students and alumni. It goes on immediately to make an explicit connection between its internationalization aims and its use of EMI:

> Major targets are
> – to broaden the *international education programs* of the University,
> – to participate in mobility programs supported by the European Union.
> The University reputation has been growing by the approx. 5000 *international students*, who graduated here. Since the 80's regular full time *programs in English* have been offered in B.Sc, M.Sc. and Ph.D. levels. Additional 3000 *international students* have joined the University programs in mobility schemes for one or two semesters. [My italics.]

As usual, English here means native English exemplified by the English language entry requirements, once again primarily TOEFL, IELTS, and Cambridge ESOL examinations (although the minimum scores required are lower than those of most of the other institutions in the entire study). But it is the Turkish institutions that are the most explicit among the 16 European websites about the perceived links between their internationalization strategy and English. Bilkent University makes a direct link between its international nature and EMI programmes, and the contribution of English to its "truly international perspective". It seems that all its undergraduate and many of its postgraduate programmes are conducted in English, with the usual English language examinations required for entry. All the undergraduate programmes include a course 'English and composition', the aim of which is "to introduce students to an academic approach to *thinking*, reading, speaking and writing" and to "develop the students' *linguistic accuracy* and range in English" (my italics). The implications of this are firstly a belief that academic thinking does not take place in the students' first language, and secondly, that the focus is on native English. This is again implied in the linked video, which includes interviews with staff and students, predominantly NESs. Some of the exchange students interviewed (three from the US, one from France, one from Denmark) praise the fact that their lecturers have studied in the US. The online student testimonials focus mainly on the fact that EMI is offered.

The Middle East Technical University (METU) presents an even stronger perceived link between internationalization and English than does Bilkent (in fact the strongest link of any of the European institutions). Like Bilkent, METU specifies internationalization as one of its main objectives, and emphasizes the part played by EMI in its internationalization strategy. For example, it facilitates their efforts to accommodate international students from nearly 80 different countries across their programmes. Its linked document, 'Middle East Techinical University Strategic Plan 2011–16', contains a substantial amount of information on English and internationalization, more so than on any other of the 60 websites. The document outlines the institutions' major strategies regarding English, which focus heavily on English language proficiency and "increasing student awareness throughout the University regarding the importance of English" in their education and professional lives. Two pages of the document are devoted entirely to this, with emphasis on academic writing, including a course on "Academic writing in *the English language*", speaking skills, and the assessment of these. One main strategy consists of:

> Str 2.2.1 Providing opportunities for students to use the foreign language in *effective communication* both in written and spoken form throughout their education in their departments. [My italics.]

It is evident from other parts of the document and website, such as their English language course content and entry requirements, that "the English language" refers to one of two particular versions of 'the *native* English language', standard British or American English, and that "effective communication" in English involves the use of this version. It seems that it has not occurred to those responsible for the University's strategy that when international students from so many different countries and L1s come together to form a HE community of practice, the optimum way of achieving 'effective communication' in their lingua franca is not likely to be the mimicking of certain versions of English used by certain of its native speakers.

METU is an extreme example, but the orientations to internationalization and English on its website are reflected to a greater or lesser extent on all the mainland European sites. When it comes to English language entry requirements, as with the East Asian institutions, there is little difference English-wise across all 16, regardless of any other differences in orientation to English/internationalization among them. And nowhere is there any suggestion that prospective NES students, too, might need their academic English skills to be assessed. Again, references to other languages tend to be kept to a minimum. It could be argued that this is because it is the English websites that I have explored. But this does not allow for the possibility that potential (or current) international students might prefer to have information provided in languages other than the local one(s) and English, and perhaps to learn or study in them. Nevertheless, the most striking finding is that in all these institutions, it is native-like English that is either explicitly or implicitly prioritized and/or required regardless of the institution's/country's orientation to the local language(s) and to multiculturalism. It seems, then, that whether or not these institutions (and countries) are in favour of English as the lingua franca of HE, for them it must be native English. Their policy makers seem to be completely unaware of the advantages for them and their staff and students, of extending their multicultural credentials to the language in which multicultural exchange takes place both on and off campus, let alone of the arguments coming from ELF(A) research (see, e.g., Cogo and Jenkins 2010, Mauranen 2012, Wright 2009).

Latin American websites

This section provides something of a contrast with the previous two. For one thing, it is rather shorter and less detailed than the previous two. This is partly because there are fewer websites involved (six) as a result of EMI currently being a relatively minor phenomenon in Latin American HE. The choice of suitable websites for the study was therefore heavily restricted. It is also because even those websites that do provide information about EMI, tend to do so in far less detail than the East Asian and mainland European websites explored above. While there is a certain amount information on all six Latin American websites as to how these institutions perceive their international nature, this information tends to be minimal and often of a very practical nature (e.g. internationalization means the number of countries with whom they have exchange agreements). In addition, there is little explicit or implicit information relating to how they orient to English and any perceived links between their internationalization strategy and use of EMI. It seems that they offer English less with any grand internationalization strategy in mind than as a practical solution to the problem of international students not having sufficient knowledge of Spanish or Portuguese to study in it. In fact all but the Mexican website, put more emphasis on the local language than they do on English.

Mexico's Tecnológico de Monterrey (henceforth TDM) is the most explicit about the involvement of English as part of its internationalization project. It aims to be both international and a leading university in Latin America, and claims to incorporate "experiences of internationalization" and "global citizenship" in its educational model. It receives international students from a wide range of countries and offers a variety of subjects in English medium as well as subjects in Spanish, for both international and local students. It explains its rationale as follows:

> Many international students study in Mexico because they want to interact and meet local students, yet *want to participate in classes taught in English because they have not mastered the Spanish language.* At Tecnológico de Monterrey you can attend regular courses taught in English and have the credits applied to your college degree back home.
>
> In addition, local and Latin students also attend these same classes in order to *improve their English skills.* Therefore, you can study in a language you're comfortable with while meeting students from around the globe. Tecnológico de Monterrey offers several options that allow you to take advantage of this opportunity. [My italics.]

In other words, it believes that for the purposes of being international (and despite its local language being a global one), it is necessary for it to teach in English medium. TDM seems also to understand the usefulness of providing students with opportunities for intercultural communication, and sees this as benefiting local students too. As an aside, some Anglophone institutions could learn from this, and start to consider the benefits for home students of integrating with and learning from international students, rather than the current heavy one-way traffic of international students being expected to assimilate to the home culture (see Chapter Seven for further discussion).

The reference to local students improving their English also suggests that it considers English an important international skill for (Mexican) Spanish L1 speakers. On the other hand, there seems to be an assumption that international students will not need to improve their English, perhaps because a TOEFL or IELTS score is a requirement for entry in the first place for NNESs:

> If you decide to take a course instructed in English, but *are not a native English speaker*, you should submit either a TOEFL (Test of English as a Foreign Language) score of at least 550 (213 on the computer-based TOEFL) or a IELTS (International English Language Testing System) score of 6.5 to the International Programs Office.

As in East Asia and mainland Europe, and despite TDM's focus on intercultural communication, it seems to be taken for granted that the kind of English in which this communication, as well as academic work, should take place is *native* English. There also seems to be an assumption that NESs' academic English skills are by definition appropriate for university study.

In spite of the focus on native English and on English as the institution's language of internationalization, even on the English language website there is as much emphasis on Spanish as on English. We learn, for example, that whereas 60 regular courses are offered in English, 3000 are offered in Spanish, and that international students will need advanced Spanish to be eligible. Texts written in Spanish are also included in the reading lists of some of the EMI courses, while the website also offers international students the opportunity to learn about Mexican traditions.

The same combination of internationalization through English and focus on the local language characterizes the other five institutions, although as I mentioned, there is less explicit linking of English with their internationalization strategies. Fundação Armando Álvares Penteado (FAAP), for example, describes itself as an "international institution" because of its partnerships with 40 other countries. And although there are courses offered in English (four in 2012, with six expected in 2013), little information about them is provided on the website, and the main focus is on Portuguese, and the need for international students to take an intensive Portuguese course while they study initially in English medium.

The other Brazilian institution, the University of Fortaleza, likewise provides little information on its EMI courses. Although it refers to "participation in the global arena" as a key concern, it again links this primarily with its agreements with universities in other countries. However, like TDM, it also sees English as a tool for integration between local and international students, and states:

> The demand for courses given in English brings together students from the University of Fortileza and the exchange program. They get to know each other, study together and exchange experiences from all over the world.

What it describes here is an academic ELF community of practice. But as with TDM, while it understands the cultural benefits provided by enabling such communities to exist, it does not make the linguistic leap and consider the implications for the use of English.

The other three Latin American institutions are similar in their orientations to internationalization. The University of Viña del Mar in Chile associates it with belonging to a global network of universities, the "Laureate International Universities", which enables it to send students on exchanges to "renowned international universities" and bring the knowledge thus gained back to Chile. There is little information about English on its website, although the impression it creates is that EMI is offered so as to attract international students who do not have sufficient Spanish to study in Spanish medium. The EMI programme includes the learning of Spanish, while the University as a whole associates globalization with plurilingualism and multiculturalism, and at the time of writing, is promoting French, Mandarin, and Portuguese.

The two Argentinian institutions, the University of Belgrano and Universidad Argentina Austral, have a stronger English focus than the Chilean, though again oriented to native English. This is illustrated, for instance, by the involvement of US lecturers in the subjects to be taught at the University of Belgrano, and more specifically by the "advanced written and spoken English" required for its EMI courses, and the Anglophone-published course literature that predominates on reading lists for these courses, even when the content focus of these course is on Argentina and/or Latin America. On the other hand, much of the teaching takes place in Spanish medium, and Spanish language courses are heavily promoted in the international sections of the website. The same is true of Universidad Argentian Austral, where the main language of instruction is also Spanish, and the fewer EMI courses tend to focus content-wise on Latin America. Internationalization does not figure in its mission statement, though the international section states that the University "aspires to blend the best traditions and experiences of the European and American universities to our context", implying that it sees the inter-nationalization of HE as above all a western/Anglophone phenomenon. And when it comes to English specifically, its entry requirements involve the same Anglo-phone examinations as are required by the vast majority in the sample. However, like TDM, it does not seem to require these for international students, only for home students, for some programmes even if they are not actually studying in English medium.

So on the one hand, most of these Latin American institutions do not make as strong a link on their websites as the other non-Anglophone institutions between internationalization and English, and focus far more on their local languages. But on the other hand, those that do see English as playing some kind of a role in their internationalization strategy are as equally oriented as all the others to native English. And this includes the two institutions that explicitly mention the cultural advantages of bringing together students from different parts of the world, including their own home students. It is not clear how much the difference in orientation between these and the mainland European and East Asian orientations to EMI can be accounted for by the fact that this is far earlier days for EMI in Latin America than in the other two parts of the world, and how far it may also be affected by the fact that Spanish and Portuguese are global languages. In the latter respect, the same is true of Mandarin Chinese, and it is perhaps for this reason that both the Latin American and Chinese websites in general devote more attention to the local language than the other websites do.

Anglophone and Anglophone branch campus websites

By contrast with those of the previous section, the Anglophone websites are far more detailed and explicit about English both in itself and in terms of its role in their internationalization strategies. Not surprisingly, perhaps, their orientation to native English is stronger than that in any of the other three macro regions, and they are particularly explicit on both English language entry requirements and the kinds of English language support on offer to international students. They also go into more detail about who is excluded from their language entry requirements than the non-Anglophone websites do, and in all cases, such exclusions involve the applicants' either being NESs or having received specific parts of their education in English medium in certain types of institutions in "English speaking countries" (e.g. Imperial College London), "a majority native English speaking country" (University of Sheffield), a country where English is "the primary language" (University of Illinois), and the like. By this they generally mean the countries of the Inner Circle, although the UK institutions also accept degrees taken in certain other countries, for example Guyana, South Africa, and the West Indies (Imperial), or those countries within the UK Border Agency's definition (Sheffield). Some institutions also accept grades achieved in English in institutions in certain post-colonial and Expanding Circle countries. For example, the University of Sydney specifies a number of post-colonial countries as well as Denmark, Finland, Germany, the Netherlands, and Sweden.

These Anglophone institutions seem to see internationalization primarily in terms of their own standing in the world, especially their rankings in league tables and international recognition for their research. They also refer to exchange, and particularly research collaboration, with institutions in other countries. However, as contrasted with the non-Anglophone institutions, this generally appears to play a secondary role in their internationalization strategy except where their own branch campuses are involved (see pp. 114–19).

One further international factor these institutions are all keen to emphasize is the diverse composition of their campuses and their positive orientation to this diversity. The University of Illinois, for example, describes itself as "one campus, many voices", while Sydney talks of providing international students with "an environment that values the contribution they can make". But when it comes to the English language in which these international student voices are heard and in which they make their contribution, the websites tell a very different story. That is, the institutions' intercultural stance does not extend in any way to the use of English. The language requirements (IELTS and TOEFL in the main) in all cases make it clear that native English is the benchmark against which NNES students are uniformly measured, with the required scores tending to be a little higher than those of the non-Anglophone universities in the study.

There is also far more detail provided about English language preparation classes for prospective students, and (sometimes mandatory) remedial classes for existing students who do not gain the required minimum score in their English entry test. Some also offer pre-sessional English language programmes, a trend that has escalated dramatically (and lucratively) in the UK in particular over the past 20 or so years. Imperial's English Support Unit, for instance, offers a pre-sessional programme that "aims to equip students with *the academic language skills* typically needed to begin postgraduate research or taught courses in science, medicine or engineering subjects" (my italics). The reference in the 'Key features' of this pro-gramme to the provision of "native speaker contact", along with the institution's native English-oriented language entry requirements, implies that the "academic language skills" to which they refer are, likewise, grounded in native English.

The prioritizing of native English is made more explicit in the two Australian websites. In presenting its EAP offer, Sydney describes its General English course as focusing on developing students' communication skills to live and work in Aus-tralia and *abroad*, and explains that the course is mapped onto the CEFR (therefore by definition assessed according to native English benchmarks). The linked video of their Centre for English Teaching goes on to explain that the Centre's main focus on academic English and Cambridge ESOL exam preparation will help stu-dents to become "world citizens". The University of Queensland's Institute of Continuing and TESOL Education offers similar courses for NNESs for "purposes such as to prepare for the *global* workplace" (my italics). One of these, offered within its 'Go Global English and Internship Programme' in order to "improve your global English communications", is 'Advanced English Communication Skills'. The outcomes for participants are listed as follows:

> Improve their ability to understand *native speakers*
> Increase their vocabulary and knowledge of *common* English phrases
> Refine their ability to use grammar *accurately*
> Improve the *accuracy and fluency* of their pronunciation
> Expand their general knowledge of world issues and current events
> Understand a range of *real-world* listening and reading materials. [My italics.]

Given the university's English language entry requirements and its focus on NNESs' understanding of NESs, we can probably assume that "common English" means 'common in native English', and that "accuracy" and "real-world" also have this in mind. Students' "knowledge of world issues", it seems, needs to be acquired in native English, while to communicate effectively in English, to be prepared for the global workplace, to live and work abroad, and to become a citizen of the world, according to these universities' positions, also require native-like English.

These institutions' positions on English do not even seem to be affected by the presence among their staff of influential scholars working in the field of Global Englishes. I referred earlier to the situation at Chukyo in Japan, where the work of the ELF scholar, D'Angelo, has not impacted on the institution's English language policy. The same is true of some of the Anglophone universities. For example, the scholar Gibson Ferguson states on his staff page at Sheffield University that his main research area is "language policy and planning with a particular focus on the spread of English as a global lingua franca and the linguistic, cultural and socio-political implications", none of which appear to have had any influence on the University's highly native English-oriented entry requirements and English language course content. Again, the presence of both Braj and Yamuna Kachru,[13] two of the world's most famous World Englishes scholars, both Emeritus at Illinois, as well as the renowned World Englishes scholar, Rakesh Bhatt, seems to have had no impact even within the Department of Linguistics to which they are affiliated. Similarly, the presence of the scholar Suresh Canagarajah, widely known for his critiques of Anglophone approaches to academic English, seems not to have affected English language policy in his own institution. Far from it in fact, for the section of the website, 'Programs Supporting International Students' describes its:

> programs to *introduce* international students to academic and social life at Penn State and beyond ... to *familiarize* students with *U.S. customs* and *culture* in addition to the educational system and academic complexities of a *U.S. higher education.* [My italics.]

There is also a Peer Mentor program to support this process, in which "mentors offer advice and insights about *academic, social, and cultural life at Penn State* to help the transition to life in Happy Valley" (my italics). The website may describe the university as "Global Penn State" and discuss the institution's internationalization strategy as focusing on "global engagement". But unlike the Latin American institutions discussed in the previous section, there appears to be no mention of what the international students bring to the University from which the home students (and staff) can learn in order to become more internationally minded themselves. Instead, it seems to require a one-way process of adjustment by the international students. The same is true of California State University LA, which states as the first goal in its mission statement: "We are focused on assisting international students to maintain a legal status and *to adjust to a new life* in the U.S.".

García, Pujol-Ferran, and Reddy (2013: 174) observe in respect of both immigrants and international students in HE in the US that "the language ideologies that valorized English as the language of power and success that were prevalent during colonial times are still very much in vogue today". They go on consider the international student situation by exploring the orientation to academic English in an unnamed 'global' US university, where they find that its academic English course "heavily emphasizes the norms and conventions that are required for reading and writing in Western, academic contexts" (p. 188). As will be clear from the above, this is exactly what I found on the US as well as the UK and Australian websites. It was also the case with the non-Anglophone websites, which indicated a similar predilection for native English. However, whereas non-native English is the norm on non-Anglophone campuses, NESs form the overall majority at Anglophone universities (if by no means on all programmes), and international students are therefore surrounded daily by so-called 'correct' English on campus. In Chapter Seven, we explore the effects of this combination of pressure to 'improve' their English and exposure to an English that they are unlikely ever to 'achieve' on international students' confidence in their English and self-esteem as academics.

We turn now to the five branch universities. The Anglophone branch campus university phenomenon has grown apace over the past few years and continues to do so despite the concerns beginning to be raised over issues such as the costs involved to the 'parent' university, and the possibility that the branches may in future decide to break free and run themselves independently.

I start with the two UK branch campuses, Nottingham–Ningbo (which was also discussed briefly in Chapter One) and Xi'an Jiaotong-Liverpool (XJTLU), as they form an interesting juxtaposition (see Feng 2012 for a detailed comparison of the two). Ningbo's website repeatedly promotes the branch's connection to its British 'base', for example "Study at a UK university in China", "Study in English in China", "Study for a UK university degree in China". XJTLU, on the other hand, explicitly characterizes itself as a "joint venture … an independent Sino–Foreign cooperative university" that "captures the essence of both prestigious parent universities". And while Ningbo emphasizes its Britishness, XJTLU focuses more on its Chineseness. This is immediately apparent from their HPs. Ningbo's is entirely in English apart from a small link to the Chinese language version, and is identical in design to that of the Nottingham UK website. By contrast, XJTLU's has its name written in large Chinese characters in the significant top left corner (see p. 86 above on MacroTheme-Rheme), while the design of its HP as a whole, for example its left-hand menu prioritizing the "Welcome message from the President" and "Mission Statement", more closely resembles the Chinese HPs I discussed earlier than those of either the Liverpool partner or the other Anglophone sites.

The branches' different approaches to their Britishness vs Chineseness carry through into their orientations to internationalization. Ningbo's 'About' link at the far right-hand side of the top of the HP leads to the following statement:

> Internationalisation is at the heart of the development of The University of Nottingham–Ningbo China. Academic staff are recruited from top universities and research institutes *across the world*. By the end of 2011, there were more than 400 teaching and administrative *staff from at least 40 countries* …
>
> Our internationalisation policy also means that students have the opportunity to study at The *University of Nottingham UK* or to go as exchange or study abroad students to study at *other top universities around the world*. [My italics.]

In other words, while internationalization for Ningbo involves staff diversity on campus and links with the world, it is also closely connected to the parent institution in the UK. The website also emphasizes diversity in relation to students. The 'International Context' section of its Teaching and Learning pages says as follows:

> There is an international dimension in all our activity. Welcoming students and staff from across the world to its campuses in the UK and in Malaysia, our teaching promotes *respect for all cultures* and development of the personal *interactions between our students*.
>
> Our courses are *internationally relevant* and provide you with the opportunity to study abroad with one of our many overseas partner institutions

> As an international university we seek to locate our courses in the *global context*. ...
>
> You will learn to find and evaluate information from a wide range of perspectives and be encouraged to build your own views with an awareness of the *wider international picture*. [My italics.]

While the UK link is not excluded, it is no longer the focus, with international-ization in respect of Ningbo's students prioritizing international relevance, vision, and multiculturalism.

XJTLU's orientation to internationalization is focused more on its relevance to China than to its UK partner or the UK as a whole. In this respect it more closely resembles the orientation of the Chinese institutions in the East Asian section above than that of Ningbo and the other branch campuses. XJLTU's HP, as mentioned above, includes a prominently sited link to a Welcome message in which Youmin Xi, the Executive President, states that the University aims to become:

> a research-led international university *in China* and a *Chinese university inter-nationally recognized* for its unique features through capitalising on the advantages of its unique model and global education resources. ...
>
> After a few years of study and training at the University, we are confident our students will be equipped with: *a global vision*, the ability to *compete internationally*, proactive attitudes and the determination to succeed. Students will become *international leading professionals* in technology and management who have an *excellent command of English*. [My italics.]

But when it comes to their orientations to English, there is no perceptible differ-ence. The XJTLU President's reference to the institutions' students' "excellent command of English" in the same breath as his reference to their international standing sets up the expectation that "excellent" equates in his mind with 'native'. And a look at both XJTLU's English language entry requirements (IELTS, TOEFL, and similar) and its English Language Centre webpage demonstrates that the expectation was well founded. The latter explains that:

> A unique *immersion English learning context* awaits students from around China and abroad at XJTLU. Student motivation and confidence is enhanced while studying English language modules delivered by the ELC for the first two years of their degree program. ... .the aim is to ensure that students develop *the study skills and the language proficiency that they need to complete a British degree* and, therefore, we offer specially designed modules focused on English for Academic Purposes (EAP). ... The English modules that students study are part of the programs which have been *validated and accredited by the University of Liverpool* and the ELC is *well supported by the University of Liverpool* when modules are improved or when new modules are developed. [My italics.]

Whereas the focus is on the campus's Chinese context in other respects, as soon as the subject of the English language is broached, the link to the UK campus, and thus to native English, becomes paramount. The same is true, if more to be expected, of Ningbo's stance on English language teaching. For example, the blurb for its Centre for English Language Education's 'Premaster English language programme' includes the following:

> you will need to be able to use English in a wide range of academic situations. On your future course, for example, you will have to read textbooks and journals, listen to lectures in your subject and make notes on what you have read or heard.

What is particularly interesting here is that no account is taken of Ningbo's staff from "at least 40 countries", many of which by definition cannot be English mother tongue countries. In the 'About' section of the website, this is presented as a particularly positive feature. And yet it seems from the focus of Ningbo's various English language programmes as well as its (IELTS and TOEFL) entry requirements, that the goal for its students is to be able to understand lectures from and communicate with NESs only, a point that is emphasized by the first-listed aim of its Pre-sessional course, which is "Introducing you to the academic environment of a *British* university".

The three US branches, Temple and Lakeland in Japan, and State University New York (SUNY) in South Korea are similar in many respects both to the UK branches and to each other. Starting with their orientations to internationalization, all three refer positively to the diverse make up of their campuses. Temple, a branch campus of the Temple University, Philadelphia, but controlling its own campus directly since 1996, talks of its multicultural student body in glowing terms:

> One of TUJ's *greatest assets* is its student body. Students come from approximately 60 countries around the world, including Japan, the United States, East and Southeast Asia, Russia, the Middle East, Africa, Latin America, and Europe. Its *diverse student body* helps make TUJ a rich, *dynamic, and stimulating* institution. [My italics.]

Lakeland makes a similar point:

> Lakeland is a global community, drawing students of varied ages, religious backgrounds, and cultural traditions, from areas around the world, building community out of the *rich diversity of its members*, in a climate of civility, respect, and free expression. [My italics.]

And State University New York (SUNY), South Korea likewise lists diversity as one of its major attractions, pointing out that the branch has over 450,000 students from 160 nations around the world and "offers a vibrant international environment where you can get a truly multicultural perspective", and that its students will graduate "with the cognitive, cross-cultural communicative, linguistic, and professional skills necessary to start a career in the global market". One might assume that "cross-cultural communicative skills" involve the ability to communicate effectively in ELF.

However, when it comes to the English language, as with the UK branches, the situation changes completely. All three require NNES applicants to demonstrate their English language proficiency in line with the main Anglophone examinations, particularly TOEFL and IELTS, although SUNY Korea also accepts proof of achievement on its Intensive English Program (IEP). I was unable to locate any information about this programme on the institution's own website, but found the following SUNY Korea online advert on the ELT Career Portal:

> We are looking for three highly motivated and experienced teachers to join our friendly professional team. We, SUNY Korea provide a pathway to university study in New York State University, U.S.A. Teaching general as well as Academic English to prepare students for direct entry into university is what we do. We cover all the major skills of speaking/listening and reading/writing as part of our program. If this sounds like you, then please read on.

The advert goes on to stipulate that applicants should be NESs, and should have a masters degree or TEFL/TESOL certificate. But there is no mention of language teaching experience.

The other two US branches have an equally native English orientation. Temple Japan's Academic English Program states the following:

> The goals of the AEP are that students will achieve the necessary TOEFL score for admission to the College of Liberal Arts (CLA) or another English-speaking undergraduate program and that they will be equipped with the skills and knowledge needed to do high-quality academic work after university admission.

Its language aims for each of its four programs are therefore all benchmarked against TOEFL scores and all four programs include a component on "TOEFL/grammar" in which students focus on "strategies for success at the test and on discrete points of grammar". On completing the third programme successfully, students will be equipped English-wise to "enter university courses in the United States, the United Kingdom, Canada, or other English-speaking countries, as well as the undergraduate program of TUJ". Unlike SUNY Korea, Temple seems to employ some NNES English language instructors. But apart from instructors from "the US and other parts of the English speaking world", it mentions only those from Japan, and even then emphasizes that its NNES instructors are "highly accomplished fluent users of English".

Lakeland's EAP program is similar in orientation to the other US and UK branches, although in some ways even more extreme. For example, its webpage highlights the fact that it is "An All-English Environment" and makes implicit links between "American, global, and the English language":

> Lakeland is not a Japanese college – it's *an American college*; therefore, students are required to use *only English* in EAP classes. Moreover, the *international atmosphere* at LCJ insures that *the "global language" of English* is being spoken outside the classroom as well. [My italics]

It goes on to point out that all its teachers are NESs, although unlike those in the SUNY Korea advert, it seems that they have teaching experience, both in Japan and in other countries.

It appears, then, that the five branch campuses, regardless of their different 'parent' countries and institutions, and regardless of whether they are branches in the standard sense, or more of a partnership, show little difference from each other in terms of their English language policies and practices and, indeed, little difference from the Anglophone institutions either.

Drawing the website findings together

It is time to make comparisons and contrasts across the macro regions and consider the findings further in terms of their ideological implications. For anyone coming to this from an ELF(A) perspective, the analysis of the 60 websites will probably have made depressing reading. While a general preference for native English, especially in the Anglophone and branch institutions, was to be expected, it turns out to be far more widespread and entrenched than might have been predicted. If these websites are an accurate representation of what happens in practice, there is little sign of any movement in the direction of the internationalization of academic English around the world, and the 'Englishization' of HE is still very much a matter of 'native Englishization'.

The research question relating specifically to the website study asked "what are the prevailing academic English language policies and practices of universities around the world that teach partly or entirely in English medium, in respect of native academic English norms?". The sub-questions focused on 1) the extent to which universities require these norms, whether overtly or covertly, 2) whether links are made between these norms and internationalization, 3) whether there are signs of difference across regions, disciplines, and branches v locally run institutions, and 4) whether there is any sign of a shift towards acceptance of the current sociolinguistic reality of English use. The answers, in a nutshell, are: 1) to a very great extent, 2) yes, 3) very few, and 4) very little if any.

Indeed, the overarching finding is that all 60 institutions across macro, micro, and different-L1 regions as well as disciplines (in so far as I looked at individual disciplines which, as mentioned earlier, I did not do systematically) on the one hand present cultural diversity as a key element of internationalization and of their own internationalization policy and practice, and on the other hand see it as going hand-in-hand not only with English/EMI but with native English. This seems to be so regardless of whether they are keen to promote their own language, as is the case particularly with the Chinese and some Latin American institutions, or whether they have a fundamental dislike of English being the lingua franca of HE, as with some of the mainland European institutions. It is also the case regardless of whether an institution's country is a member of the European Higher Education Area (EHEA), with its concern for multilingualism and the benchmarking of all L2 learning against native norms in line with the CEFR, or a member of ASEAN with its more relaxed orientation to English as its lingua franca. And given that the kinds of orientations to English to which I refer can be found in university presidents' messages, mission statements, blurbs 'about university X', course materials both discipline and ELT/EAP, English language entry requirements, and the like, I believe that they reflect the thinking, or at least the taken-for-granted assumptions about English, of senior university personnel. In terms of the 'management' component of Spolsky's (2004) framework (see Chapter Four), then, if these universities are reasonably typical, we have a situation where prospective and current NNES university students are being influenced on an epic scale to change the way they speak and write English so as to make it more like the English of NES members of the academy.

By contrast, the websites give no indication of valuing the potential contribution of NNES students beyond the rather vague notion that they provide 'diversity' on campus. And there is certainly nothing to indicate that these students are valued in relation to the diversity of their English. Instead, they are portrayed as a homogeneous group ('non-native students', 'international students') and the differences in their L1s, cultural backgrounds, and prior learning experiences ignored, something that Saarinen and Nikula (2013) found likewise in their investigation of four Finnish institutions' websites. At the same time, where EMI is mentioned at all, it tends to be in terms of the advantages[14] it brings to students in relation to their mobility and future 'global' careers on the one hand, and in terms of English language entry requirements for NNESs, and the content of remedial English language courses for those who fail to make the grade on the other. Meanwhile, any problematizing of EMI, including evidence of the awareness of the potential difficulties of studying in an L2, is meaningfully absent.

I referred in the previous chapter to Shohamy's (2006) expanded view of language policy linked to language ideology, and her "list of mechanisms between ideology and practice". I mentioned that three of these mechanisms have particular relevance to my investigation of English language policy in HE, that is, 'Rules and regulations', 'Language education', and 'Language tests'. I now briefly consider my website study findings in relation to each of the three in turn.

Shohamy considers that of all the mechanisms she discusses, "rules and regulations are the most commonly used devices that directly affect and create de facto language practices and thereby turn ideology into practice" (2006: 61). In the context of my findings, the most relevant aspect of this mechanism is standardization, a "device used by central governments to impose and manipulate language behaviour" (p. 63). Shohamy observes that it is particularly important to critique the notion of standardization in the case of languages such as English, given their lingua franca role around the world. She goes on to argue that as English is "the language of many different individuals and communities in different parts of the world, and not the possession of its native speakers" (ibid.), standardization is not a realistic proposition and, citing Pennycook (1994), that any standard devised for the purposes of intercultural communication "is bound to be based on Anglo–American mother tongue norms" (Pennycook 1994: 166). This is precisely what appears to be happening in the case of HE around the world. Whether university management are persuaded by the ideology that equates *standard* English with *native* English, and then make an unsound (and empirically disproven) link between the latter and mutual global *intelligibility*, or whether they have not considered the issues at all and simply taken the 'need' for native English for granted, this is the kind of English they all require and promote. It is of course entirely true that there is a need to ensure a high degree of mutual intercultural intelligibility in international HE. But the findings of ELFA research provide plentiful evidence of more appropriate, equitable, and effective ways of achieving this than resorting to the kinds of English in which the world's minority of NESs communicate among themselves, a point that Shohamy (2013) has more recently made herself in her critique of EMI in HE.

In discussing her 'Language education' mechanism, Shohamy (2006) addresses EMI directly. She points out, citing Auerbach (2000), that even those who are opposed to the US English Only movement nevertheless consider it common sense that English should be the medium of instruction. She goes on to discuss the role of code-switching as a natural practice among bilinguals, arguing that "[i]n this transnational and global world people constantly move back and forth from one entity to another and from one area to another and use different codes and languages within these contexts" (pp. 82–83). And yet the sociolinguistic reality of their mixing is not recognized, let alone legitimized. Shohamy is talking here about immigrants in respect of the dominant language, and particularly immigrants in the US and English. However, what she says resonates strongly with the current situation vis-à-vis global HE, where educational ideologies mean that code-switching and, indeed, any kind of linguistic hybridity used by NNESs, is considered indicative of incorrectness. In other words, the vast NNES majority studying in EMI at universities around the world are seen as making 'errors' whenever they exploit their bilingual resources. Again, ELF(A) research demonstrates that the only error involved is the ideology itself.

The third mechanism relevant to my findings is that of language tests. As was clear throughout the entire chapter, entry tests predicated on native English are the rule in universities in all the regions involved in the study. Shohamy regards language tests as "a powerful device that is imposed by groups in power to affect language practices and criteria of correctness often leading to inclusion and exclusions and to perpetuate ideologies" (2006: 93). The curious thing when it comes to EMI, however, is that in the main, the "groups in power" are themselves NNESs, many of whom probably speak English in ways that are as 'non-native-like' as those of many applicants to their institutions. And yet they still buy into the 'native English = standard English = international intelligibility' ideology, and hence into tests such as TOEFL and IELTS that perpetuate this ideology and, in turn, hold back natural processes of language change (McNamara 2011). Yet, as Shohamy points out, these tests "determine the criteria of correctness according to the native variety of language" (p. 96), at a time when native English is losing its relevance for global communication.

This is not to claim that no English language entry tests are needed, as do Hu and McKay (2012) in respect of East Asian HE. It is simply to argue that it is time for the gatekeeping practices of the existing tests to end, and for more appropriate tests to be devised that evaluate prospective university students' (both NESs' and NNESs') linguistic suitability for academic study in an intercultural university environment where English functions as a lingua franca, not as a native language, and thus do not risk 'mis-recognizing' student achievement (Leung and Lewkowicz 2012). In this respect, I found it interesting in my study that prospective and current NES students, apparently by virtue of their English nativeness, are generally assumed to be proficient in academic English, and therefore not to need to have their English proficiency tested or any kind of remedial help during their studies. Some of the US institutions, both local and branch, at least require ACT (American College Testing) or SAT (Scholastic Assessment Test) scores[15] of NES applicants, and some also ask all applicants to provide an essay in English. The UK institutions, to my knowledge, require no English language evidence from NES applicants, as do almost none of the universities in the non-Anglophone universities in my sample.

Having said all this, I believe a contrast needs to be drawn between Anglophone and non-Anglophone institutions in practice even though not, for now, in theory. This relates to Costa and Coleman's (2012) observation that administrations may be "ignorant about what is taking place in the classroom" and the need to find out how much they actually know "about the teaching habits of their academic staff" (p. 14). I made the point earlier that whereas NNESs are the vast majority of students on non-Anglophone campuses, NESs comprise the overall majority (although not on substantial numbers of postgraduate courses) in Anglophone universities. This means that whereas in the former, NNES students are surrounded by non-native Englishes of various kinds, in the latter, outside courses with strong NNES cohorts, they may hear more native English: the 'correct' version of English that is required of them, but which they cannot 'achieve'.

This is also likely to be true at the staff level. As was clear from the videos linked to many of the non-Anglophone university websites, NNES staff's speech does not, in the main, sound like that of NESs, while examples of written non-native English occur even in the most formal parts of the non-Anglophone university webpages such as their presidents' messages. Countable use of nouns that are uncountable in ENL are probably the most common examples of this phenomenon (e.g. Budapest University of Technology says in its Survival Guide for international students "Please note the following *advices* ... "), but I also spotted other kinds of non-native use of English. The same was true of the NNES staff's responses to my questionnaire (see Chapter Six). If the staff themselves use English that has a flavour of their L1, even though they may not condone this and may consider themselves to speak 'bad' English, it is likely that they are more forgiving and less denigrating when they hear and read non-native-like English from their NNES students, whether out of a sense of being in the same position or because they simply do not notice (both of which reasons were mentioned by NNES respondents to the questionnaire reported in the next chapter).

The extent to which this is actually the case is largely an empirical question. But it is one that has an intuitive truth about it and that also reflects what I have seen and heard myself on university campuses in various parts of the non-Anglophone world. And there is already some empirical evidence of the acceptance of non-native ways of doing English in the non-Anglophone world of HE, beyond the obvious one of accent. For example, Li and Wharton (2012) demonstrate how Chinese L1 undergraduate students' patterns of metadiscourse in their written English vary across two contexts, one in China, the other in the UK, and that their Mandarin-influenced metadiscourse (the use of strong assertions in their rhetoric) was not an obstacle to passing the assignment in question in the Chinese context (Bohai University). In the UK setting (Warwick University), by contrast, the students used more hedges, suggesting that "the Warwick based tutors might guide students to make use of relevant metadiscourse resources" (p. 353). By 'relevant', the authors presumably mean 'relevant to the UK context', which I would argue implies a national rather than international perspective. Their finding is nevertheless interesting and, as they point out, it supports previous findings (Sanderson 2008, Yakhontova 2006) that demonstrate not only how local context affects academic writing, but also that local context seems to exert a stronger influence than academic discipline.

While in practice there may be more tolerance and even acceptance of non-native-like English on non-Anglophone campuses even if this has not yet made its way into language policy, a strong uni-directional language discourse socialization perspective continues to hold sway in 'international' Anglophone universities. This assimilationist perspective requires NNES students to conform to and reproduce local norms and practices in their academic English. However, as Duff (2010) points out, "socialization is a bi- or multidirectional, contingent process" in which "[t]hose being socialized have agency and powers of resistance, innovation, and self-determination" (p. 171). She goes on to show how a group of Korean undergraduates in a Canadian university seek to socialize themselves "not into a local Anglo-Canadian university CoP so much as a Pan-Asian, transnational, multilingual one, a kind of hybrid/third space" (p. 182). In a sense, then, they have constructed their own international university setting, one that the university itself apparently did not provide.

It seems, then, that Anglophone university management, particularly in the UK, would do well to consider the potential implications of their English language socialization practices. UK international student fees are rising dramatically, and the UK Border Agency is making it increasingly difficult for prospective international students to obtain visas to study in the country at a time when the number of EMI universities/programmes in non-Anglophone countries, especially East Asia, is growing apace. If prospective international students start to realize that they may actually feel more comfortable and fit in better linguistically in a NNES HE community nearer home, this may become a further factor in their choice of where to study. The way in which Anglophone universities orient linguistically to their international students may thus begin to play an increasingly important role in recruitment of such students, an issue to which we return in the final chapter.

My study of these 60 university websites is of necessity limited in terms of the degree of detail I could provide. Even after making substantial cuts in relation to the institutions, countries, and disciplines that I had explored, the chapter is still far longer than originally envisaged. And yet it is clear that much more remains to be done. Earlier, I mentioned Doiz et al.'s (2013a) point that each institution needs to investigate its own context, and I see this, as well as cross-discipline empirical studies, as crucial next steps. In addition, it will be useful if those who carry out such research speak the local language(s) of the website(s) they investigate so that they can explore any meaningful differences that emerge between what is presented in English for the international market, and what is presented in the L1 for the home market (see the discussion of Greenall's study on pp. 85 above). Finally, there needs to be more research into differences in policies and practices according to the type of EMI being used. Tange (2012), in her study of five Danish institutions, for example, distinguishes between EMI in single courses, in parallel English and Danish programmes, and in English only programmes and disciplines. My aim in conducting the study of the 60 websites, however, was not to provide this level or kind of detail, but to gain an overall impression of the current situation and, in particular, the kinds of discourses being used. This, together with the information provided by staff and international students which follows in the next two chapters would, I hoped, provide a reasonably representative picture of the current state of affairs regarding orientations to English and EMI in international universities around the world. And it is to the views of university staff that we turn next.[16]

Notes

1 '4 International Colleges & Universities' describes itself as "an international higher education search engine and directory reviewing accredited Universities and Colleges in the world. 4icu.org includes **11,000 Colleges and Universities**, ranked by web popularity, in 200 countries" (http://www.4icu.org/; emphasis in the original).

2 As mentioned, this is not at all to suggest that I personally equate 'international' with teaching in English medium in Higher (or any other) Education, but purely because the purpose of my research was to explore English language policies and practices. As will be seen in the website analysis that follows, it is university management, rather than me, who make the assumption 'international = English'. I prefer to see it the other way round, i.e. 'English = international' which embraces, among other things, the possibility of other international languages as well as English.

3 Global 30 (G30) is a group of Japanese universities (currently numbering 13) selected by the Japanese government to "nurture internationally competent individuals by creating an academic environment where international and Japanese students can learn from one another", and with the aim of ultimately bringing 300,000 international students to Japan (http://www.uni.international.mext.go.jp/global30/). They all offer degree programmes in English medium. Two non-G30 universities were also included in the study: Chukyo because it has a Graduate School of World Englishes and I was interested in finding out if this has had any impact on institutional language policy; and the International Christian University because contacts in Japan told me that it has a full university curriculum in English in its College of Liberal Arts.

4 See Appendix 1 (p. 211) for details of these websites, as well as the names of all the institutions that were included in the sample.

5 Information on the number of EMI programmes and courses in East Asian universities is still very difficult to find. On the other hand, as far back as 2008, Wächter and Maiworm reported that over 400 European HE institutions had delivered more than 2400 programmes taught entirely in English in 2007. And more recently, the Institute of International Education (IIE) has reported that there were over 600 institutions in Europe teaching 4664 masters programmes alone either entirely or partly in English by October 2011(Brenn-White and van Rest 2012).

6 Unlike Greenall's (2012) Norwegian study, I am unfamiliar with the original languages of the majority of the websites in my study. This means that my analysis is, of necessity, confined to the English language versions. However, it would be fruitful for researchers who speak the various languages involved to conduct comparative analyses of these websites of the kind done by Greenall.

7 The term 'macro region' is used loosely in the case of Anglophone branch universities, as these involved branches of institutions in two Anglophone countries (the US and UK) in three East Asian countries (China, Japan, and Korea).

8 My thanks to Lanxi Hu for checking the accuracy of my comments on the Chinese university websites.

9 My reporting of the website content is in the present tense. However, readers obviously cannot assume that the material available on the days I accessed it will be exactly the same if they should access it at a later date. Web content may also vary if readers access sites via other routes than those I used as some universities seem to have more than one English language website. I would nevertheless expect the general thrust to remain similar.

10 There are, nevertheless a very small number of dissenting voices. These, however, are academics whose publications presenting alternative views are not easily found on these websites. One example is Wen Qiufang, Professor of English at BFSU (see, e.g. Wen 2012). Another is Fang Fan, a teacher at Shantou University (though currently studying for a PhD in the UK), whose publications on ELF are listed in his staff profile on Shantou University's ELC web pages.

11 The article, 'Teaching English is not about quality', can be accessed at: http://www.universityworldnews.com/article.php?story=20121114175515819

12 Just as 'foreign' language tends to mean 'English' on these university websites (as Saarinen and Nikula (2013) also found in their Finnish study), the term 'bilingual' tends to mean the local language plus English.

13 Sadly, Yamuna Kachru died in April 2013.

14 The extent to which these institutions genuinely see EMI as an advantage for students and the extent to which it is simply a marketing device is unclear. I suspect, however, that the truth lies somewhere between the two.

15 Unlike tests such as TOEFL and IELTS, which focus exclusively on English proficiency, ACT and SAT include English alongside other subjects.

16 Note that in order to protect the anonymity of the staff who provided questionnaire responses for Chapter Six, the universities explored in the Chapter Five study are not those of the questionnaire respondents.

6

STAFF PERSPECTIVES ON THEIR UNIVERSITIES' ENGLISH LANGUAGE POLICIES AND PRACTICES

Introduction

This chapter, like the previous one, is concerned with the extent to which internationalization is having an impact on university English language policies and practices around the world. The website study reported in Chapter Five demonstrated how a number of international universities across a wide range of countries represent themselves language-wise in relation to their proclaimed international status and character, and what they are doing (or not doing) in this respect, particularly in terms of EMI. Chapter Six moves on to consider how university staff perceive their institutions' English language policies and practices.

In order to gain insights into the perceptions of academic teaching staff, I administered an open-ended questionnaire to academics across the same four macro regions that the website study reported in the previous chapter. The questionnaire as a research method is not without its weaknesses. In particular, as Adamson and Muller (2012) observe, citing Lillis (2008) and Edwards and Owen (2002), "there are limitations to the strength of conclusions that can be drawn from questionnaire research, as it can present a distorted picture of reality" (p. 94), However, as they go on to argue, "in working with a geographically dispersed population of participants the convenience it offers in allowing investigators to gather data help[s] to outweigh the shortcomings of the instrument". In the case of the present research, the respondents were very widely dispersed in 24 different countries across the four macro regions:

- East Asia: Brunei, China, Hong Kong, Japan, Korea, Malaysia, Singapore, Taiwan, Thailand
- Latin America: Argentina (the majority), Brazil, Chile, Ecuador, Venezuela
- Mainland Europe: Denmark, France, Germany, Greece, Spain, Sweden, Turkey
- Anglophone: Australia, UK, US.

The use of a questionnaire was thus the only feasible way to access their views. And although the use of open questions has its disadvantages (see below), the fact that the questions were open rather than closed, and that so many respondents answered them at length, meant that the qualitative data provided by their responses were more revealing than would have been the case with the kinds of numerical/statistical data typically yielded from closed questions.

Collecting and analysing the questionnaire data

The respondents were selected with the help of intermediaries in as many countries as possible, with no stipulations as to disciplines. My only criteria were that the respondents should be engaged in teaching academic subjects (rather than English language skills), that they should teach at least some of their courses in English, and that at least some of their students should be NNESs. In other words, I did not want to start from the premise that there would be differences in orientation to English according to a respondent's country, L1, or discipline (see p. 72), but for any such differences – along with common ground – to emerge from the data itself. The research I had conducted for an earlier book (Jenkins 2007), which had admittedly looked mainly at the perspectives of English language teachers, nevertheless led me to believe that I would find a good deal of similarity in orientation regardless of the respondents' backgrounds. On the other hand, the spread of respondents across 24 countries and a range of institution types and disciplines meant that if substantial differences did emerge, I would be in a position to explore the possibility that these variables may be involved.

The questionnaire was piloted with respondents from six different countries involving five L1s as well as both British and American English, and the wording adjusted in line with their comments. The final version began with questions asking for background information about the respondent (L1 and past/present teaching experience) and about his/her institution, followed by ten open questions (see Appendix 2, p. 214–15).

Although I had originally hoped to receive around 300 completed questionnaires, after I had removed those that did not meet the criteria, there were 166 in all. According to the contacts who were administering the questionnaires, there seemed to be two main reasons for reluctance on the part of some potential respondents: first, the fact that the questions were open and, in some cases, complex, meant that they were seen as likely to be time-consuming to complete; second, although the project had been granted ethical approval, and assurances of confidentiality and anonymity had been given, some still feared that their university might be identified. I found it particularly difficult to recruit respondents in the US despite the best efforts of several good US contacts. It was not clear why this should have been the case, and I suggested to one US contact that it could be because of a general lack of interest in the topic in the country that has the largest number of international students regardless of any English language concerns these students may have. But the contact disagreed with me.

The 166 questionnaires that were completed across 24 countries and a wide range of disciplines (hard sciences, social sciences, arts, and humanities) nevertheless provided a rich source of data. For as Dörnyei (2003) notes, "by permitting greater freedom of expression, open-format items can provide a far greater 'richness' than fully quantitative data … can offer graphic examples, illustrative quotes, and can also lead us to identify issues not previously anticipated" (p. 47). An inevitable downside to this "richness", however, is that responses to open questions are notoriously difficult to analyse.

For the purposes of analysis, I used qualitative content analysis, also known as 'latent content analysis' (e.g. Berg 2009) and 'latent level analysis' (e.g. Dörnyei 2007), because "it concerns second-level, interpretive analysis of the underlying deeper meaning of the data" as contrasted with 'manifest level analysis', "an objective and descriptive account of the surface meaning of the data" (Dörnyei ibid.: 245–46). Or, as Berg (2009) puts it more simply: "manifest content is comparable to the *surface structure* present in the message, and latent content is the *deep structural* meaning conveyed by the message" (p. 344; his italics). Thus, although I began with the literal meanings expressed by the respondents, I went on to explore the deeper meanings so as to add interpretive depth and breadth to the analysis.

The analytic process therefore involved various stages. I began by looking at the data in order to identify prominent topics, and doing an initial coding. Then I carried out a 'second level coding' (Dörnyei op.cit.: 252) in order to categorize the prominent topics under a smaller number of main themes/patterns to serve as the focus of the analysis. Finally, I moved on to making interpretations and theorizing. In this way, the codes, or themes, that I identified were not ends in themselves, but served as starting points for interpretation and theorizing in line with Berg's view of qualitative content analysis as a means for researchers to "examine ideological mind-sets, themes, topics, symbols, and similar phenomena, while grounding such examinations to the data" (2009: 343).

The coding process was initially manual. This was not only because, writing apart, I am generally more comfortable working with paper copies than on screen, but also because I find it more fruitful to do so in the early stages of data analysis, particularly when there is a need to return repeatedly to the data in the process of narrowing down the number of themes. I had therefore coded and re-coded four times manually, question by question, and was already very familiar with the data, before transferring to the computer, and specifically to the qualitative data analysis (QDA) computer software package, NVivo 10.[1] This enabled me to confirm and where necessary, modify, my manual analysis, to select representative and idiosyncratic data segments for quoting, and to do word searches to see whether they supported my emerging interpretations.[2] These searches helped me to identify not only which concepts (e.g. 'good English', 'errors') were frequently mentioned and, via their collocations, how respondents oriented to them, but also which were noticeable by their absence. Thus, NVivo was helpful both in correcting false impressions that a particular item had occurred frequently when it had not (perhaps from my personal bias or expectations), and in drawing attention to what was 'missing' in the responses.

The questionnaire findings: how staff orient to university English

And so to the findings. First, I report and explore the responses question by question.[3] Then, in the final part of the chapter, I draw the questionnaire findings together and consider them in the light of the language policy literature discussed in Chapter Four.

The analysis and discussion that follows is divided into four sub-sections. The first covers four questions (1, 2, 3 and 6) that asked respondents about their own institution and their views on how the institution manages English language matters. The second sub-section (questions 4 and 5) explores the respondents' comments on written and spoken academic English. The third and most complex sub-section, involving questions 7, 8 and 9, includes the two questions that elicited most of the lengthiest responses (8 and 9). This sub-section raises issues concerning the effects of university English language requirements on students, responsibilities for intercultural communication on campus, and what it means, English-wise, to be an 'international' university. The fourth section looks at the responses to question 10, which elicited respondents' comments on, and complaints about, the questionnaire itself.

What respondents say about their institution: questions 1, 2, 3, and 6[4]

Questions 1, 3, and 6 sought specific information about respondents' institutions. Coding of these three questions was therefore organized mainly in line with the information requested, whereas the questions in the other three sub-sections were coded entirely according to the themes that emerged from the data itself. Question 2, by contrast with the other three questions in this first sub-section, also elicited the respondents' views, albeit on the situation at their own institution, so again, was coded according to the emerging themes in the responses.

Question 1 asked respondents whether their institution had any official or unofficial English language policies at university or department level, and if so, whether the respondent found these policies useful. The majority said that their own university did not have an official or stated policy, but often added that it had some kind of informal understanding or 'unwritten rule'. Some referred specifically to particular tests (entry, programme, or exit) or to remedial English teaching as examples of informal policy. Few commented at this stage of the questionnaire on the *kind* of English involved in their institution's policy. Those who did so tended to refer, usually with approval or as if they regarded the matter as uncontroversial, to their institution's concern for 'standards', 'correct' English, 'near-native English' and the like. This set the tone for much of the analysis, with such issues recurring throughout the responses, whereas less was said overall in support of the notion of a more flexible approach, particularly in respect of writing. The word 'standard(s)', for example, occurred 107 times across the 166 responses (despite not occurring anywhere in the rubric itself), and in most cases indicated the respondent's own orientation, for example "I believe that the standards should be high" (Danish), "We expect high standards since this is necessary for publishing" (Turkish).[5]

When it came to the usefulness or otherwise of their institution's policies and practices, the respondents' focus tended to be on international students, with the majority saying they find the policies/practices useful. The main reasons given were the perceived benefit to students. More specifically, the policies and practices were considered to demonstrate to students that 'good' English is expected and encourage them to improve their English. And since teaching is in English medium, the language policy was seen as helping students to study more effectively, as well as enabling them to study abroad, by which they generally meant NNES students travelling to Anglophone countries to study. Some thought that their institutions' policies help broaden students' views and strengthen their ability to appreciate other cultures and communicate with foreigners. Again, this tended to refer to NNES students benefiting from communicating with NESs (with Chinese students sometimes being singled out). Some respondents also found their institution's policies and practices beneficial to NNES staff because they encourage teachers to teach in English, and hence enhance teachers' English skills. And some think the policies and practices are of benefit to the institution itself, promoting its reputation through being able to send students abroad, and by enabling the university to achieve its goal of being international (which seemed to mean teaching in English medium and attracting international students).

On the other hand, a minority found their institution's policies and practices distinctly un-useful. The main reason given was that the policies are vague and/or tacit. Some from Argentina see them as hegemonic and neglecting NNESs' identities, and in institutions where the students and teacher share the same L1, it is seen as "silly" (to quote a Brazilian respondent) to teach in English. Others in this same-L1 situation find it pointless to teach in English when the language is not used outside the classroom. Meanwhile, some of those whose institutions' policies are limited to the use of particular tests argued that the tests themselves are not reliable, particularly some of the 'international' entry tests (see the responses to question 3 below for further discussion).

Question 2 asked respondents whether they think their institutions should have English language policies if they do not currently have any. The majority who answered this question take the view that such policies are necessary, citing the need for them in modern universities. They also gave a number of other overlapping reasons. One was that there is (in their view) a positive link between language policy and student/staff proficiency in English. For example, a Chinese respondent argued "if there are not such policies and practices, I think the quality of teaching and lecturers' performance are not guaranteed". Another prominent reason was that English (and judging from their responses to other questions, this

generally meant native or near-native English) is an important global communication tool. As another Chinese respondent put it, "since top Chinese universities
seek to cultivate talents geared to the needs of globalization, such [English lan-
guage] policies and practices should be implemented". Another spoke up in favour
of policy, "especially to non-English majors", adding that "due to the globalization, with good English language ability, they can communicate and exchange
with the rest of the world".

A further reason given was that English language policy helps international students integrate (this response was particularly prominent among respondents from
Anglophone institutions, and tended to mean 'integrate with NESs'). Many simply
said there is a need for a standard, a term which, as was pointed out above,
occurred frequently among the respondents. Overall, it was clear in the pro-policy
responses that even though the question did not specifically refer to NNESs, most,
if not all, responses had in mind policies directed at NNES students (and less often,
staff) rather than giving any thought to the possibility that NES students (and staff)
might benefit from policies directed at them too.

By contrast, certain concerns were raised. These were often similar to those
raised in question 1 in respect of existing rather than hypothetical policies and
practices. The main concerns related to the dominance of English in HE, the cost
to first language and identity, and the potential damage to NNES students who
are less able to operate in English than in their L1. A few also objected to the
idea of having any such policies in their own institution on the basis that these
were likely to be determined top down and to focus on native English rather than
to allow for local idiosyncracies, mixing of languages (code switching), and ELF.
The 'hypothetical objectors', however, formed a relatively small, if vociferous,
minority.

Question 3 moved on to the subject of English language entry requirements
specifically for NNES students, and again, respondents were asked whether their
own institution has such requirements or, if not, they think it should do. The
majority, unsurprisingly, referred to various widely known examinations, with 43
naming IELTS and 32 TOEFL (though there would no doubt have been more
references to TOEFL had there been more respondents from the US). A few said
their institutions determine entry according to particular CEFR levels. Other
examinations were also mentioned, both other Anglo-run and local examinations
such as the National University Qualifying Entrance Examination, Gao Kao, in
China. Some respondents also mentioned exit examinations that students are
required to pass in order to graduate, such as China's College English Test (CET),
for students who major in a subject other than English. Some respondents noted
that although their institution does have language entry requirements, these are
treated flexibly, with institutions in some cases offering remedial English teaching
for students who do not match their language entry requirements.

Of those respondents whose institutions do not have entry requirements, opinions were divided as to whether they should do. Again, unsurprisingly, many
who answered this part of the question feel that entry tests are useful, that it is

reasonable to have them, and important if teaching is carried out in English medium and/or the literature in the discipline is written in English. Others are less favourably disposed on the grounds that they believe examination results are unreliable as indicators of what students can do. These respondents pointed out that students may in practice perform differently from their examination score: they may have achieved a low score but have proficient English for their course of study or vice versa (see Chapter Seven where this point is also brought up by international students who participated in my interview study). Some thought such examinations were irrelevant. For example, one UK respondent found students' main problem to be the ability to communicate verbally, and believes this comes with increasing confidence during study, not with an examination score. Another, from Taiwan, felt that decisions about the suitability for study of students' English should be left to the teacher, not decided by an examination.

A few respondents raised ideological and equity issues. They disliked, in particular, the conflation of English 'proficiency' with 'native-like' English even if this is implicit rather than stated, and questioned what notions such as 'competence' and 'command' actually mean. Others felt that there was a problem of fairness across disciplines in terms of different entry requirements, or found it unfair that universities in non-Anglophone countries attach importance to English language entry qualifications in the first place. In China, for example, English is one of three subjects included in Gao Kao (the other two being Chinese and mathematics), taken in 2012 by over nine million students for entry into universities in their *own* country (Bolton and Graddol 2012: 5).

Turning to question 6, respondents were asked what kinds of English language support their institutions offer to both native and non-native English students, and what they think of the nature of this support. It was noticeable that although they had been asked about both NES and NNES students, as with questions 1 and 2 (which had not specified either), almost all respondents answered entirely in respect of NNESs. Predictably a relatively small number felt the level of support offered by their institution to NNES students is acceptable, with less than 20 per cent making positive comments in this respect, although one US respondent thought his/her university offered sufficient support for NNESs but that it "do[es] not adequately take advantage of the available resources". Others, by contrast, talked of a mismatch between the institution's expectations and the support offered to enable NNES (particularly international) students to meet these expectations. In several cases there is no official support at all. For instance, "except for teacher's advice and help, there's none", observed a Brazilian respondent, while an Argentinian respondent said "they are told that something is wrong but are given little or no help – such as explaining what was wrong and why". Some were critical about the quality of the support on offer. An Australian respondent, for example, complained that "more and more of this support is being offered online and by non-academic support staff for financial reasons". And several argued that support is too generic, and should take more account of differences in academic norms across disciplines.

Predictable too was the assumption of many respondents that the goal of English language support is, and should be, to help NNES students conform to norms of native English. This led some to argue that their institution needs to employ more native English teachers. By contrast, a minority expressed the view that support should focus on areas other than language skills, such as the teaching of communication skills and the developing of students' confidence. Some in the UK felt that support should be used to encourage international students to integrate better with home students, though there was no mention of the need for official support aimed at encouraging integration in the opposite direction.

The responses to questions 1, 2, 3, and 6 provide a snapshot, albeit brief, of the kinds of English language policies (or lack of them) and practices currently occurring in a range of EMI universities around the world. The overriding impression from the questionnaire data discussed so far is of some kind of native English being seen as a given for English in HE, with relatively few dissenting voices. We turn now to look more closely at what the respondents believe this means for written and spoken academic English specifically.

Orientations to written and spoken academic English: questions 4 and 5

Question 4 concerned the extent to which the respondents believe NNESs' academic writing should conform to native academic written English. It emerged that around half considered **conformity important**[6] or desirable (although apart from a handful of respondents who referred to the CEFR's descriptors or to specific grammatical features, they rarely attempted to explain what they meant by 'native academic English'). A Thai respondent, for example, answered:

> Yes, I expect all written works to conform to the native academic English because academic is a rigid business and I don't want the students to think that as a non-native they could try what fits them, they just can't.

A Turkish respondent likewise said:

> I expect their English to fully conform to native academic English. I expect to have mastered the language and be able to perform at the level of a native speaker.

The desire for conformity was particularly evident among respondents in Anglophone settings. Many of the UK respondents tended to argue that as NNESs study for the same qualifications as NESs, written English requirements should be the same for both, with no allowances made for NNES students. For example, one respondent stated "I expect it [NNESs' written English] to conform entirely to native academic English as (a) it is an English University, and (b) that is the standard expected in science following University". Another said:

> I think we have to treat equally all students regardless the level of English. Both native and non-native English-speaking students should meet some academic standards and this includes very good academic writing skills.

Several of the US respondents said likewise. For instance, one stated "I expect students to conform to standard academic English as used in the US", and another that:

> I expect both native and non-native English speakers to be able to write (or learn to write) formal, professional English, and assess student writing against my view of that mark.

Native academic English was often linked to notions of a standard/standards and of correctness/errors, particularly grammatical (none of which occurred anywhere in the questionnaire rubric) although these terms, like 'native academic English', tended to be used without qualification. For example, a Chinese respondent simply stated "students are required to write clearly and correctly", while another said "I will require students to use correct English". A Danish respondent talking specifically about students from "Eastern Europe, Russia, Ukraine and even more so China", replied "none of these groups as a rule lives completely up to the standards of native academic English". Another, from Ecuador, argued "if students want to become professionals in an international community, they must have high standards for themselves and others". It was evident from his/her answers to other parts of the same questionnaire (e.g. references to the need for NNES students to be "near native correct", and to their "errors"), that the respondent equated high standards "in an international community" with native academic English. The same was true of several others who referred, for example, to "international (academic) English" (Argentina), "global standards of academic English" (Malaysia) and the like as if 'native' and 'international' or 'global' are self-evidently synonymous in respect of English.

Many respondents referred specifically to a need for 'good' written English (the word 'good', collocating mostly with 'English', occurred 154 times across 90 of the questionnaires, or well over half, even though it did not appear in the questionnaire rubric). Again, in most cases there was an assumption that 'good English' means native English. For example, a respondent from Hong Kong said:

> Sometimes it [students' writing] does conform to native academic English ... but that is only the case with at best the top 20% of students. The majority do not have good English.

For a small number, conformity to native academic English even boiled down to whether this should be American or British English and a concern that one or other should be used, or that students should "not mix the two models up" (Bruneian). This preoccupation, as the interview data in the next chapter demonstrates, causes added (and arguably unnecessary) problems for NNES students, especially those whose L1s do not have Latin script.

Sometimes respondents justified their desire for students' conformity to native English on the basis of external factors. Among these were their university's English language requirements. As one respondent said, "I encourage their written work to conform to native academic English. That is the expectation of the university" (Brunei). This is so even if they disagree with their university's position. A Japanese respondent explained, "my main job is to prepare my students for future study in 3rd and 4th year so I have to acknowledge that those teachers will also use NES norms". Others pointed out that their students would have to conform if they went on to study elsewhere. A Chinese respondent said "I think they [students] should try to conform to native academic English in their work, since they will probably have to do so in their near future when they pursue further degrees". And a Singaporean respondent argued:

> For those students who wish to pursue further academic study in English-speaking countries, conforming to NAE [native academic English] at an early stage can make them quickly adapt to the new study environment.

On the other hand, a Brazilian respondent referring to future study in Anglophone countries, said "I do not want them to write like Americans or Brits, even though I know this will be demanded from them if they are given the chance to attend universities in these places".

The other main external reason respondents cited for insisting on conformity to native academic written English was the possibility that students might in future want to publish their work in international forums, where publishers in most cases require native-like academic English. As one Hong Kong respondent put it, students "may want to publish their work in academic journals and so their academic writing assignments could provide some kind of training to prepare them for their entry into the academic community". A respondent from Argentina likewise argued that students need "a good mastery of native academic English" so that they can "publish articles in appropriate academic style".

By contrast, around half the respondents emerged as more flexible in their expectations of their NNES students' academic writing, expressing a willingness to accept some kind of **variation from native academic English**, or at least saying they are 'resigned' to such variation. These respondents are mainly, though not exclusively, from non-Anglophone settings, where there appears in general to be greater awareness of what it means to write in a second (academic) language, especially among respondents who are in this situation themselves. Typical of many, a Chinese respondent stated "I don't expect them to conform to native academic English completely, because it's an impossible task for non-English speaking students". Another (NES Japan) said "I don't expect it to conform to (that closely) NS level, which is clearly a fantastically optimistic goal", and added "I am happy, and it is challenge enough, for students to produce work that moves towards at least the shape and style of NS writing".

A Taiwanese respondent linked his/her (non)-requirement of native English to students' confidence, saying s/he does not require students to conform to native English "because I want to improve their confidence by writing more". Another, also from Taiwan, pointed out that it was the first time his/her (mathematics) graduate students had to write papers in English, "thus, encouragement for further trying in English writing is the focus in this class. I won't care much on whether their works match native academic English". This may in fact be the situation of the majority of NNES graduate students studying in English medium at present, in that it seems that much undergraduate teaching outside Anglophone and post-colonial settings is carried out in the local language, with a switch to English at postgraduate level.

Of those who accept some degree of non-conformity to native academic English, a substantial number (around a quarter of all respondents) said they prioritize content, meaning, intelligibility, and the ability to communicate over language and, as a UK respondent put it, make allowances for "less than perfect expression". For example, a Brazilian respondent said "In general I assess content only. If I can understand what the student meant, I'll accept the paper". Another respondent, a NNES based in the UK, explained "I would expect them not to make obvious grammar mistake but I don't expect them to 'sound' native: ie, if they use a slightly strange word but still get their points across, I don't mind".

While a Japanese respondent commented:

> I do not consider conforming to native academic English is the most important factor when grading my students' papers because what is most important to me is for them to express their understanding of the content.

Other respondents did not demand grammatical conformity but had certain holistic requirements. For example, "I expect they organize their reports logically and communicate properly, but I am not very strict on grammar or syntaxes" (Spanish). Similarly, "we do teach and strongly encourage students to acquire an academic register when they write" but "we do not usually force them to write in an Anglo-American fashion that emphasises linearity or starting every paragraph with a topic sentence, if that is what you mean by 'native academic English'" (German). Finally, a Danish respondent argued that there comes a point when the conformity issue becomes completely irrelevant: "When it is so difficult to follow that assessing the content becomes a problem, the native/non-native issue kind of fades away".

Fewer respondents considered variation from native norms in terms of the possibility of legitimate *non-Anglo* ways of using English, in other words, the existence of other varieties of World Englishes and of English as an international lingua franca. The word 'variety' (or 'varieties') occurred in less than 20 per cent of the questionnaires (across all questions), and in some cases did not even refer to the notion of *language* variety (e.g. it was used in the phrase "a variety of subjects").

And while a substantial minority of respondents did seem to be aware of and positive about other ways of using English than native, very few of these actually linked this awareness to academic writing. Thus, only a handful of responses to question 4 referred specifically to the notion of language varieties, and most of these still revealed some kind of attachment to Anglo written norms. One, a Bruneian, said, for example, "I subscribe to the idea that there will inevitably be use of Southeast Asian or Bruneian idiosyncratic vocabulary, structures or phrases" but went on to say "in Academic essays they [students] would be expected to minimize these".

Among the very few respondents who did seem to take seriously the notion of legitimate non-Anglo written norms was a Singaporean who described English as "more of a 'toolbox' language" that "does not constitute the exclusive monopoly of any particular nation or people". Likewise, an Argentinian declared "I expect students to conform to 'international' academic English rather than 'native' academic English", signalling an understanding that the two are not the same, though not explaining how. And a Swedish respondent said "I require some type of academic international English, which is rather different from native English" but added intriguingly "I always mark deviations from Western practice. Asian students really write in a different language that might be called Chinese or Pakistani English". And a Brazilian respondent observed that s/he still assesses his/her students' written English in accordance with native English because "I don't have a non-native academic variety I can turn to yet", but added that s/he believed before long, "the variations which are more and more present in oral English will begin to appear in academic written English and be equally taken as legitimate".

Finally, two respondents queried whether there is in fact any such thing as 'native academic English' in the first place. One, from Brunei (NES), pointed out that it is "a vague term requiring precise definition". S/he went on to argue that "'native' standards are in any case irrelevant" as many "'non-native' academics speak and write better than the 'natives'", though to some extent spoiled his/her argument by adding "we expect conformity to international norms of written English", a notion equally as vague. The other (UK) said:

> A few years ago I would have been very critical of Ss [students'] writing that does not conform to 'native academic discourse', but I have since reached an understanding that there is no such thing as 'native academic discourse'.

Some of those who fell into the more flexible category raised two other objections about requiring their students to conform to native written academic English. Firstly, a few NNES respondents questioned their right or ability, as NNESs themselves, to judge the English of others. A German, for example, argued "being a non-native speaker I can hardly ask them to write like a native". A Danish respondent made a similar point: "being a non-native English speaker myself ... I have some tolerance to the students written work, partly also because I don't necessarily detect academic English that does not comply with the native norms of academic English". And a Swede who had said s/he does not find academic English writing "particularly difficult", thought this may be because "my standards are low to begin with as a non-native speaker". Another Swedish respondent took a similar, if more extreme, view: "I'm not sure I could judge what idiomatic English might be; we all speak broken English". And a NNES in the UK put it equally bluntly, saying that correcting students' English "feels weird because I don't feel fully qualified to correct someone else's English (native or non-native), when mine could be just as rubbish (or much more)!!!".

The second objection, which was raised by just a few respondents, concerned issues of equity. For instance, a Malaysian said: "NO, I do not [expect my students' writing to conform to native English] as it would be an injustice to them – most of them are bilingual students who communicate in English as a Foreign Language". A respondent from Argentina pointed out that NESs do not necessarily follow the 'rules' of native academic English themselves:

> I have noticed when there is a native student or visit in our class, they tend to disregard any formal structure or vocabulary as if saying: "well, what you have just corrected wasn't THAT wrong. We use it sometimes".

And the Singaporean who had described English as a "toolbox" (see above), also said "I find it rather insulting to judge people in accordance to an idealized native speaker. The word 'conform' is rather strong and actually loaded with ideology".

One final point: it will be evident from the above that the prevailing view among both 'conformists' and most of those with more flexible approaches, NES and NNES, is that NNES' academic written English is by definition inferior to that of the natives. On the other hand, a few respondents commented that academic writing is a problem for both, while three argued that NNESs' academic English can be superior. One of these, a respondent in Brunei (NES) said "many Asian 'non-native' academics speak and write better English than I do". And two respondents from the US and the UK (one an NNES, the other ambilingual) declared that some of their NNES students have better academic English than that of their NES students, one mentioning German students specifically, while a couple of others made the same point but in response to other questions.

It is clear from the amount said that many respondents were very exercised by the topic of academic writing. By contrast, even though a similar number answered question 5 on NNES students' spoken English, they tended to say far less. Their responses nevertheless followed a broadly similar pattern to those of question 4. That is, some respondents supported more normative positions in respect of native English speech, others were more flexible, and still others had non-conforming perspectives. However, there was a general tendency for respondents to be less attached to native spoken than written English.

Of those who held **more normative expectations** of their NNES students' spoken English, the main factor that emerged was that 'correct' (i.e. near-native) speech is their first priority. An Argentinian respondent's expectation, for example, is "fluent and accurate language and appropriate use of technical disciplinary vocabulary", while a German respondent specified "correct grammar and lexis". A Chinese respondent said "at least they can use correct words and sentences to communicate with teacher and other students", while another referred to "fluency, accuracy and expressiveness". Similarly, a Turkish respondent said "we expect that they express themselves in a clear and correct manner", and another that "I expect them to perform at the level where they make themselves understood by a native speaker", a point also made by other respondents. Focusing likewise on native English speech, a Chinese respondent said s/he considers that "to keep up with the spoken English changes in native countries is the ultimate goal", while a Greek respondent cited the CEFR, saying that "on graduating, fluency and comprehensibility at C level [i.e. *near* native] are desirable, *not necessarily* a native speaker's competence" (my italics).

A few of the more normative responses referred specifically to pronunciation. For example, a Chinese respondent stated his/her expectation that "their pronunciation is basically correct". One from Argentina argued that students' pronunciation should be "native-like", and another that it "should have no distracting or irritating features from the point of view of pronunciation", although it was not clear who the respondent had in mind as the potentially distracted or irritated listener. A respondent from Hong Kong stated that students should have "good pronunciation", in this case in order to qualify as teachers of English and "provide a good role model for their own students". In fact most of the others who referred specifically to pronunciation were also teachers of English. Almost without exception, they seemed to find it unacceptable for their students to maintain a noticeable non-native English accent. And for the normative group as a whole, a native accent was generally preferred across all disciplines, although intriguingly, a Thai respondent said "Thai accent is fine if pronounce the words correctly". A respondent from Argentina was even concerned that students should not "mix" British and American English accents and lexis, a concern that was also expressed by others in relation to written English (see above).

We turn now to the larger number with **more flexible expectations** of their students' spoken English, of whom the majority favoured communication over correctness. Many commented in ways similar to this (NES) economics lecturer in Korea:

> Communication is the goal. Accuracy mistakes, in so far as they do NOT interfere with communication is irrelevant. If I can understand them and most other students can understand them, then communication has been achieved. In my courses, English ability is not as important as understanding of material and the ability to communicate that knowledge.

Similar comments include the Danish respondent who expected "a reasonable fluency that makes it possible to assess the contents of what they say", and the respondent in Japan (NES) who argued:

> To me a very important factor for communicating effectively in a content area is for a student to use appropriate content specific terms and general academic vocabulary ... As long as they can do that, perfect grammar is not necessary.

A Chinese respondent simply said "just spit the words, have the desire to say something, anything".

Some respondents in the 'flexible' group also referred to intelligibility, a term which, in the main, they seemed to use to mean the same as 'communication'. For example, a respondent in Australia said s/he expects "intelligibility of content at least". One from Malaysia said "as long as they are able to communicate in an intelligible manner, I would not insist that they change the way they speak to that of a native speaker". And another, from China, referred to "intelligibility to class-mates and to teacher(s) including frequent international academic visitors", which seemed to imply intelligibility for both NES and NNES listeners.

A final area of concern among those who took a more flexible approach was their students' confidence, a factor that several respondents mentioned. A Thai respondent, for instance, said:

> I don't want them to be intimidated and I want them to feel that they use the language as a means to connect to other human beings and not that it's something that will weigh them down.

It seems, then, that rather more of the respondents take a flexible approach to their students' spoken than written English, and to prioritize the message over the medium. As one Danish respondent put it, "I can see that I make much less demands of their spoken than of their written work". The few with **non-conforming positions**, take this to an even greater extreme with several arguing that non-native English accents are entirely appropriate for NNESs. For example, a Brunei (NES) respondent said:

> I encourage them to maintain their own accent. I emphasise that they should not try to imitate me as they are not me. They should speak well and clearly, but not try to pretend they come from the UK.

Also, a Chinese respondent replied: "I expect them to be able to appropriate English as theirs and struggle for global intelligibility as much as possible".

This orientation towards non-Anglo-accented speech (and, indeed, to other aspects of spoken as well as written English) characterizes a view of English still rare both inside and outside HE: a view that ownership of the English language, and the right to determine its forms in international contexts (including international universities in Anglophone countries) no longer belong to NESs alone. The issues involved in this view of English were discussed in Chapter Two, so I will not repeat them here. Suffice it to say that only a few respondents to my questionnaire seem to be aware of the issues, and while there was overall a greater tendency for staff working in non-Anglo than in Anglo settings to express willingness to make allowances for NNES students' English (particularly spoken, less so written), there was little evidence of a willingness to see differences from native English as legitimate English forms rather than errors. We saw glimmers of this in references to international/global intelligibility, communication, and the like in the responses to questions 4 and 5. But unequivocal expressions of a belief in the legitimacy of non-native English were rare indeed. The strongest in respect of question 5, came from a Singaporean, who argued in favour of "an internationally intelligible model of English that does not need to be affected by either a British or American model"; and from a Brazilian respondent who affirmed: "I expect them [NNES students] to see themselves as legitimate users of English, not eternal learners of an interlanguage", and "to be open to variety in accents and non-conformity to native models whatsoever.

Effects, responsibilities, and requirements: questions 7, 8, and 9

With the next three questions, we move into more abstract realms. Question 7 focused on the effects of universities' language-related expectations, question 8 on who holds responsibility for successful intercultural communication on campus, and question 9 on the implications of universities calling themselves 'international'. While some of the 166 respondents did not answer one or more of these three questions (nine in the case of question 7, and 11 in the case of questions 8 and 9), the responses of the many who did were often substantially longer and more searching than those to the other questions. It seems that despite the potential complexity of these three questions, many of the respondents found it easier to think more expansively and/or critically about the broader issues when they were removed from a focus on concrete English language matters. Having said that, the respondents who talked in more critical terms generally had a lot more to say than those who talked positively or neutrally about their institutions. In respect of question 7, for example, a small number of those with positive or neutral views simply made brief comments such as "The effect must be positive", "no expectations", or "no effect". Meanwhile, across all three questions, more were likely to say they did not know, or did not understand these than the earlier questions. As a Swedish respondent said in answer to question 8: "Don't know. Quoting Winston Churchill, we must just keep buggering on".

Question 7 asked respondents to consider the positive and negative effects of their university's language-related expectations of both NNES and NES students. A range of **negative effects** emerged from the responses, with a number of respondents talking of their institutions' requirements causing NNES students to struggle and to lose self-confidence. Comments about students finding the requirements "discouraging", "demoralising", "demotivating", "stressful", and the like occurred often. For example, a UK respondent considers the requirement "probably reduces their [NNESs'] self-confidence and their willingness to participate in class", adding "English students tend not to interact with them because they find it 'difficult'". A NES in Korea said "university-wide, I think it is discouraging for non-native English speakers", while a (NES) Japanese respondent described students' "shock at the expectation that I/we put before them in their first year". And an Argentinian answered:

> Well, we know the effects for sure, because students have told us that our (or some teachers') high expectations in the field of language can be DEmotivating as if students felt they would never attain THAT high level.

A Malaysian respondent believed "many universities in Malaysia, including my university, have unrealistic expectations of its non-native English students" who have not studied in English medium before. Several from other countries spoke of students not coping and even dropping out because of their institution's language expectations and the pressure these cause. For instance, "the expectations are so high that students tend to feel unable to cope with them" said one Argentinian, adding that "there is a lack of extra academic support for students to feel 'accompanied' in the process of learning", and that "it is very usual that they give up to study at private places with lower academic demands – resigning themselves to the fact that their degree will not be as valued as that of [name of University]". Another Argentinian made a similar point: "in some subjects I consider linguistic demands to be excessive and counterproductive", likewise adding "it is not the high linguistic level required that I consider wrong but the lack of support" on offer in terms of both linguistic skills and academic literacy to enable students to achieve it.

One major problem for NNES students that emerges from many of the responses to question 7, in line with those to questions 4 and 5, is the institution's and/or the respondent's equation of a 'high standard' of English with native or near-native English. Some respondents mentioned this as their own expectation, others as the expectation of their institution, although in many cases they seemed to condone (or at least not to problematize) it themselves. It occurred, for example, in references to the benefits for students and their institutions of certain Anglophone entry examinations such as IELTS and TOEFL, and in comments about the advantages for NNES students of having NES teachers. Some, on the other hand, were openly critical of this stance. As a NES respondent in Argentina put it:

> the expectations of the students' English in the area of linguistic abilities are too frustrating for the students because some teachers still have an ideal English native speaker in mind. The straightforward consequence is that there are many dropouts, but those students who persevere are afraid of participating in class.

And a NES respondent in Japan argued that having a first year programme staffed with native English teachers creates the impression that the best way for NNESs to improve their English is to be taught by the natives. S/he added:

I also worry that our use of TOEIC and the pressure for students to improve their score has a negative effect on students' confidence, and again creates an image that advancement is measured by a native English yardstick.

To which it could be added that for international business students, as in this case, such a yardstick does not even reflect the ways in which they are most likely to use English in their future careers.

Others, while not voicing dissent from a 'high standards = native English' position, like the two Argentinians quoted above, nevertheless expressed criticisms of their institution in terms of a gap between its requirements and the level of support on offer for NNES students to achieve them. One US respondent, for instance, talked of "a marked mismatch between teachers' and institutional expectations and the exposure and classes students receive for academic purposes". Many referred also to the fact that it is time-consuming for NNES students to work on their English as well as their academic discipline, and that their institution does not seem to realise this. As one UK respondent put it:

The university expects non-native students to achieve the same standard as native speakers but seem not to appreciate that these students often need more support and time than native speakers.

And like several others, a Chinese respondent argued that as a result of institutional requirements, "most students spend too much time on learning English and forget their major subjects".

An Argentinian referred to "overtraining linguistic forms instead of broadening their knowledge of the different disciplines". And some respondents even argued that it is unreasonable in the first place to expect NNES students to achieve the same 'standard' of English as NES students and that a 'lower' level of English should be accepted. By (rare) contrast among the answers to question 7, a Bruneian respondent described his/her institution's expectations as "not *perfect native* English models and pronunciation, but an internationally intelligible form of English" (my italics), a point also made in a small minority of responses to questions 4 and 5.

A number of others, like the Japanese respondent quoted above in relation to TOEIC, also mentioned the negative effects of their institution's in-sessional English examination requirements. One Chinese respondent, for example, argued that "exam-oriented education might do harm to student", and another that "my university requires most students to pass College English Test band 4, which have a great impact on their English study", adding that "they lose their passion immediately after they pass this exam". A respondent from Hong Kong noted that his/her university's requirement for some students to take IELTS before they graduate means that students "pay more attention to English learning during their university studies" (and therefore, presumably, less time on their university studies themselves). S/he went on to say that the university is considering introducing an exit test for all its graduates, and that if this happens, some students will "feel pressurized". The issue of exit tests raises more general questions about equity on two counts. Firstly, is it fair that NNES students should have to pass examinations in English language as well as in their discipline, while NES students the world over are able to graduate without a second language? And secondly, even if there were certain cases where English language exit examinations could be justified, is it reasonable that the English required in these examinations should have to be an idealized native version?

Another rather different negative point was also raised. That is, although NESs were rarely mentioned in the responses to question 7 as a whole, some respondents in Anglo contexts referred to a perceived negative impact on them of the presence on campus of international students. An Australian, for instance, said:

> Anecdotal evidence suggests that Native English speaking students avoid non-mandatory tutorials because they believe that the tutors spend too much time helping [NNES] students.

A US respondent thought that "native English students don't get enough attention because I'm too busy trying to help the non-natives". A few also expressed concerns about the impact on themselves as supervisors of NNES students. As one respondent from the UK put it:

> My personal expectations are that a non-English speaker should not take more than twice as much effort to supervise, since my employers do not give me any more credit for the extra hard work involved. [There is a need for] more recognition of the huge effort needed to supervise these students.

This is an issue that I am sure will resonate with many UK supervisors of international students. The problem, as I see it, is not due to the students themselves (at least, not those in my own experience), but is a university management generated problem. That is, management want to recruit large numbers of international students, not least for the income they generate in fees. But they fail either to recognize what it means English-wise to be an international campus and adjust the institution's practices accordingly, or to employ sufficient staff to supervise the students, which disadvantages both the students themselves and their supervisors. We will return to these issues in Chapter Seven.

However, a lot of respondents discussed their institution's expectations of students' English in **more positive terms**, again mainly focusing on NNES students. Some made general points such as "from what I've seen, I believe the expectations are reasonable" (US), and that the expectations are "of great benefit for them" (Ecuador). Others spoke specifically about how they saw their institution's expectations enhancing students' (by which they usually meant NNES students') global communication skills. A respondent from Hong Kong, for example, talked of enabling students to become "world citizens", while one from Taiwan said "this is a good mean to provide English improvement and to engage with the international community". Some respondents argued that their university's expectations benefit NNES students by giving them the opportunity either on campus or in the future to engage with NESs. One Chinese respondent said, for example, "it is good for students, which can help them to communicate with English-speaking people", and another that "our Chinese [medical] students can communicate with US doctors and patients freely". Meanwhile, only a couple of respondents referred to such benefits for NES students, one, an Australian, arguing that "interaction with students from a different culture enhances the Native English speaking student's ability to communicate with clients from a non-English speaking background".

The majority of the positive responses, though, saw links between their institution's expectations and improvements in NNES students' English language skills. Respondents argued that students become aware of good English and its importance and are encouraged to improve their own English as a result. As one from China put it, "I think our stress on the students' ability to communicate in English has a positive effect on the students and they tend to spend more time on learning English". Some were more specific. For example, a US respondent said:

> Overall, I feel that my university's expectations improve the level of spoken and written English for native and non-native speakers. I think our expectations are the norm for an American university.[7]

And a UK respondent felt "it has positive impact on improving the quality of students' written work". Many others from a range of countries said much the same, in most cases ignoring the negative aspect of the time element mentioned by some of those who take the opposite view. Another respondent from China also cited the university's expectations as having a positive effect on NNESs, but interestingly added a negative outcome for native English speakers: "they don't have to improve their Chinese". In general, then, these respondents found their university's expectations of their NNES students reasonable on the grounds that "they encourage non-native speakers to improve their skills", or at least there are not "any expectations which may impact either positively or negatively non-native English students" (both UK). Meanwhile, one of the few to refer to NES students, let alone negatively, said of his/her UK university's expectations, "precious little effect on our native speakers; more on our non-native speakers, who have to meet our language requirements".

Some respondents also believed their university's English language expectations benefit NNES students in terms of study and work abroad, being able to learn about technological developments in other parts of the world, and the ability to publish in English and present at international conferences. Others talked more generally about the benefits to students' future careers. For example, an Australian argued that "high English standard expectations prepare [NNES] students for the rigours of professional practice", and a Spanish respondent commented "I think it [the university's expectations] is positive. They are well prepared and can have a job at the end". A Swedish respondent believed that "becoming fluent in business/

science/engineering English is of great value for one's career" though was not sure whether it is the university's expectations as such or "the years students spend here" that are responsible. Another from Sweden argued that "the benefit of learning and practicing to communicate advanced topics in English is necessary and valuable both in academic and industry".

A final theme that emerged from the question 7 data was the respondents' perceptions of **universities' motivations** for their expectations of students' English. On the one hand, some see this as related to concerns about reputation. As one Australian put it:

> High expectations of English especially at graduation, if met, may enhance the reputation of the university nationally and internationally and therefore make the degree it offers more valuable for local as well as international students.

Others, in non-Anglophone countries, mentioned the importance for their university's reputation of high English language skills of the students sent for study abroad. On the other hand, a motivation that was not stated directly, but which seems to underpin a large number of the question 7 responses, is the equation of internationalization with English which, in turn, leads universities to have certain English-related expectations of their students. But as this is the focus of question 9, we will consider it later on.

Despite the fact that the wording of question 7 specifically mentioned both NESs and NNESs, few respondents interpreted it that way, the vast majority focusing exclusively on NNES students. Overall, it seems, their universities' (and in many cases their own) English language expectations are entirely an NNES issue, with the main problem being seen as NNES students' difficulties in achieving a high standard of English (which, as discussed above, seems usually to mean 'native-like'). The occasional references to NESs tended to refer to their being neglected because NNES students need more attention, or to their finding communication with NNESs 'difficult'. And in one case, the university's expectations were considered positive not only because they encourage NNES students to improve their English, but because "they also value the abilities of the native English-speaking students", suggesting this (UK) respondent may believe that NESs can, by definition, do academic literacy, and that native English is, by default, the best.

We turn now to the two questions (8 and 9) that elicited the most extensive responses. First, question 8, which focused on the respondents' views of the respective responsibilities of NNES and NES students and staff in achieving successful intercultural communication (henceforth IC) on campuses where English is used as a lingua franca. Their comments generated three overlapping themes. The first of these is what I have called a **multilingualism–multiculturalism approach**. At the furthest extreme are the few who questioned the notion of English as the primary lingua franca of HE at all, and believed that everyone involved shares responsibility for successful intercultural communication within a framework of multilingualism and multiculturalism. For instance, a Danish respondent commented:

> I see a clash between a basic assumption that English is the solution to the communication problem in academic transnational encounters (very much found in our students, who often identify "being international" with speaking English) and the reality which is much more diversified.

Another, also from Denmark, argued that it would be good if staff were competent in languages other than English and Danish, so that students from elsewhere could submit their writings in those languages. S/he went on to say that "it would be even greater if staff and students could learn to accept and work around multi-lingualism", and added "why not let Chinese students work in groups in Chinese?" (see Chapter Seven for further discussion of this point). By contrast, a couple of other Danish respondents were critical of Danish home students who "switch over to Danish when they speak to fellow Danes" in breaks, periods before and after lectures, and in group work, or more generally "stick together" rather than mixing with international students who (presumably) do not speak Danish. This nevertheless links to another point made by some in the multilingualism-multiculturalism category: that for successful intercultural communication to take place, staff and students should be willing to learn the language of the country in which they are working or studying. A German respondent, for example, spoke of the importance of:

> willingness to learn the national language (at least to a certain extent). Both native speakers and non-native speakers shouldn't be too militant when it comes to language issues in their own communication but rather help each other and appreciate the different perspectives several languages can add to a department.

Another Danish respondent likewise said "I think it is a good idea to uphold the demand that non-Danish speaking staff should learn Danish". A Bruneian respondent argued similarly that "'Native' English-speaking staff should have some familiarity with languages that students bring to the university (e.g. Brunei and Standard Malay)", as well as being aware that their local English does not travel: "problems arise when expatriate [native English] staff use culture-bound idioms from US/UK/Australia and expect these to be understood by Bruneian students". And in the same vein, a Hong Kong respondent considers that all on campus, native and non-native, staff and student, "should keep an open mind and strive to achieve effective communication using a language that is spoken and understood by all, whether it is English, Cantonese or Putonghua – in the case of my University".

Meanwhile, two respondents from Argentina approached the issue of responsibility for IC from a political angle, one arguing:

> In the case of English in countries like mine, I think that those teaching and learning the language [English] should be careful to understand and discuss

openly the question of power. Because of the power that English-speaking countries have achieved in the whole world, learning English can have potentially adverse effects on the culture and language of our learners. Therefore, as educators we have the responsibility of helping students develop a critical mind so that they do not end up assuming a submissive attitude towards the foreign language [English].

The other criticized teachers for their "strong prejudices against Spanish, their own and the students'!!" and for "forever downgrading Spanish and exalting native speakers of English", pointing out that "we're all native speakers of a language".

There was general agreement among those in the multilingualism and multi-culturalism category that all staff and students, whether NES or NNES, have a responsibility to develop intercultural competence. Some spoke specifically about their own contexts, such as the German respondent who prioritizes "first of all, a general openness to the other culture/other cultures". Others spoke more generally. For instance, a Chinese respondent said that university staff and students should know their own culture and show an interest in other cultures. A Greek respondent described "risk-taking and curiosity about the 'other'" as "a must in order to encourage intercultural communication". And a UK respondent (NNES) argued:

> There are aspects other than language that allows intercultural communication such as respect for our beliefs, customs, way of life … So our responsibility is to study who the other person is and make the most to understand and respect that.

The second main theme emerging from the question 8 responses is a stronger **prioritizing of the English language for IC, but still within a multicultural framework** where there also is, or should be, mutual interest in each other's cultures. This group of respondents saw English as the most important language on campus, but did not hold to the 'English only' position that regards English as the *sine qua non* of HE. And while many in this group could be described as 'English mainly', some of them were closer in perspective to the respondents described above, in that they saw English and other languages more as complementary, and even, to an extent, on an equal footing. A Danish respondent, for example, argued:

> The university should educate students for both an international (i.e. English speaking) and a local (here, Danish-speaking) labour market, and this is a job that all staff should be willing to take part in, not only those of us (few in my dept.) who happen to have the local language as their native one.

A UK respondent spoke of the importance of "realising that language is about more than sound and structure and is primarily about communication. Becoming more aware of how subjective prejudice shapes attitude in this respect". Another in the UK (NNES) pointed out that culture as well as language is implicated in successful IC:

> Students should do their best to improve their English as much as possible through their study at [name of University] and social life. Staff should be interested in learning different cultures and languages and it is especially important for native English staff who have never lived outside the UK.

Others in this group took a more English-language focused approach to successful IC. As a respondent from Ecuador put it:

> I would expect all students and English speaking staff to model correct usage of the language and to value cultural diversity. They should use and practice English at all appropriate moments and be open to learning more about languages and cultures.

Another, from Japan (NES), commented likewise:

> Apart from the necessary linguistic proficiency (on the part of the non–native English students and, if applicable, staff), I think a willingness to cooperate (also and especially on the part of the 'natives') is key to achieving effective intercultural communication.

According to this perspective, on the one hand, all are responsible in terms of valuing "cultural diversity", being "open to learning more", and "willingness to cooperate". But on the other hand, "correct usage" is seen as equally important and the *linguistic* onus tends to be on the NNESs. Meanwhile, the assumption seems to be that the language in which they "cooperate" is by definition English, or English mainly. In other words, there seems to be an equation of IC with the English language.

The latter assumption was common among those who prioritized English within a framework of multiculturalism. Another Japanese respondent, for example, argued with reference to the G30 (Global 30) project (see Chapter Five), that IC is likely to become increasingly important in Japanese universities in the future, and therefore that "it is of the utmost importance that they [staff] equip students with the necessary skills to function in an intercultural environment". But given that the G30 project's prime concern is to "nurture internationally competent individuals" by means of teaching them in English medium environments, it seems that 'inter-cultural' refers here to communication in English rather than to IC per se. A UK respondent likewise argued that IC is "crucial", adding "the more interaction the greater the intercultural experience and the greater the development of a global society". But since the respondent was talking about the UK university system, one not known for its multilingualism, we can probably assume that, as with G30, the medium in which this "crucial" IC is conducted is English (or at best, English mainly) and, again, that IC simply means communication in English.

Some of the respondents in this group nevertheless referred to the importance of tolerance, understanding, and the acceptance of difference for successful intercultural communication to take place. Considering this in terms of staff responsibilities, one Argentinian said:

> In particular, I believe one of the main qualities a teacher must have in any subject is tolerance of differences of habits, values and opinions. This is, in my view, one of the foremost ingredients in developing intercultural communication.

Another argued that staff should acquaint students with cultural differences so as to enable them to be "open-minded and tolerant towards errors that do not hinder communication in contexts where English is used as a lingua franca". And a NNES respondent in the UK said "I think culture is more powerful than just language. I think natives have to be tolerant and patient. Another UK respondent, also a NNES, was more direct: "more understanding needs to be shown to the international staff/students. Stop picking on the accents and mistakes". And a respondent in China also thought "the native should be more tolerant and open-minded", adding "even English has borrowed so much from other languages".

Notwithstanding the point made above about the linguistic onus tending to be on the NNESs, the respondents in this second thematic grouping are to an extent divided as to where the responsibility for successful IC lies. Some believed all are responsible:

> Both students and staff should develop flexibility to adjust their language to their interlocutor's needs, tolerance, ambiguity to overcome the strain that the unfamiliar might produce, and cultural awareness in order to understand the system of beliefs of their own culture and to understand and respect different cultures. [Argentinian]

Another respondent from Argentina argued "both native and non-native English staff and students should be responsible for using the language in a way that will be understood by all people". A UK respondent (NNES) also talked about shared responsibility:

> It is an equal responsibility between staff and students to achieve effective intercultural communication. There is a need to encourage interaction between Home and international students and allow them understanding the value of intercultural communication. This is two ways process.

A US respondent likewise said "all faculty and students should have some awareness of cultural differences in communication". And a Thai respondent spoke of the need for everyone to "collaborate in order to design English-medium courses for the students as well as to familiarize the students with intercultural communication", commenting that this will both facilitate effective IC in the University "and enable us to be a perfect part of ASEAN flow". Another Thai respondent believed "one of the important factors is that the individual students and staff need to be aware the culture of the international interlocutors".

A minority even saw the main responsibility as that of NESs. For example, an Argentinian argued that "the onus is on the native ones to be welcoming, to show a strong and genuine interest in non-native citizens' experience of English" and "to understand that their variety of English and the cultural and institutional aspects of their society are no better than any others, but the result of historical developments". A US respondent saw successful IC specifically as a staff responsibility: "I think the greater responsibility lies on the staff and faulty because of their greater power". A UK respondent took a similar view, arguing that it is the staff's "responsibility to try to be as self-reflexive as possible in all matters of teaching, marking, discussion, etc.". This is an interesting point that has links with the issues of equity raised in some of the responses to question 7. A few UK respondents also made points about NES staff's responsibility specifically in respect of their use of English, and the need to avoid local (i.e. national) forms in *international* communication. For example:

> Try harder, avoid colloquialisms and think more actively about choice of words and multiple ways of saying things.
>
> I suspect it starts with an awareness (e.g. for staff to avoid overuse of idioms) and then moves on to develop a respect and understanding of the benefits for all of such interactions
>
> Remembering to speak clearly and distinctly and avoiding as far as possible colloquialisms or narrow cultural references. Making it clear, politely but perhaps repeatedly, when one has not understood another person – ideally re-expressing what the other speaker is thought to have meant.

However, another UK respondent (NNES) was aware that such practices are not necessarily commonplace:

> Many students have confided to me (perhaps because I am also non-native) that the English malaise of the unfinished, trailing phrasing and the excessive "polite" hesitation makes sentences infuriatingly imprecise and often difficult to follow. I agree with their observation.

A few UK-based respondents also considered the responsibility of home students. One described how home students tend to complain "if they get a 'foreigner' for a lecturer", and argued that as well as providing workshops for NNES lecturers, the University should "educate the [home] students", though adding that "in this fee-paying climate, it will be more difficult to persuade them to be tolerant and try to accommodate, as they will believe it is compromising their learning".

The latter point has implications for the final sub-theme, those who considered IC from an English language perspective, but went beyond a view of non-native English as defined by its errors and the need for tolerance of them, to seeing it as acceptable difference. Their focus, therefore, was on how to achieve successful IC by means of a more flexible approach to the English language. A respondent from the US argued that NES staff and students "need to have an idea of the global reach of English" and what this means to those who do not speak it as their first language "but may use it in a number of ways". S/he went on to argue that university staff "need to situate their language and its use in the wider world and realise that language status is not a neutral phenomenon and language hegemony has global implications".

The respondents in this group talked of mutual intelligibility as a two-way process, in which familiarity with, and accommodation to, each other's Englishes play key roles. An Argentinian argued that "on both sides they should benefit from English being the medium and not strengthen the fact that the participating varieties are necessarily different". A Malaysian observed:

> Staff and students will have to understand that different students come with different varieties of English and different cultures and must try and understand the differences and commonalities in the English used.

And a Singaporean respondent's solution to successful mutually negotiated IC was to "take note of misunderstandings that occur as a result of language differences and try to veer towards a model that all can understand", rather than to native English.

We turn now to the final main theme, the **normative approaches**. In contrast to the more liberal and nuanced views that typified many of the responses to questions 7, 8, and 9, a substantial number of respondents took a far more normative approach to IC, and focused exclusively on NNESs' English language skills as bearing the responsibility. Interestingly, the language in which they expressed this view is often remarkably similar. The following are typical examples. A Japanese respondent, for instance, considered that successful IC depends on NNES staff gaining "sufficient proficiency in English". A Chinese respondent said the same, arguing that it is unreasonable to expect NESs to learn Chinese (in order to work or study in Chinese universities!). Other Chinese respondents made similar points, including that "they [NNESs] should aim high and do more", "using English properly and clearly", and "non-natives should improve their English levels". A Danish respondent suggested that NNESs should "follow additional courses when needed, take care to listen carefully as well as to express yourself as well as you can!!!". Meanwhile, a Spanish respondent commented "they [NNES students] can also have a very good knowledge but they cannot communicate in English. They should have to improve their English", a Taiwanese respondent said that "for the students, taking it [English] as an important skill and being diligent", a Turkish respondent that "high entrance standards and a good preparatory class is what it takes", and another that NNESs should "perform to the expectations of an institution with high standards", with English being "a means to reach that goal both for the faculty and the students", which "inevitably leads to effective intercultural communication".

Similar comments were made by several of the UK respondents, such as:

> I think we should try to improve students' use of English where it is parti-
> cularly weak ... I think students also have a responsibility to try to improve
> their use of language where they know it is weak.

Whereas the respondents in the 'English within a multicultural framework' the-matic grouping tended to see accommodation and familiarity with difference as the solution to successful IC on campus, those belonging to the normative group saw the solution as the use of English only. A Japanese respondent, for example, argued:

> The university staff ... needs to institute a strict English–only policy in class
> because students easily switch back to Japanese otherwise. As for students
> they should understand the importance and meaning of having English–only
> courses in their career-development and do their best to develop the habit of
> learn content matter in English.

A Turkish respondent believed "all activities should be in English as it was in the 60s", and a Taiwanese respondent likewise suggests that all courses should be taught in English. In this respect, a Chinese respondent felt that students should read more papers in English, while a Chilean respondent thought the presence of NES staff on campus would be helpful.

Members of this normative group also tended to hold the view that there is 'no alternative'. While this was implicit in much that they said in respect of the pre-vious two sub-themes, it was sometimes stated directly. One reason given by sev-eral respondents was the fact that English is the language of scientific international communication, and thus, whatever a student's or staff's career stage, they will find that 'proficient' English is now required international practice. Others believed that it is the only way for NNESs, especially in Anglo contexts, to receive an education as good as that of NES students. As one UK respondent put it, "it is grotesquely unfair on students to let them start a PhD when they will spend the first year struggling with reading and writing. This means they don't receive a fair educa-tion". This is, on the surface, a reasonable point. But it avoids the issue of what 'proficiency' involves, or should involve, in a twenty-first century international HE setting, and does not consider that changing the way education is delivered might make it more "fair" than expecting near-native English from international students.

Question 9 went on to explore the respondents' understanding of the implica-tions, English-wise, for universities that describe themselves as 'international'. More specifically, it asked them to consider what kind of English 'international' uni-versities should require of their staff and students. Four main themes emerged, of which the first concerns the **amount and scope of English that is implied by a university's claim to be 'international'**. Perhaps inevitably, given the questionnaire wording, many responses across the (geographical) board referred to English as the main language of international academic communication, with internationalization typically seen as linked specifically to English. Others mentioned English as the working language of international universities, and a need for the whole community in any such institution to be able to communicate fluently in English across language boundaries. At the 'English only' extreme, some argued that both academic and non-academic communication should be in English, while others talked of the importance of NNESs having opportunities to communicate with NESs and/or to study abroad in Anglophone settings. And from this perspective, there was also a view that NNES staff should have overseas experience (meaning in Anglophone universities) and be able to lecture in English.

The second question 9 theme was a **normative approach** to the type of English that a substantial number saw as necessary for an international university. Several again mentioned English language proficiency, referring to the need for 'good' English, a 'high' or 'sophisticated' level of English, and the like. For example, a Swedish respondent said:

> The aim is to develop English skills so communication becomes effortless. For the students (and staff ...) to speak and write *proper English like a native* is another matter which would require significant efforts. For instance, a native English speaker would have a much larger vocabulary and would master synonyms and nuances. [Respondent's italics.]

Similarly, a Chinese respondent:

> I think a university to describe itself as 'an international university' should require its students and staff reach the level of academic English proficiency of giving lectures and presentations, writing and communicating with *native speakers* freely. [My italics.]

A Turkish respondent believed an international university "should expect native-like competence from its students as well as its faculty". And a UK respondent linked lower standards with NNESs:

> Should an international university expect a lower standard? No. ... To be 'international' means that students from many backgrounds are enrolled – they will have many native languages. There should be adequate support to them so that they can receive an education of the highest standard of English.

Another UK respondent considered that in an international university, "non native speakers should be subject to the same language requirements and expectations as native speakers". Meanwhile, another Chinese respondent linked English proficiency to the university's reputation, saying "this requirement should be high or otherwise the reputation of the institution declines". In this respect, a German respondent stated that unless the language requirement is high, there is a risk that German professors will "end up in baby English". And while a number of respondents referred to English that is "globally understood" and the like, they conflated this with native English.

The third theme emerging from the question 9 responses was a **more open approach** towards international university English. A Japanese respondent, for example, said "university community members should be encouraged to speak their own variety of English ... in our university, this means they shouldn't be afraid of using their Japanese variety of English". S/he went on to say:

> We have many international students from other parts of the world as well, so what our university should aim for is an 'international' English that reflects features of diverse varieties of English that its members bring to campus.

A Brunei respondent (NES) made a similar point: "being an international university has meant moving away from a more British language framework, and more international students also means more varieties of forms of English" (even though in theory, if not in practice, they "must still officially require British English").

While other respondents, like the last two, saw 'international' English in terms of diversity, some saw it as more unitary. An Argentinian respondent, for instance, said:

> It is undeniable that a new kind of English, an international variety of English, is emerging all around the globe. Many call it globish. In this sense, universities cannot look the other way and continue requiring proper British or American varieties without accepting the existence of this new variety of English.

On the other hand, a UK respondent argued more pessimistically that no such world standard of English exists as yet, and so "we have nothing better to steer students or teachers to", adding:

> I can't see us getting there any time soon. As long as English is regulated internationally by bodies such as Cambridge ESOL, IELTS and TOEFL, which are accepted by governments round the world as benchmarks for English, it will be very difficult to move towards a world standard or to recognise regional differences. We're not even allowed to do this with UK dialects!

A Brazilian was equally pessimistic:

> tradition still prevails. It's easy to eyewitness that there's very little tolerance to other Englishes (especially in academic writing), and the common practice

seems to be a disregard for students' cultural differences. As it frequently happens, we see international students being forced to 'adjust to the system' though mandatory courses which potentially, will either 'anglicise' or 'americanize' their writing and, consequently, their ways of thinking.

By contrast, some of this group did see change on the horizon. A German respondent argued, for example, that "the era of reliance on UK- and US-based notions of correct English is coming to an end". S/he went on to say that English has become "a language that transcends these cultural spheres", and that "using English as a means of scientific communication between non-natives ... poses different requirements than speaking like a native". S/he compared the traditional university situation to that of academic journals that call themselves 'international', asking "if most of their authors are from the UK or US, how does that qualify as international? Real internationalisation requires bidirectionality".

With the fourth theme, a **multilingual approach to the international university**, we move on away from a focus on English or even Englishes, to one in which other languages are crucially involved. A Greek respondent summed up this position by saying "for me, an international university should have a policy for multilingualism and multiculturalism". S/he went on to argue:

> If English is to be the recognised official language of the university, it should be seen more as a tool of communication between everyone involved rather than a standard language with its own independent rules that everyone should adhere to.

A Chinese respondent argued that "both English and Chinese should serve as the official languages", and that all staff and students should be able to communicate in both. And an Argentinian respondent said similarly "I believe a truly international university should be bilingual". An Ecuadorian respondent thought an international university should provide its students with the opportunity to learn other languages, while a US respondent said "I would assume an international university would not have a monolingual/English focus", though added "I'm not really sure if any university in the US could even begin to describe itself that way".

Comments and complaints: question 10

The final question asked respondents if they wished to make further comments on either the topic or the questionnaire itself. This question elicited the least number of responses (119) and of these, many simply said "no thanks", "I enjoyed answering the questions", "very interesting questions", "good luck with your research", and the like. However, those who did have something more to say raised interesting points, sometimes at great length. Their responses divided into four broad areas: comments about the importance of the topic and how the questionnaire had enabled them to reflect on it; language-ideological arguments; issues not raised by the questionnaire; and complaints about the open-ended format.

Starting with the **importance of the topic**, several respondents commented that the questionnaire raises important and ambitious questions. An Australian respondent, for example, said "this is an important area to research and ameliorate", and a Chinese that "it is meaningful to do such research". A UK respondent considered it to be "an interesting topic which will probably increase in relevance over the next few years". And another from the UK said:

> As a university we are hoping to recruit a lot more international students so it is an area that is vital for our future. I would love [name of University] to be known (in the UK and overseas) as a university where international students will enjoy coming to.

Some of those who found the topic interesting and important expressed a desire to see my findings. A Dane said, for example: "I'm curious about the results of your investigations so please let me know when and where results are getting published. Perhaps this could make me think less pessimistically about it all", while a Swedish respondent said s/he had no further comments, but added "I would like to see what comes out of your study". And a UK (NNES respondent) said "I just want to tell you I enjoyed answering this questionnaire. Good luck with your research. If I could know the outcomes of the research when it becomes available, I really appreciate it".

A number of respondents commented that the questionnaire had enabled them to reflect on issues that they had not previously considered, or even been aware of as 'issues' at all. For example, a respondent from Argentina said:

> It's an interesting experience to reflect on the topic of university language policies through a sort of 'guided tour'. I had never stopped to even consider what is being done at [name of University] or in Argentina in general ... Thanks for the opportunity!

A Chinese respondent simply stated that "the topic is really good and it helps me to retrospect my teaching experience in the past few years", and a Swede that "I have come to think of these issues by filling in your form".

The second main theme to emerge from question 10 concerned **language ideology**. The strongest expression of this was a Brazilian respondent who argued that there is a need to politicize the entire discussion about university English.

> First, I'd like to congratulate you for bringing up this discussion at a world level. This is a very sensitive topic and as it involves a multi-billion [dollar?] industry which, in many ways, has consolidated a lot of its privileges throughout time, it is good and about time to discuss and open our minds to

the simple fact that there is still a long path to tread. The first important thing this study does is to positively 'politicize' and 'ideologize' the discourse.

Other respondents argued that students should have a choice as to whether they learn English or learn *in* English, or spoke in support of the importance of the local language as well as English. And one of the few who had heard of ELF believed it (rather than American or British English) should be the default language in HE.

The third main theme was less of a unified theme and more of a series of **comments relating to the topic**, that some respondents felt had not been sufficiently covered by the other questions. The main points they raised related to the needs of NNESs students and staff, and in particular that universities should recognize the language needs of international students, and should help NNES staff to teach in English. Some also focused on English language testing saying, for example, that universities should conduct their own tests, and not use the generic Anglophone 'international' ones such as IELTS and TOEFL. Others spoke of the pressing need to find a way of distinguishing between English proficiency level and English variety. Finally a few questioned the meaning of the term 'international university'.

The final theme involved **complaints about the questionnaire format** itself. Some said they found the questions too abstract, complex, and deep to tackle adequately in a reasonably short time. Others commented negatively on the open-ended format and said I should have asked closed questions. And a couple (themselves both L1 English speakers) objected to my use of the terms 'native English speaker' and 'non-native English speaker', arguing that these tend to be used in prejudicial ways and that a neutral term such as 'expert speaker' is preferable.[8] This, of course, takes us right back to the whole issue of who can be considered expert in English in the context of an international university.

Interpretations of the questionnaire findings

As the questionnaire analysis and discussion has demonstrated, there was a considerable amount of common ground in respect of staff perspectives on university English both among the respondents and across each individual's responses to the ten questions. Overall, the findings reveal:

- an assumption that English is the language of the internationalization of HE and therefore the most appropriate language to serve as a common medium of instruction among speakers from different L1s
- that native English, specifically 'standard' North American or British academic English, is widely seen as the most acceptable kind of English
- a focus on NNES students as problems in terms of both language and IC
- a lack of focus on NES students as problems in either respect
- a distinction between NNES and NES respondents in terms of level of awareness of the lived experience of NNES students studying in English medium.

In order to draw the questionnaire findings together and interpret them more broadly, I adopted a three-pronged approach combining three separate but overlapping conceptual frameworks. The first of these is the 'beliefs' component of Spolsky's conceptualization of language policy (2004: 70), the second is Woolard's (2005) ideologies of 'authenticity' and 'anonymity' (see pp. 72–73), and the third is Wodak's (2006) notion of "Us and Them", an approach to exploring discourses on language policy rather than a conceptual framework per se.

As explained in Chapter Four, Spolsky's (2004) 'beliefs' component is one of three that together comprise his conceptualization of language policy (the other two being 'language practices' and 'language management'). Members of a given speech community, argues Spolsky, share "a general set of beliefs about appropriate language practices, sometimes forming a consensual ideology, assigning values and prestige to various aspects of the language varieties used in it" (p. 14).

In the case of my questionnaire respondents, the speech community was composed of academic teaching staff working in global academia. And as the questionnaire has demonstrated, regardless of whether they are L1 English speakers or not, and working in Anglo settings or not, there was a "consensual ideology" among the majority that native English is superior to non-native. This was equally so for those who are tolerant of NNES divergences from native English as for those who are not. For even the respondents who argued, for example, that allowances should be made for NNES students' English, and that intelligibility or conveying meaning are more important than form, tended to couch their arguments in words that reveal an underlying 'good English = native English' perspective even if they did not actually state it. As mentioned earlier, the word 'good' occurred 154 times, in almost every case referring to native English. Words such as 'correct', 'excellent', 'perfect', 'proper', and the like were also used in this way, while NNES English was generally considered in terms of the user's 'proficiency' or 'competence' within a framework of 'errors', all words which occurred frequently, while as also mentioned earlier, the word 'standard' (occurring 107 times) mostly collocated with 'high' in order to refer to native English.

In addition, the majority of the comments expressing more flexible approaches towards NNES students' English were revealed as practical decisions, particularly the need to show a degree of tolerance, rather than as reflections of an ideology that sees non-native English as acceptable. Many of the 'tolerant' respondents, for example, made comments similar to that of the respondent quoted above (p. 143), who observed that although 'good' English is desirable, this does not mean that s/he expects "perfect native English models" from the NNES students. And as I pointed out in the earlier discussion, when it came to focusing specifically on students' English usage rather than on the more abstract questionnaire topics, and especially on academic writing, the tolerance of divergence from native English was diminished.

A relatively small number of respondents were in favour of regarding NNES students' English, where it differs from native English, as legitimate variation. Indeed, the only ones who took this view consistently across all questions were a very (sociolinguistically) political Brazilian, a couple of Argentinians, a Dane, and a Bruneian (the latter being the only NES among them). As well as this, one respondent argued consistently in favour of multilingualism and a few others (all NNESs) for the local language(s) as well as English to be used habitually on campus, rather than English being their institution's primary/only lingua franca. In terms of 'beliefs', then, there was a "consensual ideology" among the majority of the respondents, regardless of how they respond to it in practice, that native academic English is appropriate in HE while non-native variation from it is not, and that the former has high status while the latter does not.

Woolard's (2005) ideologies of anonymity and authenticity (see Chapter Four) concern, on the one hand, the belief that a dominant language or variety is universal (in the metaphorical sense), neutral, and therefore widely available and understood (anonymity), and on the other hand, the notion that a particular community of speakers represents the authentic voice of a language. In the case of English, the combination of these two ideologies has led to the widespread perception that English is (and should be) global, that authentic English is that of British and/or North American NNESs, and that these native communities' English varieties are standard, common, and unmarked: in effect, as 'global' as the language itself.

Both ideologies are heavily represented among the university questionnaire responses. In respect of the ideology of anonymity, it is striking that so few questioned the role of English as the universal lingua franca of HE at all. Even though the questionnaire did not ask specifically about this, its open-ended nature, and particularly the completely open final question, provided respondents with plentiful opportunity to talk about the things that most concerned them. And many of them did so at length on other topics, but not this one. It seemed that the majority simply took it as given that English is (and, for most, should be) used in their institution.

The only debate to be had, then, was what kind of English is acceptable. And in accordance with the notion of authenticity, native English, British and/or North American, was unanimously preferred. In addition, most respondents not only saw non-native Englishes as non-preferred, but also as simply incorrect English. Meanwhile, many of their comments about the need for NNES students to 'improve' their English also hinted at the idea that native English is available to them if only they are willing to put in the time and effort to learn it. This takes us back to the ideology of anonymity: not only is English 'universal', but so is native English.

While many respondents, particularly those who are NNESs themselves, were tolerant of their NNES students' English and said that they make allowances for it, this did not mean that they consider it legitimate. Very few of those with flexible approaches went beyond tolerating NNES students' 'errors' to an acceptance of these differences from ENL as "non-native sources of innovation" (Woolard and Schieffelin 1994: 64), or to an acknowledgement of bilingualism (and therefore code-switching) as the norm, or the need for NESs to adjust their local English in international communication settings (including Anglophone). And the fact that almost all problematizing in the questionnaires, with a tiny number of exceptions, focused on NNES students (even when a question did not, itself, focus on NNESs) suggests that NES students are seen, by definition, as using legitimate (anonymous and authentic) English, while NNESs are not. This even extended to comments made about IC, where there was a strong tendency, particularly among respondents in Anglophone contexts, to put the onus for successful communication on NNES students, and also to blame them for communication problems with NES students. This is very much at odds with the views of the international students I interviewed (see Chapter Seven). Meanwhile, the notion of NES students' English as unproblematic concurs with the findings of the website study, in which it emerged that NNES university applicants are routinely required to gain particular scores on English language entry tests, whereas NES applicants are not (see Chapter Five).

The questionnaire findings thus provide a sense of linguistic inequality in HE English language policy and practices: in other words, a sense of "Us and Them" (Wodak 2006: 178). This is not to suggest that my questionnaire respondents consciously view the relationship, English-wise, of a NES "Us" and a NNES "Them", or that they would wish to do so. However, this view of linguistic life appears to be so deeply entrenched in many areas of life, often subconsciously, that it is very often considered to represent basic common sense, as I believe is the case in HE.

Wodak discusses five "discursive strategies" that she sees as "useful in the analysis of discourses on language policies" (ibid.). These strategies, she argues, "are all involved in positive self- and negative other-representation" and "serve the justification or legitimization of inclusion/exclusion and of constructions of identities" (p. 179). She presents them in the form of the following five questions:

1. How are persons named and referred to linguistically?
2. What traits, characteristics, qualities, and features are attributed to them?
3. By means of what arguments and argumentation schemes do specific persons or social groups try to justify and legitimize the inclusion/exclusion of others?
4. From what perspective or point of view are these labels, attributions, and arguments expressed?
5. Are the respective utterances articulated overtly? Are they intensified or are they mitigated?

Looking at these questions in terms of my questionnaire findings, while there is no evidence of "positive self- and negative-other representation" in the "naming" of NNESs, there is plenty of evidence of this kind of thing in relation to Wodak's second question. Terms such as 'good', 'high standard', 'proper', 'perfect', and the like occur regularly throughout the questionnaires in respect of native English. By contrast, NNESs' English is mostly characterized as 'poor', 'incorrect', containing 'errors', and NNES students themselves as lacking sufficient 'command', 'competence', and 'proficiency' in English (there were 148 instances in total referring in some way to NNESs' lack of command/proficiency/competence). The prevailing view was that NNES students whose English is not sufficiently near-native should make efforts to improve it, a view that was justified (Wodak's third question) by the 'common sense' argument I mentioned, according to which native English represents an unquestioned (and unquestionable) 'natural linguistic order' in HE. Interestingly, this argument, whether overtly or covertly articulated, was voiced from the perspective of both NNES and NES respondents. It seems that, as with the NNES respondents in my earlier study (Jenkins 2007), many of these NNES staff were complicit in the subordination and negative stereotyping of their own English, a point made by Lippi-Green (2011) in respect of NNESs' pronunciation specifically. Very few, by contrast, offered any resistance to the 'native English is best' position.

Overall, then, the respondents had strong beliefs and ideologies about English. But in many cases, they had a pre-internationalization perception of university English. Most had not thought much, if at all, about the implications of the internationalization of HE for the lingua franca of this internationalization, that is, English. In particular, there was almost no awareness of ELF. And while I would not expect the term itself to be familiar to any except the few respondents who work in related areas of linguistics, I had expected some awareness of the phenomenon itself, of the fact that so much communication in academic settings takes place entirely among NNESs, and some sense of what NNESs are contributing to the evolving twenty-first century English language (beyond errors!).

The findings of the questionnaire study are summed up in the University-English Ideology Continuum (Figure 6.1). At the two extremes, are total conformity to Anglophone norms and total acceptance of diversity, that is, multilingualism, on campus. Most respondents fell between the two, almost all seeing English as the 'natural' medium of instruction. Many regarded conformity as important, but were willing to accept (or were resigned to) a certain amount of divergence from native English norms. In the middle are the largest number, those who were most flexible about the kind of 'lower proficiency' English they accepted provided the content itself is clear. They nevertheless still conceptualized any divergences from ENL as errors, and most were more tolerant of spoken than written 'errors'. The smaller group to their right in the figure are those who were flexible about their NNES

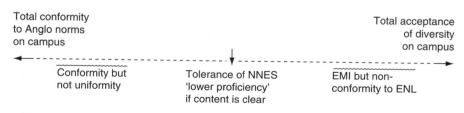

FIGURE 6.1 The University-English Ideology Continuum

students' English *and* saw it as legitimate when it differs from native academic English. But again, some of this group were more likely to be flexible about spoken than written differences from ENL, so did not fully believe in the legitimacy of non-native Englishes.

Other broad points of interest emerged from the analysis. One of these was that there was little noticeable difference in orientation across macro regions/countries, with the exception of a substantial distinction in orientation between Anglophone and non-Anglophone contexts. That is, respondents working in non-Anglophone contexts, especially NNESs, were more likely to show awareness of NNES students' (and staff's) difficulties in studying (and teaching) in EMI environments, and particularly of the time involved in improving their English as well as studying their academic subject, something the NES respondents seemed largely unaware of. This was also true of most of the NNES respondents working in Anglophone countries.

There was also little evidence of different orientations to English across disciplines, with more normative-minded and more tolerant respondents spread equally among the hard sciences, social sciences, arts, and humanities. And while some respondents, across both countries and disciplines, cited their institution's normative orientation, including the requirement for students to pass examinations, as the reason for their own normative approach, in most cases there was little evidence that they disagreed with their institution in this regard. That said, as the University-English Ideology Continuum demonstrates, there were also a few respondents who argued in favour of NNES versions of English as acceptable variation rather than 'incorrect' English in need of improvement (or tolerance). These few, unlike the majority, however, tended to be familiar with ELF research.

The Chapter Six findings as a whole, like those of Chapter Five, illustrate the strength of standard native English ideology among the majority of the sample across the regional, L1, and discipline board. To a great extent, respondents had not considered the issues before, but had simply taken it for granted that native English should be the lingua franca of global HE. These findings thus demonstrate the need for awareness raising among the university faculty of the facts concerning the spread of English and the implications of its lingua franca use in HE. In this respect, it was encouraging that so many of the respondents who said they had not thought about the subject before spoke of the importance of the issues raised by the questionnaire. This indicates that there may be a certain amount of receptivity ready to be tapped into, a finding that also emerged from the conversations with international students, to which we now turn.

Notes

1 I am immensely grateful to Ying Wang for teaching me how to use NVivo.
2 While word counts were occasionally used to "demonstrate the magnitude for certain observations" (Berg 2009: 345), they never served as a basis for quantitative analysis. Instead, my approach was broadly similar to that of Adamson and Muller in their (2012) questionnaire study of journal reviewers, in which "[d]ata is not analysed quantitatively

but some frequency of common responses is referred to, as in 'most common responses'. Less frequent responses are also cited if of interest" (p. 97).

3 The coding of the main themes and first-level sub themes for each question is shown separately in Appendix 3 (pp. 216–19).

4 Note that when I refer to a respondent as 'Chinese', 'Spanish', 'from Thailand', and so on, this means they are L1 speakers of Chinese, Spanish, Thai, and so on unless otherwise stated. I have also indicated where those working in Anglophone settings are L2 English speakers. However, in both cases, I have not done so where there is a risk that it could reveal a respondent's identity.

5 Throughout the discussion of the questionnaire findings, apart from correcting typos, I have reported the exact words used by my respondents, and have also eschewed the convention of adding *sic* where an item is not standard according to Anglophone norms.

6 Bold type is used to highlight the main themes that emerged from the analysis of questions 4, 5, 7, 8, 9, and 10.

7 According to this respondent's answer to earlier questions, if his/her institution's English language expectations are indeed "the norm for an American university", then the norm means minimum scores in TOEFL and SAT/GRE (Scholastic Aptitude Test/Graduate Record Examination), all run by ETS, and for undergraduates, passing "English 101" (a basic composition course).

8 I admit to feeling ambivalent about these terms myself, and have in the past suggested alternatives (see Jenkins 1996b, 2000), as has Rampton (1990). However, it is not the terms themselves that concern me. After all, whether one is an L1 or L2 speaker of English is simply a fact of many English speakers' lives. Rather, it is the way the term 'non-native speaker' is sometimes used to disadvantage people (e.g. by advertising jobs for which it is essential to be a native or near-native English speaker), and to stigmatize people whose English is different from so-called 'standard' native varieties. However, I continue to use the terms myself because, as yet, there are no widely recognized alternatives. In any case, it seems to me that the term 'native' is beginning to lose its advantage in respect of English (see Chapter Two and the Afterword for further discussion of this point).

7

CONVERSATIONS WITH INTERNATIONAL STUDENTS

Introduction

Whereas the studies reported in Chapters Five and Six range widely around the world, Chapter Seven turns to one single country, the UK. I chose this setting partly because the UK is currently the second most popular destination for international students (the US being the most popular), and partly because it is the context in which I have had my most substantial contact with international students, particularly at master's and doctoral level. I therefore felt that my familiarity with the kind of setting in which the interview participants were studying would facilitate a more natural, relaxed style of exchange and lead to the establishment of an easier rapport. And although it is not possible to generalize from qualitative research of this kind, even from one participant group to another let alone one country to another, I anticipated that some of the key issues raised by the students in my study were likely to apply to international students in other Anglophone settings such as the US and Australia as well as elsewhere in the UK. This was in fact confirmed during the course of the study to the extent that several participants described similar experiences elsewhere.

The interview, or more accurately, conversation study was carried out in order to attempt to answer my third research question: what are the perceived effects of current English language policies and practices on international, EU and home students? The sub-questions (see Chapter Four for details) focus on the linguistic expectations and requirements of international students, the students' perceived effects of these on their academic identities and self esteem as well as on home students' intercultural communication skills, and their perceptions of any differences in orientation to non-native English in Anglophone versus non-Anglophone contexts.

I decided to include conversations with international students[1] in my overall research design because it seemed to me that while a lot has been spoken and written about international students, they had not yet, to my knowledge, been given very much opportunity to engage in the debate to any great extent themselves, particularly in respect of the English language and EMI. Where their input has been sought, this has tended to relate primarily or entirely to cultural rather than linguistic issues. UK-based examples of this kind include Trahar and Hyland's (2011) focus group study, Montgomery's (2010) monograph, and studies by Schweisfurth and Gu (2009), Tian and Lowe (2009), and Wu and Hammond (2011). Some of the research exploring international students' perspectives on cultural issues focuses on students from one particular L1, for example Chang and Kanno's (2010) study of Taiwanese students, and Tarry's (2011) of Thai students, as well as some of the contributions to two volumes on Chinese learners: Jin and Cortazzi (2011) and Coverdale-Jones and Rastall (2009).

Two other recent edited volumes, while mainly conceptual rather than empirical, and focusing primarily on staff orientations, likewise include chapters exploring international students' perspectives in the UK. However, one of these, Clifford and Montgomery (2011), is concerned with internationalizing the HE curriculum for global citizenship, and given the (to my mind bizarre) fact that the 'international curriculum' is not generally seen as involving language issues, the volume barely touches on English. Ryan's (2013) edited collection, many of whose contributions are again UK-based, likewise focuses mainly on cultural matters. This volume also provides a useful demonstration of current differences in orientation to linguistic and cultural issues in discourses about international universities. For whereas its culture-related contributions typically approach culture as a two-way process of accommodation involving both home and international students and staff, its few references to English language, with the main exception of Wicaksono's chapter, tend to approach it as a one-way phenomenon in which the 'problem' is international students' level of English, and therefore international students who need, with remedial help, to make all the linguistic adjustments. For as Turner (2012: 11) points out in relation to Anglophone HE, "[d]espite the fact that internationalization is a key strategic aim of university policy across the sector, this does not seem to apply to language, language use, and pedagogic practice" and "leaves the field open for the already widespread discourse of remediation to predominate".

The majority of empirical studies focusing on international students in the UK to date, then, have been concerned more with cultural than linguistic factors, and few have sought international students' perspectives on English in the international university. The number of studies exploring English has nevertheless increased over the past few years. In the UK context again, for example, recent studies include Henderson (2011), who reports on group interviews with international and home undergraduates (the latter, though, in the majority), and Hennebry, Lo, and Macaro (2012), who administered a questionnaire to 43 students, and interviewed a small sub-set of their respondents as well as six staff. Others have focused on one particular aspect of international student life, such as Carter's (2012) study of the PhD viva, Copland and Garton's (2011) research into a pre-sessional programme, Pilcher, Cortazzi, and Jin's (2011) study of Chinese students' experience of the master's dissertation, and Trahar's (2011) exploration of international students' doctoral experiences. Turner (2011), meanwhile, is a book length treatment of English language issues that impact on international students in HE, although mainly conceptual and descriptive rather than empirical in approach.

While each of these makes a valuable contribution to the field, none is a substantial empirical study providing international students from a range of L1s with a discursive space in which they could engage in conversation about their full range of UK English language-related experiences in private (rather than in focus groups) for as long as they wished. And the same seems to be true of such research in other Anglophone contexts. For example, a considerable amount of research on international students has been conducted in Australia, but again the focus has tended to be on non-linguistic matters such as internationalizing the curriculum, intercultural issues, and global citizenship. This is the case with most of the Australian contributions to the edited volumes of Carroll and Ryan (2005), Clifford and Montgomery (2011), and Ryan (2013), the majority of which, as mentioned above, are also conceptual rather than empirical. Little is said about language, and even less from international students' own perspectives.

On the other hand, Ryan and Viete (2009), in an article on international students in Australian HE, do focus on linguistic as well as cultural issues. They consider factors such as the impact of native English norms on international students' self-identity and self-esteem, both of which are highly relevant to my own study. But theirs, again, is a conceptual piece drawing on the authors' own experience and previous research rather than providing new empirical evidence. Fraser (2011), by contrast, is an empirical study that explores perceptions of the intercultural communication skills of both native and non-native students and of academic and administrative staff, and involves questionnaires, follow-up interviews, and workshops. Her project is unusual in that rather than seeing international students' language skills as the default problem, her starting point was "a commitment to a 'two-way' approach, paying attention to the speaking and listening skills not just of international students but of local people" (p. A118). She draws the intriguing conclusion that developing NESs' intercultural competence may be the most effective option, and refers to the potential for her research to demonstrate "the return on investment from a two-way approach to improving speaking and listening skills in the multicultural university" (p. A119). However, Fraser's study was not designed with the aim of exploring her international student participants' linguistic experiences in depth, and the perspectives of the small number interviewed therefore form only a small part of the overall discussion. In general, though, most of the few who explore English language as opposed to cultural issues affecting international students in the Australian context, as with the UK context, take a deficit perspective towards international students' English, and focus on how to 'help' NNES students increase their proficiency – a point made by Benzie (2010) who, nevertheless, sees social integration with NESs as part of the solution.

By contrast with Australia, studies of international students conducted in the North American context look more frequently at English language issues, often from a language socialization perspective. Some scholars such as Duff (2010; see also p. 123 above) and Horner, Lu, Jones Royster, and Trimbur (2011) take a nuanced view of language socialization in respect of international students rather than assuming it to be a one-way assimilation process on the part of the students. But again, these are conceptual pieces rather than new empirical studies. Sherry, Thomas, and Chui (2010), on the other hand, is an empirical investigation of international students' experiences, albeit an exploratory internet survey, while Marshall (2010) provides a much more in-depth investigation of international students' English language experiences at a Canadian university and the negative effects on their identities of "re-becoming ESL" (p. 41). From a similar perspective, Lee and Maguire (2011) conclude from their in-depth interview study of two Korean international students at another Canadian university that their two cases "call for a re-examination of hegemonic approaches that have become normative ways of framing, representing, and describing 'English Learners' and their learning challenges from a deficit view" (p. 368).

However, the majority of North American studies that focus on international students in relation to the English language, particularly in the US context, seem to do precisely this. In other words, they tend to frame the issues they explore with their interview participants as unproblematic: simply a matter of identifying NNES students' academic English 'deficiencies' and helping them to overcome these so that they are able to assimilate to American ways of doing academic English. The same deficit assumptions about international students' English can be found even in studies whose authors consider NES discrimination to be a major factor, such as Lee and Rice's (2007) interview study with 24 international students in a university in the US Southwest. But it is especially so in studies involving international students who work as international teaching assistants (ITAs), where there is a strong tendency to treat academic American English as if it was fixed in time and space, and to problematize the ITAs' English but not the expectations of their (largely) NES undergraduate students (e.g. Ates and Eslami 2012, Chiang and Mi 2011). This, in turn, limits both what researchers (are able to) ask their international student interviewees and the interviewees' freedom to explore their own and the interviewers' views in depth and, perhaps, in new ways, as I hoped would be the case in my interviews.

Collecting the conversation data

My own study involved lengthy conversations (mostly 1–1½ hour) with 34 post-graduate international students at a UK Russell Group university[2] during summer 2012. I chose postgraduate students partly because they are currently the majority of international students in the UK, and partly because they would be able to draw on previous HE experience, whether in EMI or non-EMI classrooms and Anglophone or non-Anglophone settings.

The participants came from 15 different countries: Austria, Chile, China, Germany, Italy, Japan, South Korea, Malta, Mexico, Romania, Saudi Arabia, Spain, Thailand,

Turkey, and Vietnam. Of the 34, 15 were female and 19 male, while 20 were doctoral students and 14 master's students. Their disciplines ranged widely across the hard and social sciences, arts, and humanities, with a strong emphasis on the first two. However, in order to ensure the participants' anonymity in the event that any reader should be able to identify the institution, I am not naming the precise disciplines or indicating which participants (nationality, gender) came from which broad area of study.

Most of the participants were recruited via student contacts using their wider social networks, while a few of those who came for interviews then put me in touch with further participants in the institution. In addition, once the interviews had started, and word about them had spread among the participants' peer groups, two others approached me directly and asked if they could have an interview too. In one case, I sensed that the student simply wanted the opportunity to have a long conversation with a NES, and in the other case that she wanted to discuss her experiences in the university with me.

The approach I took was in line with Talmy's (2010) conceptualization of interviews as 'social practice', which he distinguishes from conventional orientations to interviews as 'research instruments'. The latter, he observes, treat interviews as a "resource" for "collecting information" and their data as decontextualized "reports" that "reveal truth and facts and/or the attitudes, beliefs and interior mental states of self-disclosing respondents" (p. 132). The former, by contrast, conceptualize the interview as "a site or topic for investigation itself" and its data as "accounts of truths, facts, attitudes, beliefs, interior states, etc. coconstructed between interviewer and interviewee" (ibid.). My understanding of my role in the process was also informed by Kvale and Brinkmann's (2009) metaphor of the interviewer as 'traveller' rather than 'miner', travelling with the participants in the context of the conversation under way, rather than mining their lived worlds in order to become "the great interpreter" (p. 218) of their "real inner meanings" (p. 230).

While aware of the power differential between the participants as postgraduate students and me as a senior academic, and that they too were aware of it, I was also aware that they had all kinds of knowledge and experience that I lacked, and approached them as equals in the context of our conversation. They were therefore welcome to decide what and what not to discuss, to ask as well as answer questions, and to choose when to draw a particular topic or even the entire conversation to a close. This meant that rather than being 'semi-structured in-depth interviews', as is often the case with qualitative research interviews, mine were completely unstructured. I had neither a formal list of questions to ask the participants, nor even a set of topics to cover, merely "some sense of the themes" relating to my research questions (Legard, Keegan, and Ward 2003: 141). It seemed that many of the participants, too, saw the event as a conversation, some thanking me at the end for the "conversation", others telling my contacts that it had not been "like an interview".

This is not to claim that our conversations were without any direction. For as Richards points out, "there is no such thing as a completely 'non-directive'

interview", and even in interviews that "are allowed to develop more naturally ...
the interviewer is aiming to elicit information and must design responses with this
in mind" (2003: 51). Berg (2009) likewise notes that interviewers engaged in what
he calls the 'unstandardized interview' must "develop, adapt, and generate questions and follow-up probes appropriate to each given situation and the central
purpose of the investigation" (p. 106). This requires active listening, that is, the
"ability to listen actively to what the interviewee says ... and how it is said", while
"upholding an attitude of maximum openness to what appears" (Kvale and
Brinkmann op.cit.: 138). It means, in turn, that the interviewer has to decide
which of the many aspects of a participant's contribution to pursue so as "to go on
with the interview in a fruitful way that will help answer the research question"
(p. 139). And this demands "an ear for the interview theme and a knowledge of
the interview topic, a sensitivity towards the social relationship of an interview, and
knowledge of what he or she wants to ask about" (ibid.). Thus, despite the highly
informal nature of my 34 exchanges with international students and the fact that
I did not try to prevent the conversations from going 'off message', whenever the
opportunity arose I homed in on anything a participant said that had particular
relevance to the theme of my research.

The only formal part of the event took place at the very beginning, when each
participant was invited to join me at a table in order to read the participant information sheet and complete the consent form. I also took the opportunity to ask the
participants for some basic personal information, primarily their nationality, L1, and
discipline and programme of study, as well as how long they had been at the university and in the country, whether and (if so) where they had studied in English
medium previously, and whether they had attended a pre-sessional academic English language course or similar. We then moved from the table to sit more infor-
mally on comfortable chairs arranged so as to face each other diagonally for the
conversation itself. This demonstrated both physically and symbolically that the
'interview' would be informal, and prepared the participants for the conversational
approach that was to follow. I turned on and tested my digital audio voice recorder
(Olympus WS-331M), and the conversation began, often with me picking up
on something the participant had said during the formal stage, less often with
the participant asking me a question or referring to something s/he or I had said
previously.

Once the conversation was under way, I often 'went with the flow', responding
to what the participant said, whether to agree, disagree, sympathize, or whatever.
In other words, notwithstanding what I have just said about eliciting information
related to my research focus, I engaged in each conversation to a great extent as I
would have done in any naturally occurring conversation with my own postgraduate students over a coffee, drink, or meal. This inevitably meant that each
conversation covered a certain amount of different ground, and that in most cases
there were stretches of talk that had no bearing on my research focus. Having said
that, the participants had read my information sheet and asked questions about the
research, and some had also emailed in advance of the meeting to ask what we

would be talking about. They knew, therefore, that my primary interest was in their views of their institution's English language policies and practices and the impact of these on their own academic lives. Most also seemed interested in the topic at a personal level given its relevance to their current and future lives. Not surprisingly, then, despite the diversions, a reasonable amount of each conversation was broadly 'on message'.

Each session drew to a close either when the participant chose to end it or when it seemed that neither of us had more to say. At that point, I asked if we had covered everything the participant wanted to talk about, and unless s/he started up the conversation again, as sometimes happened, I turned off the voice recorder. We then parted company in the same informal manner in which the conversation had taken place. Afterwards some participants emailed to say that they had enjoyed our conversation and/or to ask me follow up questions and/or to send me items such as ELT materials to which they had referred during our conversation.

Analysing the conversation data

After all 34 conversations had taken place I listened to the recordings to gain an initial sense of their shape, key features, and themes, as well as any patterns and contradictions emerging across the whole dataset. I then listened again in order to take detailed notes of the stages of each conversation and topic(s) covered, and transcribed the stages that related to the research focus (i.e. not those where the discussion moved away from it to something else entirely). Next, I categorized their content. For this, I again used qualitative content analysis (see Chapter Six for details), although this time entirely manually. Given what was said earlier in the chapter about approaching the conversations as social practice rather than research instruments, this may seem rather odd. However, as Richards points out, a social practice approach does not mean ignoring content. Rather, categorization serves as a useful starting point so as to impose "some degree of order" on the data (2003: 273). And as Mann observes, even though "we need to develop more sensitive, informed and data-led accounts for the ways in which interviews are constructed", dispensing with content would result in "a form of qualitative interview navel gazing ... We still need to focus on 'what' is said; we just require more attention on 'how' this is constructed and how interaction is managed" (2011: 21). Talmy and Richards make a similar point in their observation that "the active interview is a theory of interview that foregrounds not only the 'content' drawn from interviews – that is, the *whats* – but also the linguistic and interactional resources used to (co)construct it – or, the *hows*" (2011: 2; their italics), and that we need to look at both in order to analyse how an interview is achieved.

My initial content categorization produced 40 emergent categories relating to the research focus (though, as with all qualitative approaches, no doubt relating also to the researcher's sense of what is important). I reflected on these in order to identify the most significant, combine categories that overlapped substantially, and group them into distinct, coherent themes accepting, though, that this is a somewhat arbitrary process as there are inevitably relationships and overlaps across main themes. It nevertheless resulted in five overarching themes each with a number of sub-themes, and with the first two main themes eliciting by far the largest amount of discussion. The five were:

- understanding the English of others
- concerns about academic English writing
- English language entry tests
- issues of fairness
- orientations to English/ELF.

Having identified the 'whats', I returned to the data to explore the 'hows': that is, how the participants and I had co-constructed meaning in respect of each theme. As Talmy (2011) observes, more conventional approaches to interview analysis often involve "decontextualized content or thematic analyses, in which respondents' utterances are treated as independent of, and unaffected by, their interactional context" (p. 28), as was the case with most of the studies of international students mentioned earlier in this chapter. Talmy calls instead for "heightened reflexivity ... on the role of the interviewer in occasioning interview answers" (2010: 143). Such reflexivity was crucial in my own case, given my interest in exploring whether the student participants shifted their positions during the course of our interaction, and more specifically whether hearing about ELF(A) and my position on English affected their positions on their institution's language policies and practices.

In order to explore the student participants' positions, I drew on two analytic frameworks: firstly, Eggins and Slade's (1997/2006) speech functions analysis framework, and secondly, positioning theory (van Langenhove and Harré 1991, 1999).

Eggins and Slade's (1997/2006)[3] model for the description and analysis of casual conversation which develops Halliday's (1984, 1994) systemic functional account of dialogue, involves in essence three major conversation moves: 'open', and 'sustain', itself comprising 'continue' and 'react'. Opening moves initiate talk around a particular proposition. Examples are statements of fact (giving factual information) and opinion (giving attitudinal or evaluative information), and open and closed questions of fact (respectively demanding factual information and demanding agreement with it), and of opinion (respectively demanding opinion information or agreement with a particular opinion). Sustaining moves "keep negotiating the same proposition" (p. 195) and are achieved either by the speaker who has just been talking ('continuing' function), or by another speaker taking a turn ('reacting' function). Continuing functions involve 'monitoring', 'prolonging', and 'appending' moves. Monitoring involves, for example, checking that interlocutors are following what is said, or inviting them to take a turn. Prolonging moves occur when a speaker adds to his/her previous contribution, for example, by means of elaboration (clarifying, exemplifying, or restating the prior move). Appending moves involve a speaker losing a turn, but once s/he regains the floor, expanding on his/her previous move. Finally, reacting functions involve two kinds of move: 'responses' and 'rejoinders'. Responding reacting moves involve negotiating the initiating speaker's proposition, while rejoinders query or reject it. 'Responses' are either supporting or confronting. In the first case, an interlocutor accepts his/her position as a respondent and negotiator of the initiator's proposition. In the second case, the respondent may refuse to participate in the exchange by responding with silence or offering a confronting response such as contradicting or challenging the initiator.

Eggins and Slade define casual conversations as "interactions which are not motivated by a clear pragmatic purpose and which display informality and humour" (p. 20). They see talk that has some kind of pragmatic goal in mind, which they call "pragmatic conversation" (ibid.), as different from casual conversation in that it tends to be shorter, to involve a higher level of formality, and not to display humour. They illustrate their point with a service encounter, specifically a simple transaction in a post office. This is of an altogether different order from my conversations with international students, which, although less informal than conversations among friends, were still highly informal, lengthy, and involved a substantial amount of humour. In addition, Leung (2012) provides a precedent for the application of Eggins and Slade's speech functions framework to an educational setting in his analysis of two classroom exchanges between an EAL (English as an Additional Language) student and her teachers. The speech functions analysis framework thus provided a useful means of approaching my data,[4] enabling me to explore the participants' engagement in our conversations, particularly in relation to their initiation of topics, and their supporting or confronting responses to those I had initiated. It also allowed me to incorporate evidence of the influence of my own utterances on their contributions in so far as this was demonstrated by their discourse moves as they supported and confronted my position or returned to topics we had discussed earlier, indicating that their position had now changed.

While the speech functions analysis framework enabled me to explore the participants' discourse moves, positioning theory, with its concept of 'positioning' "as a dynamic alternative to the more static concept of role" (van Langenhove and Harré 1999: 14) was able to account more specifically for the ways in which they positioned themselves in the interaction. More specifically, it had the potential to demonstrate that the positions they expressed were fluid and context-dependent, and therefore liable to change within the space of our single conversation. For as van Langenhove and Harré (p. 16) point out, quoting Hollway, "[d]iscourses make available positions for subjects to take up. These positions are in relation to other people" (Hollway 1984: 236).

Positioning is thus "the assignment of fluid 'parts' or 'roles' to speakers in the discursive construction of personal stories that make a person's actions intelligible and relatively determinate as social acts" (van Langenhove and Harré 1999: 17). It involves both 'first order positioning', that is, how people locate themselves and others, and 'second order positioning', which occurs when a first order position is challenged in some way and has to be renegotiated (p. 20). Such challenges and repositionings were frequent features of the current conversations, with many of the students saying they had not thought about such issues before, and positioning themselves in respect of them for the first time. Indeed, during the listening, transcribing, and categorization process, it became evident that the most striking feature of the conversations as a whole was the way in which the students' positions on English and on their institutions' English-related policies and practices emerged from the interaction, whether voluntarily, in response to my position, as a result of their position being challenged, or by their own repositioning.

In the next section we turn to the data itself, in order to explore both the themes that emerged and the ways in which positions were articulated and negotiated in respect of them.

Emerging positions on university English

The analysis in this section combines the 'whats' and the 'hows'. That is, within the discussion of each theme and its sub-themes, I have incorporated exchanges to demonstrate how the students' positions that are outlined thematically were reached interactively within the conversation. This is not to say that I have been able to provide extensive analysis of large numbers of exchanges. This was not feasible within the space allowed, and in any case, as Talmy points out, "one need not perform an extensive analysis of the 'hows' in order to analyse the research interview as social practice: what is necessary is a reflexive recognition of the situated accomplishment of the interview [and] the co-construction of data" (2011: 33–34).

My aim, therefore, was to provide examples of how some of the positions that were articulated by the majority of the students were constructed in individual cases within the context of the interaction. This includes drawing attention to some of the contradictions that emerged during the course of the conversations. For as Liebscher and Dailey-O'Cain (2009) point out, "[l]anguage attitudes are created through interaction, and it is through interaction that they are later negotiated" and thus, "expressed orientations are not permanent, but highly context-dependent, and can even change from one moment to the next for a single individual" (pp. 200–1). Such changes in orientation were a noticeable feature of the present study, with students' positions changing in response to something I had said, often because they had simply not thought about such matters before, or because they perhaps felt freer to express certain positions and attitudes after hearing mine.

We now look in turn at the five main themes and their related sub-themes, starting with the two themes that appeared to exercise the students the most.

Understanding the English of others

This first theme comprises the participants' understanding of the English of NESs and other NNESs, as well as others' (NES and NNES) understanding of their

English, in both academic and social contexts. The two broad categories of NES and NNES each divide further into staff and students.

The sub-theme that emerged as the most salient by far to the student participants, and was mentioned by the majority of them, concerned their difficulties in understanding the English of NES staff and home students. The main reasons given were that the latter speak too fast, use a lot of idiomatic language including slang, or "street words" as a Chilean student put it, and phrasal verbs, and expect NNES students to understand their jokes. The following exchange with a Chinese participant took place immediately after a discussion of the pre-sessional course. The student had said that it was "not directly good to the lecture" because the lecturers on her MSc programme did not speak in the way that had been presented on the pre-sessional, and went on to explain why:[5]

Exchange 1: Lecturers' jokes

S: some of my teachers they use the vocabulary or they use some very difficult vocabulary

J: do you think it's that or do they do things do they use very idiomatic English language (1) sort of what the native speakers know [but

S: [mm mm mm yes and some jokes he made and ah ah I can't UNDERSTAND and other people ha ha but I don't know why=

J: =yes a lot of students have said that to me that the lecturers tell jokes and [everyone's laughing

S: [Yeah, yeah

J: and one of them said so I just laugh [@@@@

S: [@@@@

J: it's difficult isn't [it

S: [yeah yeah and er I ask my friend why you are laughing and erm [@@@

J: [@@@ they're pretending (.) they don't really understand the joke at all

S: mmm

The student began by mentioning vocabulary as her difficulty. However, most of the other participants up to this point in the study (this was conversation 18) had referred to their British lecturers' idiomatic vocabulary as the main problem, with several saying specifically that they would find more formal language easier to follow. I therefore questioned the participant's meaning of 'vocabulary'. And while it could be argued that I was 'putting words into her mouth' by mentioning idiomatic English, what is interesting here is that she chose not to follow my lead. Initially she interrupts me to briefly voice her agreement (though the two repetitions of "mm" followed by "yes", and the fact that she discussed problems with idiomatic language later, indicate that this was not simply token agreement). However, she then turns swiftly to a different aspect of the topic in hand, lecturers' jokes, and expands on my reference to "what native speakers know" by describing her and her friend's difficulty in understanding these (a 'develop: elaborate' supporting move in Eggins and Slade's terms). Her added intensity on the word "understand" emphasizes the nature of the problem, while her support of my comment "it's difficult" with not only agreement but also a point of her own ("I ask my friend … ") provides evidence of her engagement.

Most other participants said likewise that they do not understand their lecturers' jokes, but laugh anyway, another Chinese participant adding that if they do not laugh, the home students will think they are "very strange". And many said that when they ask their international student friends why they are laughing, it turns out that they, too, have no idea what is funny. A Korean participant who had said "everyone laugh, but I can't understand that, but I just follow the laughter @@@", went on to discuss the issue in terms of cultural difference in what people find funny: "the laughing point is different". He felt that his British lecturers, many of whom did not know other languages, were unaware of this and therefore assumed that their humour was international. Others thought it was simply that their lecturers consider their own local English appropriate for HE in the UK and/ or are talking to the home students, even in situations where international students are in the vast majority. Another Korean, for example, noted that his master's cohort consisted of over 100 international students and only five home students, but that his lecturers still seemed to be talking to the five. Some participants found the 'when in the UK' argument reasonable, although most changed their position at least to some extent during the course of the conversation. Meanwhile, some of them said that they had got used to their lecturers' culturally specific jokes as well as their idiomatic language (though rarely their speed of delivery) over time. But most felt, nevertheless, that their lecturers should understand that local jokes and other local uses of English exclude international students, and should try to avoid them.

Several participants also talked of lecturers speaking too quietly or mumbling, which, as they pointed out, makes understanding particularly difficult for NNES listeners. Some said how helpful they found it when lecturers allowed them to record lectures, while others were highly critical of lecturers who expressly forbade this (Law was singled out) despite being told how beneficial the recordings are as aids to understanding. And a small number mentioned lecturers who are easy to understand because they adjust their speech for the benefit of international students. However, it emerged that even those lecturers who do make adjustments for international students seem not to carry this through to questions and answers. The next exchange took place after I had asked a Mexican student whether he and his fellow students had any problems understanding their lecturers.

Exchange 2: Questions and answers in lectures

S: mm not problems understanding the lecture but there is problems with communicating with the lecturer (.) sometimes

J: [how

S: [when they ask questions. I think that the the lecturer prepares er obviously prepares the presentation of the of the [course the class (.) prepares the

J: [yeah

S: lecture (1) but when it comes to the questions (2) erm they don't have time to prepare the answer so the answer just comes without any filter

J: yeah yeah

S: so (.) sometimes it it it's a little bit er er complex interaction between student and er professor (.) because sometimes the professor doesn't understand student and student doesn't understand professor so it's like a loop of bad communication er and that's why I think that's why sometimes they go with other fellow students to go through er the slides=

J: =do they sometimes ask YOU to help them?

S: well we have (.) we have in our programme we have a facebook community

J: ah so you all get onto facebook and ask what the lecture was about=

S: =erm what's this about what's the question about

J: okay so does this happen quite a lot?

S: it happens it happens

J: so the lecturers aren't so good then (.) I mean they're not so clear if er you have to have a facebook discussion (.) to find out=

S: =well in [discipline] it is more about (.) it's not exact sciences so er many things are left for you to analyse (1) so: erm:: (2) in (a part) the lecturer is (doing his job) like er: letting you go outside of the classroom with more questions than answers because you have to look and do your research but when it comes to the::: QA (.) questions answers session (2) er: sometimes the the the message doesn't get through (1) so=

J: =which is unfortunate because when somebody has a question to ask (.) if a student wants to ask a question that means there's something they don't know they don't [understand and that's the most important time in a way for the

S: [yes

J: lecturer to explain really clearly=

S: =[yeah

J: [I mean do you think the lecturers need – the native English lecturers need some training in how to make themselves understood to international students?

S: I think I think it would be really helpful because the students on the other hand the students are doing their BEST to try to communicate (1) I remember one of of our students my fellow students that: erm in the beginning of the semester er he used to write the questions beforehand (.) and then when it came to the part do you have any questions he read the questions from the from the notebook (3) from the notebook he had to prepare the questions beforehand

J: mm mm

S: but then the the the lecturer has to be has to understand the situation of the student (.) so I think that it would be useful for international students to have the lecturers like if the lecturers can get some (1) erm some kind of course

Again, it was the student who initiated the topic, referring to "a loop of bad communication" and illustrating the problem with an anecdote about a fellow student. In this case, the lectures themselves are apparently comprehensible because, as the student perceptively notes, they are delivered through a "filter". But his lecturers are apparently unable to access this filter when they extemporize in question and answer sessions. Although the suggestion of lecturer training came from me, the speed with which he responded in support of my point (twice), his expansion of it with an example (the student who wrote down his questions in advance), and the language he uses ("useful", "really helpful"), together indicate that he took the suggestion seriously. Meanwhile, his points about the students "doing their best" and the need for lecturers to "understand the situation of the student" imply that he feels more effort is needed on the part of lecturers both to understand what students are asking them and to be more intelligible in responding. Several other students mentioned similar problems with questions and answers specifically, a Turkish student saying that his lecturers used so many idioms in their answers, that he "did not understand anything".

Many students also spoke of finding seminars problematic, often more so than lectures. The following exchange with a Thai student was preceded by a discussion of the problems that Thai students have in understanding lectures.

Exchange 3: Seminar discussions

J: and erm (.) when you're (1) what (.) do you have seminars?
S: Oh: @@ seminars the first year is VERY bad for me very bad because very fast er it it er I think it's normal problem I mean common problem er for Thai students
J: seminars
S: er yes seminar because the British students discuss together and Thai students have some problems about listening so they er cannot catch what they say
J: so (.) the British students do all the talking?
S: OH: they're talking all the time [@@@
J: [@@@
S: because they're talking (.) they (feel free) so (.) very fast
J: and the tutor (.) the lecturer?
S: er: (1) sometimes
J: talks a lot very fast?
S: sometimes (.) because he discuss er (.) it's different from when er they give lecture (.) [different (.) it's different
J: [yeah
S: but when they discuss they try to explain er their ideas so they don't er: (.) so it is an issue (.) I mean (.) mm hmm
J: so it's difficult for all the international students (.) do you talk about it together?
S: @@@
J: @@@

S: when I talk talk to my Thai friends they told me they're quiet
    [@@ they can NOT
J: [@@
S: follow er they cannot er: can don't catch what they say
J: [yeah
S: [if if they understand but they have to: er: provide the answer sometimes
    (they're) very slowly and they talk about another topic @@@
J: @@@ they they're on the next topic
S: yeah
J: when you're @ ready to start the last topic @@
S: yeah @@ oh, don't laugh

This time I was the one who made the opening move by introducing the topic of seminars. But whereas my initial question was entirely neutral, the student's response immediately turned the focus onto her and other Thai students' difficulties in participating in seminars. What is perhaps not sufficiently clear from the transcript is the student's sense of humour. Comments such as "Oh, they're talking all the time", and "my Thai friends they told me they're quiet", were delivered with great comic effect. For although she was serious about the nature of problem, she also saw the funny side of it, especially the notion that by the time Thai students are ready to contribute to a seminar discussion, it has switched to a new topic.

The student went on to observe that although some home students do seem to be aware of international students' problems, and do make adjustments when they interact with them in other settings, they do not do this in seminars. Many other participants referred to home students' dominating seminars, speaking too fast especially when they disagree with one another (or "quarrel" as a Chinese student put it), using a lot of slang, telling jokes, and preferring to speak with each other. Most, however, did not think the home students did any of this intentionally, but because of a lack of awareness, though a Saudi student felt it was also because they were trying to show off their knowledge. The participants tended to say at first that they blamed themselves for not being able to understand the home students in seminars because, as a Turkish student put it, "this is your country". However, as the conversation progressed and they reflected more on issues such as what it means to be an international university and to speak an international language, they often changed their position. For example, the same Turkish student said just over 13 minutes later that he did not feel relaxed talking with British students as he did not understand them, adding "so if I don't understand you, why should I communicate with you?" to an imaginary home student.

Not surprisingly, then, the majority of participants said they found it easier to communicate with other NNESs, particularly students, and even (with some exceptions) staff. Many observed that although there are sometimes difficulties in understanding certain NNES students' accents in the early stages, any problems are easily resolved. One reason for this, they felt, is that they spend a lot of time studying and socializing with each other rather than with NES students, and therefore quickly became familiar with each other's L1-related ways of speaking. Another reason some gave was their awareness from personal experience of the need to adjust the way they speak in order to facilitate intercultural communication. Some also referred to feelings of solidarity and "shared issues" among NNES students because of their similar situation, and the confidence they feel when communicating with other NNESs as contrasted with their lack of confidence when NESs, students or staff, are present. A Korean talked of losing his confidence in speaking if even one British student was present because of a feeling that he was being judged. For although the students often said they believed their own English to be 'bad', they also believed other NNESs could still understand it and did not care about their grammar errors, NESs far less so. This was also true of their written English, with several believing that NES staff were unwilling to make sufficient effort to understand their writing style, rather than that the writing itself was unintelligible (see the second theme).

By contrast with NNESs' intercultural awareness, many participants were of the view that NESs tend to have limited appreciation of what is involved in studying and socializing in a foreign language, several accounting for this by the fact that NESs often do not speak foreign languages themselves.[6] Meanwhile, contrary to the widespread perception of NES staff that international students study and socialize in L1 groups, the participants spoke of home students not mixing with them despite their attempts to "get in", as one put it, but preferring to stick with each other inside and outside the university because they feel "more comfortable" together. An Italian participant, for example, said "you try to get to know them well, but understand there's no interest in your culture" and in the end "you stop", while another Mexican observed that friends back home had told him he should look to other international students if he wanted "real friends" here. Several said they found this disappointing and not what they had expected. Some went on to suggest that it may partly explain why home students seem to find NNES students' English difficult to understand, as well as why they do not develop awareness of how difficult it is for NNES students to understand them.

For all these reasons, a number of students argued or, as in the case of the Mexican in Exchange 2, agreed with me that home students and/or staff need some kind of training in intercultural communication. This, they variously suggested, would enable NESs to understand the English of NNESs more easily, to appreciate what it means to study in a foreign language (and the immense achievement involved), and to learn how to adjust their own speech (speak more slowly, avoid local idiomatic language etc.) so as to be more intelligible to NNES students. One participant even argued that home students should have to take a two- or three-week pre-sessional course in intercultural communication "so they can feel the psychology of international students", and another that "it must be compulsory for British students".

This is not to suggest that the participants' comments were unremittingly negative or that they made no positive comments in relation to understanding the English of NES staff and students. Some students mentioned specific lecturers who seemed to understand that international students have specific needs and attempted to address these, rather than lecturing as if the room was filled with home students. A few compared their NES (mostly British, also US) lecturers favourably with NNES lecturers from certain L1s, although such comparisons were relatively rare, and in general, international staff were as or more likely to be preferred. Several talked positively about their communications with their PhD supervisors. And some had good words to say about specific home students with whom they had established friendships, although those who made this point tended to be EU students rather than those from further afield. Generally, though, what the participants said about NES students and staff in respect of this first main theme came as a surprise to me in that it was far more negative than I had anticipated.

Concerns about academic English writing

The subject of academic writing was clearly of great importance to the participants with all but one either bringing it up themselves or responding at length if I raised it, and the majority describing writing as by far their greatest problem, "a different game", as one put it. But when it came to how their writing is dealt with, not only were there differences across the 34 participants in terms of what should be required of them and how staff should respond to their writing, but several also changed their position or expressed contradictory positions during the course of the conversation.

The majority described receiving some kind of correction by their supervisors or, less often, by British friends and flatmates, although a Turkish student said he had simply been told that his writing was "not intellectual", but not "how to fix it". Most also expressed their appreciation of the correction, saying that it helped them to improve their English, and in a few cases that improving their English had been one of their aims in coming to study in the UK. However, many also talked of inconsistencies, with different staff having different requirements often relating to minor grammatical points (e.g. "if I forget an -s") or the use of American spelling, both of which most of the students considered trivial in terms of intelligibility. In fact, most were of the view that their tutors understood their meaning when they made grammar errors even if they claimed not to, one pointing out that tutors would be unable to correct the errors if they did not know what was meant.[7] And while it seems that some staff are flexible about American English,[8] the majority of students spoke of staff fussing over, for instance, the lack of a 'u' in words such as 'colour' ("just a few letters … silly"), or at best insisting that students keep consistently to all British or all American (I gather from colleagues in the US that the situation is the same in reverse in their universities). But as one student pointed out, staff seem unaware that for those who come from an L1 written in a different script altogether, the differences between British and American English are barely perceptible.

More surprising were instances of inconsistencies within the same member of staff. For example, a Chinese PhD student's supervisor corrected the preposition "on" to "in" in the first draft of a chapter. The student duly made the various corrections required by the supervisor including changing the "on" to "in", and resubmitted his draft to the supervisor. He was amused but baffled when it was returned to him with the "in" changed back to "on". I mentioned this incident to a Vietnamese participant who told me that the same thing sometimes happened to him. Likewise, another Chinese student spoke of showing an outline to her tutor, being told to change something, making the change, and then being asked by the tutor, "why did you change this?".

Another East Asian student told me that he was about to meet with his supervisor for feedback on a chapter, but was not optimistic because he was "familiar with her refusals". When I asked what he meant, he said: "if she refuse, I go back and rewrite", and that despite being in his first year of doctoral study, he had already done so "many times". In his view, this was because the supervisor expected his writing style to be "British", an expectation that several other participants also said they had encountered. Worse still, it seemed that the supervisor's practice was to not read the student's work in advance, but go through it on her computer at the supervision itself, asking the student to explain it to her as she went along (as he said: "how can I explain 5000 words?"). What was particularly intriguing, although by no means confined to this one student, was that he had begun the conversation by describing his supervisor in extremely positive terms: "[name] is a wonderful supervisor". As the conversation progressed, however, it emerged that he was deeply aggrieved by the lack of time and effort he felt she was willing to invest in him in return for his high fees.

Such ambivalence in respect of responses to their writing and its correction was a frequent feature of the conversations. On the one hand, the majority described their writing as bad and in need of the tutor's help so that they could improve, and many talked initially of appreciating the corrections their tutors and supervisors made to their written work. On the other hand, most of them changed their position at least to some extent in response to hearing about ELFA and my view of writing for an international readership. For example, they said that they found some of the comments on their writing overly negative, or that they suspected marks had been deducted from their assignments purely because their academic English was not native-like. They tended to regard this as unfair, especially as they believed the tutors understood their meaning despite any non-native grammatical features, or would do if they were willing to make more effort to understand. They were particularly scathing about marks being deducted for grammar in examinations, which a Mexican student described as "really stupid". Some, such as the Thai student in the following exchange, even talked of marks being deducted in examinations for the use of American English:

Exchange 4: University examinations

S: all of them they want British one=
J: =British spelling?
S: so (.) in my exams I have to make sure that I put u and put s and not zee

J: and you have enough to think about in an exam I mean if you're in not a first language if you're not a native speaker of English doing an exam must be SO difficult=

S: =very difficult (.) my first exams I was panic (.) I said oh my god I don't know what how to deal with this (.) just three questions and I have to write everything down as fast as possible that's why I feel it's very difficult

The focus of our discussion (initiated by the Thai student) at this point had initially been on British and American English. But my comment about NNESs having "enough to think about" elicited a supporting response (a 'develop: elaborate' move) from the student in which she demonstrated her agreement by repeating and strengthening the force of my word "difficult", and expanded on it by describing an early examination experience of her own. I responded to her description of her panic by saying I felt it was unfair that international students had the same time limit as home students in examinations, because of the added difficulty of writing in a second language. This time, the student's response is rather different:

S: at first I thought this very unfair but (.) I think I do understand what they're trying to do=

J: what @

S: it's just like okay if (.) I want to study in England I want to study HERE I must have (.) enough potential

J: but you HAVE but the point is you're studying in a second language ...

S: but for me I have no problem about writing

Instead of supporting my argument, the student disagrees – a 'reacting rejoinder move' in which she both counters my argument, and goes on to say that in any case, writing is no longer a problem for her. We then had a lengthy discussion of what it means to be an international university during which I suggested that British universities should change the way they conduct examinations to take account of the extra difficulties for NNES students, and should find a way to enable NNES students to demonstrate their ability in their subject as well in English as they could do in their L1. At this point, the student changed her position substantially:

S: I I've heard that one of erm one of the universities in London they said that they have different assessment between the international [student and:

J: [really? which one is this?

S: erm:: I'm not sure (.) not LSE (.) [UCL

J: [I think this is good I mean the other thing is I think they should let you take dictionaries in [things like this

S: [they allow us to use it but=

J: =what you can take a dictionary in?

S: but we have no time [@@@

J: [@@ no time to look at it @ (1) I mean it's good if you can have a dictionary there but you know this is the trouble if you can't look at it (.) do they let the British ones take it in as well?

S: erm (.) no=

J: no just the international=

S: =and the problem is like (.) this is (.) I think it's very big problem it's just like okay when you say when you write something or you give us a question (.) sometimes I don't understand [it's like

J: [what the question?

S: exactly what they want (.) what they understand (.) I understand this way but maybe they understand in another way and I explain it in my way (1) that's the problem (some) language boundary

J: so they need to think a little bit better about how they explain their questions (.) erm (.) you know for international readers of the question=

S: =and even if we have a dictionary our dictionary say something but maybe it's not the correct interpretations (.) it's not what they want

J: no

S: that's BAD

This time, the student's moves are all supporting responses. She begins by elaborating on my point with an example of an institution that has made the kinds of changes I was talking about. My reference to dictionaries elicits further elaboration from her in which she talks of a problem mentioned by almost all the other students too: the time factor in relation to assignments, examinations, and milestones. In the case of examinations, she points out that allowing international students to use dictionaries is no help if they do not have time to do so. She then initiates a new topic with "the problem is … it's a very big problem", that of NNES students not being able to understand examination questions in the way they are intended. She ascribes this to "language boundary" differences, and argues that those who set the examinations should "think a little bit better about how they ask their questions", describing the situation emphatically as "BAD".

Other students talked of staff judging the content of their writing on the basis of their grammar. As mentioned earlier, many believed (or knew) that staff deduct marks for 'grammar mistakes' rather than assessing their work entirely in relation to its content. Many pointed out that they would be able to achieve far higher marks if they were able to write in their own first language because there is little recognition of the effort involved in writing in another language so allowances are not made for the fact that they are non-native users. Some even felt that their intelligence was being judged in relation to their use of English. A Vietnamese participant who had challenged most of my points, nevertheless argued that NESs think more native-like English, or what he called "higher level English", is a reflection of the

NNES's academic ability, and that "it's not fair". And a Chinese student observed that whereas Chinese people come across in their mother tongue as "the smart ones", she feels that in English people think their language is "baby talk" and therefore that they are "not smart".

Some students also objected to what they saw as a double standard in operation according to which home students in certain disciplines (including some sciences) are allowed to write creatively while international students are not. A Chinese student, for example, talked of how the NES students are allowed to "write ironic" whereas the NNESs "have to conform". Another talked of how NNES students lose their own voice in their writing, or "lose ourselves" as she put it, because of the obligation to follow a pattern. And several students talked, mostly with displeasure, of their tutors or supervisors changing their writing style to make it more like their own or more 'British'. This contrasted with their more ambivalent attitudes towards the correcting of their grammar.

The following exchange with an EU student occurred after I had told her how angry it makes me when reviewers of my submitted publications alter my style and grammar.

Exchange 5: Creativity in written English

S: but probably as a reviewer when you read a VERY good article you know you don't you CAN'T really find much you know to comment on you know (.) MAYBE that's some people who don't really see any sort of content-wise remark remarks to make then they will you know you know @ try to interfere with your writing

J: but it IS interfering I mean I think that's a very good word to use (.) they interfere with your writing with your style

S: Mmm

J: and I mean I would never do that with my PhD students either (.) the only thing I'd ever say is if something isn't clear

S: yeah

J: if I was if I don't understand it (1) and because I've got a lot of experience with international students and different ways of writing I think well if I don't understand it properly probably other people won't and for sure the external examiner won't [@@@

S: [@@@

J: so I always tell them if I think people won't understand it but I never change anything. You know (.) if there's an s where there shouldn't be in British English or isn't one where there should be in British English or you know things like that I never comment

S: yeah

J: and I say to them you know if you want it to be looking like British English you'll have to go and get someone to tell you that because I'm not going to @

> S: @@ yeah (.) and also it's part of the (.) as you said it's part of the the style the STYLE sort of you know you're creating your own you know er identity as a as a an academic you know (.) in writing as well=
>
> J: =because you have a voice in your writing
>
> S: yeah (1) yeah and to be HONEST I do I do you know I do agree with erm sometimes you know I find that my writing is I find it a bit RIGID and I find it that you know if I am to be very aware and cautious of the fact that I HAVE to use English you know in a in a er: correct grammatical grammatically correct manner then some of my you know that creativity and that you know that DRIVES words you know writing is LOST somehow (.) because I you know it's about self constraint and you know self censorship as well and (.) yeah and (.) when that happens you know I feel like after you know after a while re-reading my my (1) my essay or article I feel like hmm this is sounds like quite RIGID it's quite rigid yeah
>
> J: (2) because it's lost [YOU [it's lost (the sort of person in it) it's just
>
> S: [yes sort of yeah
>
> J: it's just a sort of @ correct English=
>
> S: =yeah I think [I think so
>
> J: [correct BRITISH English=
>
> S: =I think so I think that (.) that's a danger sort of danger I think

This exchange is notable for the way in which each of us strongly supports and builds on the other's points. Interestingly, though, it is the student who makes the strongest statements. She is the one who describes others' revisions of one's writing as interfering, mentions the subject of identity in writing, talks of the rigidity of her writing to ensure that it meets her institution's requirements ("correct English"), and of the consequent loss of creativity, and she sums all this up as "a danger". However, she does not say any of this until after I had responded to her word "interfere", exemplifying it by explaining across three turns my English language policy with my own PhD students. It is of course possible that the student did not mean quite the same by "interfere" as I did, and that my ensuing point was based on an inaccurate interpretation of her meaning. Nevertheless, her instant receptivity to the position I expressed and her various elaborations of it indicate that she had already formed certain views on the subject prior to our conversation, but only felt free to articulate these once she knew it was 'safe'. In fact earlier she had even discussed her writing problems ("hugely long sentences", grammar, and paragraph structure) as well as the need for English writing to fit in with the demands of publishers. This demonstrates that just because NNES students do not express certain views, does not mean that they do not hold them. And in the case of writing specifically, it does not mean they are necessarily happy with the British English status quo simply because they do not deny this or even express their appreciation of staff that correct their grammar.

Among the entire group of conversation participants it seemed that the only staff that did not require their students' writing to be native/British-like worked in the

Management discipline. In fact one Management student said she had been told specifically *not* to "try to write British way", that it was fine provided the supervisor understood, but "beautiful sentence, correct grammar, no". This is perhaps understandable given that Management tends to involve more intercultural communication than many other disciplines. Not surprisingly, in this respect, those working in the field of Business English were among the first English language professionals to support the notion of ELF, and Business ELF (BELF) is now a thriving field of research.

In the case of doctoral students, supervisors' highly negative comments on the student's English often related to publishing requirements, particularly if the supervisor wanted to co-publish with the student (which, according to a couple of students, entails the supervisor adding his/her name to the student's work). Sometimes, when publication came up as an issue, I showed students the English language policy of the *Journal of English as a Lingua Franca*, which states that native English is not required and instead that the journal simply expects submissions to be intelligible to a wide international readership. All who saw this expressed great surprise that such a policy could exist, and most said they would welcome it if it became widely accepted. However, most of them continued to express the view that their own and other non-native English is bad, saying, for example, that they wanted to write "perfect" (= native) English themselves. They thus demonstrated a difficulty in accepting the notion that other kinds of English than native could be acceptable.

Proofreading was mentioned by most of the participants, with those not in the fortunate position of having British friends to check their dissertations or theses either forced to go to the expense of paying professional proofreaders so as to ensure that their English was sufficiently native-like or risk being marked down. As a Mexican student said, "if you don't have a friend to proofread, it's like if you submit a paper with errors, they say sorry, we can't understand that". Some found, however, that proofreaders did not understand the subject so were liable to change the meaning as well as the grammar and style. Meanwhile, several were of the view that if they did not use proofreaders the content of their writing was evaluated in part on the basis of their English language use. In this respect, one Chinese PhD student, who had studied for her master's at another UK university described a friend's master's dissertation experience at the other institution. The friend had failed her dissertation and been told to improve it and resubmit. According to my student participant, the only action her friend took was to have the dissertation proofread. She then resubmitted and passed.

As far as the teaching of academic writing is concerned, opinions were very divided. Two students described in-sessional dissertation-writing courses as "useless", while no others mentioned in-sessional English language teaching at all. On the other hand, some said they had found the pre-sessional course helpful for improving their writing skills. When I asked how, though, they were only able to think of basic aspects of writing such as paragraph structure and grammar. Some even went on to describe how the homogenizing approach to English writing taught on the pre-sessional course was not reflected in the writing they were subsequently required to read and produce on their content courses. They mentioned, for example, that it was not true that professional academics' paragraphs only begin with topic sentences, or that sentences (and even whole sections of articles) never begin with "But", "And", and the like. One student described being told by an academic tutor that her writing was too mechanical, and that she should not structure each paragraph in the same way (the way she had been taught on her pre-sessional writing course). In fact, the two who were most positive about the pre-sessional course turned out to be students whose visas had not arrived in time, had been unable to attend the pre-sessional, and were reporting what they had been told by others. One of them added that she had worked hard on her English since arriving, and that by the end of the first term of her master's, she felt her academic writing skills were better than those of peers who had attended the pre-sessional. And several students said that with hindsight the main benefits of the course had been the opportunity to make friends, get used to life in the UK, and become familiar with the accents of other international students, who were the people they were most likely to encounter on their academic courses.

Finally, despite all their concerns about the current academic English writing situation and their ambivalence towards 'correct' English, the majority also commented that although they did not like the situation, they accepted it. As with their understanding problems, many blamed themselves for not being good enough. Some felt that expecting NNESs to write like NESs is reasonable as this is required by publishers. Others said they were resigned to the status quo: they are in the UK now, so must follow UK universities' ways of doing things: NESs cannot (a couple said "should not have to") change, and NNES students "cannot change the environment" so must change themselves. It remains to be seen whether they continue to accept the prevailing native English ideology in UK HE as inevitable, if – or more likely, when – knowledge about ELF(A) is more widely disseminated, or whether they then reflect more on what it should mean, English-wise, to be an *international* university.

English language entry tests

Almost all the participants had taken an English language university entry test at some point prior to their study in their current institution. This was most often IELTS, although three had taken TOEFL (two as well as IELTS) and one had taken CAE (Cambridge ESOL's Certificate in Advanced English). Most of the Chinese participants also mentioned the English component of Gao Kao, an examination that they have to pass in order to enter Chinese universities as undergraduates. Because of the students' heavy focus on IELTS, the present discussion also concentrates on it.

Some participants only discussed the IELTS examination itself, while others also commented on exam preparation courses they had taken. In most cases the students' points were largely, or even entirely, negative, though a few began by describing IELTS in more positive terms, saying for example that it was "more real" in terms of some of the task types used than other exams such as TOEFL. However, they tended to reposition themselves after they had heard other points of view, both mine, and those of other international students with whom I had spoken. And in such cases, the level of detail and exemplification that they provided in their repositioning suggested that they identified easily with these other points of view rather than that they were saying what they thought I, the researcher, wanted to hear.

For the majority of participants, regardless of whether they had taken formal IELTS preparation courses or prepared on their own, one of the main criticisms of IELTS was that it had limited relevance to their subsequent UK university life in general and to their academic study more specifically. This was the case even for those who had gained high scores such as a Thai student who had gained IELTS 7.0 overall. Because of this, she found the whole process pointless: "that's why I think why do we have to take IELTS test?" A Chinese student told the story of a Chinese friend who had gained nine, the top score, but had still been unable to cope with the kind of English she found on campus and had returned to China. Others felt that preparing for and taking IELTS had not helped them improve their English in relevant ways. One, for example, observed that IELTS teaches you only "one way to do English", a way that tends to turn out not be suitable in practice. Another used the word "homogeneous". In this respect, a German student spoke of a master's seminar in which an East European student had given a presentation using items of vocabulary that the German student (who had, himself, taken IELTS) believed to be "exactly what is necessary for passing the IELTS test", but that were inappropriate in the academic context. Likewise, an Italian student described how in her first assignment she had used all the discourse markers that she had been taught on her exam preparation course, only to be told "no, no" by her supervisor.

Some criticized IELTS for preparing students to communicate only with British people rather than for international communication, leading them to expect to hear mainly British accents on campus – a criticism levelled also at TOEFL in respect of American accents. Interestingly, a Turkish student began by saying that if you have no problem understanding NESs then you can communicate with NNESs too. A few minutes later, after we had discussed where his classmates came from, he changed his mind, noting that he had initially experienced problems understanding his fellow Indian, Pakistani, and Chinese students until he had become familiar with their accents. He even went on to say that he could "count on one finger" the British people with whom he communicated habitually on campus, adding that the IELTS exam "should prepare you to communicate with everybody not only the national", which represented a complete reversal of his original position.

Many students did not believe that IELTS scores provide a reliable indication of students' ability to study in a UK university, saying that those with high scores do not necessarily do well in their academic study in the UK, and vice versa (a point also made by some of the staff questionnaire respondents). A German student also questioned the exam's validity, criticizing its focus on certain kinds of reading text, the use of "really badly done" accents (in his case an Australian one) in the listening test, and the boring choice of discussion topics in the writing test, as well as the promotion of "the same structures again and again" in IELTS preparation course books. In these respects, others spoke of the artificial nature of much of the IELTS exam, in which students are required to read texts they would not normally read, and listen to British people in conversation with each another (whereas it could be argued that the effort would be better spent teaching British people to adjust their speech in intercultural communication). In addition, they are expected to accomplish these tasks within strict, and what most thought to be unrealistic, time limits. In real life, by contrast, they can re-read a text they have not understood fully on the first reading, and ask speakers to repeat what they have just said rather than hear it only once. Even in the case of lectures, they often have access to a recording and/or powerpoint slides, or can at least ask each other for help, if not the lecturer (see the first theme above). In any case, as several students pointed out, the IELTS listening test does not prepare them for understanding real-life lectures.

For such reasons, many found the IELTS test unfair, and to some extent also a matter of luck. As a Chinese participant put it in relation to the speaking test, if you are lucky and familiar with the topic, "you can just talk blah blah blah", whereas if you are unfamiliar with it, you may not have much to say. Meanwhile, some also believed IELTS was merely a test of technical exam skills ("learning how to play the IELTS game" as a prospective PhD student once said to me), rather than of the ability to use English effectively in an academic environment. According to this view, students who had learnt the necessary exam skills did well, while others who had not learnt them did not, even if their English was more effective than those with the technical skills.

Several of these points were covered in a single long discussion about IELTS in a conversation with one of the Chinese participants. Because the entire discussion lasted for over seven minutes, I have singled out two sections of it to explore more fully. The first relates to English language improvement, and the second to communication on campus.

Exchange 6: IELTS issues

In this part of the discussion, the student had just told me that he had taken IELTS:

J: erm so how was it (2) did you do a course before you did the exam?

S: er: actually yes I attend er er a course to make me familiar with the (basic exam)

J: and was the course useful?

S: er: (1) I think it's (.) okay it er (.) let me know more about the basic examination and er how it works (.) something like that (.) but for the (1) er: English IMPROVEMENT I don't think it's very useful

J: @[@
S: [@ yeah yeah (.) I I but I can I can KNOW how to er change from TOEFL method to IELTS method er I I mean the er the way to answer answer to do the test=
J: =so it was just like technique switch from doing TOEFL to [doing IELTS
S: [yeah yeah
J: you just learnt the new technique how to pass IELTS=
S: =yeah yeah exactly
J: er but not very useful
S: erm not very useful to for the English IMPROVEMENT

Although much of this section is composed of a more traditional question and answer format than characterizes much of the rest of the conversation, it is nevertheless the student who focuses the discussion on the only benefit of his preparation course (familiarizing him with the exam itself, and in a subsequent turn, helping him to understand the differences between IELTS and TOEFL) and on what the course did not do (improve his English). On two occasions, he also repeats my word "useful" and expands on it, indicating that he supports my point. And both times he also produces the word "improvement" with extra intensity, thus emphasizing his own point that the course did not improve his English. Even his simple agreements with me are not token 'yeses', but repeated "yeah yeah" on two occasions, and the stronger "yeah yeah exactly" on a third.

Later on the student and I turned to the fact that IELTS is based on native English speakers. The next part of the exchange comes immediately after the student had talked about preparing for the oral test by speaking with NESs:

J: isn't it funny because IELTS is to prepare you for study in a British university and that means an international university doesn't it
S: @
J: and it prepares you just to spend your time talking with listening to native English [speakers
S: [@@
J: and when you get here you spend most of your time with NON native English speakers
S: @@@ yeah
J: because that's an international university so it doesn't really prepare you for what happens in the university does it
S: er:: I think it's er: should be helpful to improve the English I I mean the IELTS exam because what (.) doing the preparation of the exams we SHOULD er er learn more or listen more speaking more about the er English but er when I come here I find some things er maybe a little different yeah it's different er er er: because like you said it's VERY international (.) people from India from Poland Greek their their pronunciation their English is a little bit more or less different from native speakers such as

Indian I I can hardly understand that before but er it's much better NOW because I communicate with that guy very much every day

This time I was the one who initiated the topic, that of IELTS preparing prospective international students for communication with NESs. The student responds to my first three turns with laughter, each time for longer, and on the third occasion adds "yeah". It seemed at the time that he genuinely found the contradiction I had raised amusing as well as agreeing with it. But it is not until his fourth move that his agreement is signalled beyond doubt, when, in an extended turn, he supports my point about the university being international, intensifying it with "very" in describing the international environment he found on arrival in the UK, how the accents he heard were different from those of NESs, and that they were difficult to understand at first. He also makes a point that was discussed in relation to the first theme that NNESs tend to learn to understand each other's English quickly because they communicate with each other regularly.

It is of course not uncommon for students to be critical of the examinations they have to take, and we cannot assume that every negative point these participants made about IELTS (also TOEFL and CAE) were entirely well founded. But what was interesting was not only that the same points were made over and over by different students, but also that those who had gained high IELTS scores were equally as critical as those who had not.

Issues of fairness

Fairness came up in relation to many of the issues the students and I discussed. While three fairness sub-themes emerged from the data, the one that concerned the students the most related to their perceived disadvantage vis-à-vis home students, and especially what they saw as the unfairness of being treated in the same way as home students for the purposes of assessment. The two other sub-themes were, respectively, the (lack of) effort on the part of staff (this was often mentioned in conjunction with a reference to high fees), and a lack of empathy towards international students on the part of both staff and home students.

Turning to the first, and main, sub-theme, several participants were particularly exercised over the assessment of their work. Despite the various comments to the effect that they were resigned to their situation (see the end of the first theme), they were critical of the fact that they were assessed identically to NES students. In this respect, the time element came up often. A Korean student, for example, said that in order to gain the same mark as a home student, it took international students four times as long from being set an assignment to submitting it, because of the extra time it took them to read and write. He saw this as "a big advantage for native speakers". When I mentioned the Korean student's point to some of the other participants every one of them expressed complete agreement. Others focused on support, arguing that international students should be allocated more tutorial time than home students because of the added difficulty of working in an L2 as well as their far higher fees. More help with master's dissertations was mentioned particularly, some saying they found it unfair that home students were entitled to as much dissertation supervision as they were.

A number of students focused on the extra time they had to spend on their assignments specifically because of the requirement to use native-like English. A Chinese student began the discussion of his written work by saying he had learnt a lot about English grammar from his supervisor's corrections and was grateful to her for helping him improve his "bad grammar". But after hearing about my approach to PhD theses (ignoring grammar deviations from native English and only indicating intelligibility problems) and the reasons for it, he shifted his position, saying: "language is just a tool for communication and if we can understand each other well, it is not necessary to change the method of writing". He added that the obligation on international students to use native-like English takes up a lot of time that could be better spent on research. Others spoke of the requirement to use native English (sometimes only British, not American) even in their exams and the extra time this takes them. And several thought they should be allowed longer than NES students for both exams and coursework because having the same amount of time is "unfair for us", as a Turkish student put it.

Some students mentioned presentations, whether as part of master's courses or for their PhD. If the presentation was assessed and/or was a milestone in their PhD, they felt, as with assessed written work, that it was unfair for them to have to follow the same timetable as NES students. In their view, this did not take account of the added difficulty for those studying in a foreign language. One suggested that in order to introduce more balance, NES students should have to give their presentations in a foreign language too. Some mentioned being criticized for grammar and pronunciation mistakes in their presentations even though it had not affected the supervisor's understanding of the content. One even talked of his supervisor pulling faces during his presentation because, he thought, she did not like his non-native English accent. But above all, they spoke of finding assessed presentations extra stressful because of what they saw as their disadvantage alongside their NES student peers.

In the following exchange, a Mexican student and I had just been talking about what is expected of her, English-wise, in her academic writing. She had said she was not sure, and I had asked her how she could find out. But instead of responding to my question, she turned the conversation to another topic, speaking, which she had mentioned briefly earlier, and now expanded on it at length.

Exchange 7: Giving presentations

S: but (.) like I told you my MAIN concern is about my speaking not my writing so for example in J-in this month I have to give er my presentation (1) like forty-five minutes and *I'm very very very scared* because I (.) well first of all I'm not used to (.) to give presentations (.) in English (.) I mean I I've

given some but just short ones like ten minutes fifteen minutes and that's it
(1) but to to think about forty-five minutes I *I'm shocked=*

J: =it's long isn't it (.) but (.) for me too

S: @@

J: and I know lots of people everybody gets nervous and native speakers get
very nervous native English speakers get very nervous if they talk for so
long (1) as well

S: (2) yeah=

J: =so make sure you have a good powerpoint [@@

S: [yeah yeah @ I will just have
to make sure my powerpoint is (well prepared)

[...]

J: is this for your course or is it at a conference

S: no this is for my (.) erm (1) transfer? upgrade=

J: =you have to do forty-five minutes for your upgrade?

S: something like that

J: because we ask ours to do TEN=

S: =oh my god

J: =five minutes ten minutes not a presentation just overview of the research

S: no we have to do a proper [one

J: [and who's watching this

S: everybody who wants to (.) yeah

J: you have your upgrade in front of every[body?

S: [yeah

J: (2) not a viva?

S: no it's not a viva it's it's a presentation about your research about what you
have done so far and the results and (.) explain everything since the the erm
the beginning introduction methodology results discussion (.) and then of
course questions=

J: =so other students can ask questions?

S: yeah

J: staff can ask questions

S: yeah

J: so who is the EXAMINER (.) who actually says whether you've passed=

S: your supervisors they are there I mean er all of them have s-HAVE to be
there

J: (2) so how many supervisors

S: I have three

J: three [supervisors

S: [plus one panel chair so [that's I think

J: [so okay four of them decide whether you
pass=

S: =yeah @

J: and it's it's decided on the presentation and the (.) answers

S: and:: after the presentation and the questions answers everybody leaves and you stay with your supervisors and then [they give

J: [so with the panel?

S: with the panel and they give us X more and what's your future plan to finish your PhD and discuss about the results you have done so far if they think it's enough or: they think you have to do more in order to get your transfer so (1) yeah (1) it's yeah *it's very (.) stressful* @ anyway I I just want to get over it @

[then followed a discussion of the written report that the student had to submit to her supervisors prior to her presentation]

J: =so (.) erm I'm still puzzled a bit by this forty-five minute presentation because they KNOW what you've done without (.) forty-five minute presentation

S: yeah (2)

J: I mean if they can read it=

S: =I think it's more (2) but I think they want to see how can you express it to the rest of the people

J: do you I mean is that reasonable do you think?

S: (2) well really I hope I wish I wouldn't have to do that but I think it it IS reasonable because if you go to a conference you have to be able to to explain it to everybody I mean of course NOT in forty-five minutes but in fifteen minutes you you have to be able to [explain

J: [most conferences papers are about twenty minutes (.) and (.) most people most people don't give papers till they've finished their research @ I mean what do you I mean (.) does it seem to you that there's any disadvantage because you're a non–native English speaker compared to you know doing this than it would be even though they get very nervous it's much easier to present something in your first language

S: yeah I think it is (1) *it IS a disadvantage* I think

J: so yeah do you think it's an unfair way of (1) doing an upgrade?

S: (2) yes (1) [@@

J: [@@ (1) have you what do the other students think

S: (1) yeah they all get very stressed when it's time er: for their upgrades (1) and *I feel like very er very jealous or er disadvantaged with the native ones* because I mean I know they will feel nervous I know they can get blocked I know what they feel I feel that even when I'm talking in Spanish (.) but (.) *STILL there's there's an advantage (.) of being a native (.) speaker* (2) and I feel like there's in that way I feel I won't be as good as them when I will be giving my upgrade (.) I mean yeah

J: and it's just the presentation (.) [part of it (.) this this is the only part that

S: [yeah

J: that's (.) a concern (.) that's a worry for you

S: yeah

J: and all the students are the same are they?

S: yeah (.) yeah *the non-native*

J: do the native students ever say anything (1) about it? (2) you don't talk to them really? [@@@

S: [@@@ we don't talk that much but I have talked to some and (2) I mean (.) yeah they get nervous they do=

J: =yes [of course

S: [everybody does=

J: =everybody giving presentations gets I get nervous and I've done hundreds @

S: oh that's good to know @@@ (needn't be) just student

[...]

J: but it's it's not just about the nerves is it for for presenting it's the sort of extra (1) almost like it's (1) I've never done it I don't think I could present in another language (.) I wouldn't be capable (.) erm (.) but it seems like an extra weight (1) they look to me I mean my students just to give like a fifteen minute presentation it's this big weight on them because it's in English

S: *yeah I feel EXACTLY the same yeah a very very big weight yeah yeah* (1) and because when you are nervous if you are speaking in your language (.) you can still have er the mind connected to your mouth but *when it's in a different language your mind doesn't connect with your mouth* and and that's a problem (1) I mean for me

I have included the above long extract from this even longer discussion of student presentations because of the insights into the international student experience that it provides. However, space allows me to pick up only on a few key points. At the discourse level, a notable feature of this exchange is the extent of the students' use of 'develop: elaborate' reacting responding moves in which she agrees with and then expands on and/or exemplifies my comment or question. In terms of content, two points in particular emerge in relation to fairness: firstly, the student's position that she and the other NNES students are disadvantaged in presentations relative to the NES students; and secondly, the strength of her fear at the prospect of giving her first long presentation in a foreign language. In both cases, her lengthy elaborations and the kind of words and expressions she uses (indicated in italics), such as "very very very scared", and "very jealous [of the NES students]", demonstrate the strength of her feelings at that point in the conversation. Even when I introduce the expression "big weight", she does not merely repeat it, but emphasizes her repetition with the word "exactly", itself stressed, and expands on it by describing the additional difficulty of being nervous in an L2, that is, that "your mind doesn't connect with your mouth". The only point she makes in favour of the 45-minute upgrade presentation is that she needs to be able to give conference presentations. After hearing my comment on conferences, however, she picks up on my questions about disadvantage and unfairness, and elaborates on these, which suggests that she has adjusted her position and no longer finds the upgrade presentation quite so "reasonable".

The second and third sub-themes, the perceived lack of staff effort and empathy in respect of international students, have already been touched on in various ways, so I mention only the key points here. As regards staff effort, many students talked of tutors and lecturers saying they were too busy, often with their own research, to give time to international students. One area of particular concern among the students was their written work, and the lack of time they felt staff were willing to spend in order to understand it or help them with it, rather than simply criticizing their non-native grammar and saying it was unintelligible. Most who mentioned this point also felt that in view of the high fees they pay and their practical disadvantages by contrast with their NES peers, this was unreasonable. A Chinese student, for example, said he was "disappointed" because the staff are "too busy" and "don't want to put any effort on us", and added, "sometimes I feel like they just want our money". Some thought that the institution should recruit more staff specifically to enable more time to be available for international students. Another Chinese student thought this would mean staff would have "more patience" with them. But the most common point made in respect of fairness focused on money. Many of the participants talked of the staff expectation that they, the NNES students, should make all the effort to fit in and be understood, rather than that staff should make efforts to meet them half way. As a European student put it, "it's a paradox, isn't it. You want to get the money for all the international students but don't want to accommodate them".

The third sub-theme, empathy, relates closely to the previous one in that some of the students felt staff and home students are simply unaware of what is involved in studying in a foreign language in another country or, as one put it, of "the psychology of the international student". Some talked of feeling "uncomfortable" when staff insisted that they talk together in English in same-L1 groups. This was particularly true of the Chinese participants, since they were more likely to find themselves on courses with a very large proportion of Chinese students. Some said they thought their lecturers did not understand how unnatural it feels to have to speak in a foreign language with people who all share your first language. Others spoke of being afraid to speak in classes where there were home students because they sensed that they were being judged by both staff and home students. Some also said staff tended to address questions to the home students and not expect, let alone wait for, contributions from the East Asian students (a point raised in Exchange 3 above). A Saudi student also mentioned the issue of international students who are studying full time in the UK but also have children here with them, how hard that makes life for them, and how little awareness there seems to be of this factor.

Although it did not relate primarily to language issues, one case nevertheless stood out for me in relation to lack of empathy. It concerned an East Asian student who had been enrolled on the wrong PhD programme because of an administrative error on the part of the institution, and found himself placed with a completely unsuitable supervisor. By the time the error was discovered it was several weeks into the academic year and the student needed to act fast. However, his supervisor told him that if he wanted to switch, he would have to find a new supervisor himself. In other words, he, a new student in an institution, system, and academic culture with which he was unfamiliar, and using a foreign language, was to approach staff he had not met before and carry out a complex negotiation with them. As he said to me, "how can I find by myself?" And this was despite how obvious his distress must have been to the supervisor: "I was very sad. I used to cry in front of her. My tears drop. I can't stand any more". In the end the student stayed where he was, researching a compromise topic that did not interest him, and spending much of his time working in isolation because of lack of shared common ground with the other PhD students in the department. Meanwhile, as he pointed out, the institution was paid a large sum of money by his government.

Orientations to English/ELF

In this sub-section we explore firstly the participants' orientations to native English and ELF, and then their perceptions of and desires for their own English.

Not surprisingly most participants expressed a positive orientation to native English, describing it, for example, as 'correct', 'fluent', 'clear', 'perfect', 'beautiful', 'international', 'best understood', 'original', or simply 'the best', whereas non-native English was mostly characterized as incorrect, imperfect, and as one student put it, "lower level because it's non-native". When the students and I explored such notions further, however, it emerged that they were not necessarily clear about what they meant by them, and tended to fall back on the circular argument that native English is best merely by virtue of being native. On the other hand, most realized the contradiction in their claims that native English is the most widely understood kind, and the experiences they had previously described of finding NNESs easier to understand than NESs on (and off) campus. Some participants also spoke perceptively of the effect of their purist orientation to their L1 and their earlier English language learning on their attitude to English. A Thai student even attributed to her educational background the fact that she "loves" and desires an RP accent. The following exchange with another Chinese student is typical of points made in this respect by several students:

Exchange 8: Native English ideology and prior education

S: I'm trying to er eliminate my English I mean grammar mistake er both in my speak and my writing my speak and writing

J: so you think your English should be more like native English?

S: yeah I will try to=

J: =you want to be like the (.) twenty per cent

S: @[@@ I am trying to but I think I know it's very difficult to speak a very er

J: [@@

S: I mean typical Eng-British English as er native speaker=

J: =but is that useful? would it be useful to speak like British people we've just talked about British people are less easy to [understand
S: [ah yes yes even though I make some mistake in grammar er: I mean the group in [name of department] they also can understand what I am saying (.) yeah
J: WHO can't understand
S: they CAN
J: they CAN understand yeah so if they can understand you (.) and often they can't understand the British people why do you want to sound like the British people
S: because I want to improve better better (.) er:
J: but why is British English better than Chinese English
S: yes yes what I want to say is that I er unconsciously er unconsciously er set the British English as my er criteria I mean (.)
J: okay so in your mind::=
S: =yeah in my mind
J: British English is best=
S: =yeah I agree with that because (1) when (.) er when started to learn English I was told this is right this is wrong that's the rule it should have been this or else you will (.) get a lower mark @@
J: yeah yeah
S: that's really why (.) I think
J: so it all goes back to your schooldays=
S: =yeah yeah it's about the [teaching
J: [telling you all the time this is proper English (.) this is [what you should do
S: [yeah yeah

The exchange begins with the student expressing his attachment to native English, and speaking of his desire to write and speak like NESs. When I introduce the issue of usefulness and refer back to our discussion of the proportion of NESs worldwide ("the twenty per cent"), and to what he had said about finding NNESs easier to understand, he interrupts me with a supporting move in which he agrees and points out that his research group understand him despite his grammar mistakes. After a brief misunderstanding between the two of us, because I understood his pronunciation of 'can't' as 'can', he reverts to his original point that native (British) English is his "criteria".[9] Now, however, he identifies his position as originating in the way he was taught English at school, and realizes that the emphasis of the teaching on British English rules and categorical orientation to "right" and "wrong" still affects him "unconsciously". It does not change his position to the extent that like many other participants, his desire to acquire native English remained. But it helped to explain this.

Hearing about ELF and related issues, particularly the number of NNESs and NESs worldwide and the phenomenon of English language change, caused some participants to adjust their positions on English. For example, a Korean student who had spoken strongly in favour of native English joked, on hearing about ELF, "please tell my supervisor", and then more seriously "I'm very happy some academics respect non-native English". Another described it as "good news for me". And another, who had previously described native English as "proper English", began talking of the time he had spent working out the English article system as time wasted. Some were surprised on hearing about the phenomenon of English language change and shocked by an example of eighth century English. One said "Oh *no*, is it [English]? Which year?", and another simply "wow, wow, wow!". Meanwhile, like a number of the staff that responded to my questionnaire (see Chapter Six), many of the students talked of hearing about these issues for the first time: "I didn't know that before", said a Thai student, "I never thought of that. It makes sense", said a Chinese student, and "I learn brand new stuff. That's a quite sensation for me" said another Korean. Such comments are very reminiscent of what many of the staff respondents' said in answer to the final question in the questionnaire, which suggests a degree of receptivity to ELF among both academic staff and international students.

Most of the students who expressed enthusiasm for ELF nevertheless reverted subsequently to their earlier characterization of native English as best, even though the various contradictions they expressed on the way may have been signs of change (Kvale and Brinkmann 2009). For despite the participants' evident interest in ELF, only in rare cases did they appear to adjust their positions substantially at the time. Of these, two felt that ELF needs to be more widely publicized. One, an Italian student, told me that I "need to spread the news", though she thought "it will take a couple of generations" for it to take effect. The other, also European, seemed to know something about ELF already, which may explain his more positive stance towards it, as well as his orientation to NESs: that their view of their English as standard is "colonial", "deep in the psyche", "a superiority thing". He likewise thought I should "document what's happening", but that it would be difficult to convince NES staff and students about ELF.

The majority, however, remained ambivalent. This showed up particularly in their perceptions of and goals for their own English, which often conflicted with the positive comments they made about ELF in theory. One participant, the Italian mentioned in the previous paragraph, having previously described the Italianness in her writing as a "problem", later changed her position, saying she did not want to come across as British: "I am proud to show my heritage". Another European said, likewise, that she did not want to lose her national identity in her English. But in most cases, even when participants had expressed agreement with ELF's orientation to English, for themselves they still wanted a native version, perceived this as 'best', saw their own English as "bad", "very poor", and wanted it to be native-like even in cases where NNESs were more likely to read their work and hear them speak. Some said it would give them confidence, while the majority simply could not decouple the notion of 'good' English from that of 'native' English, and said they regarded signs of Chinese, Korean, Turkish, and suchlike in their English as errors, however much they liked ELF in theory. A Saudi student, for instance, described it as "a wonderful idea", and repeated several times that she thought it was "a good principle". However, it would not do for her, because, she observed, "I care about English" and want "perfection", and this means native English, not an English influenced by her first language. The same position was taken by most of the Thai writers in another study (Buripakdi 2012), leading the author to conclude that "[t]he way the writers conceived of Standard English in relation to Thai English unveiled the powerful construct of English discourse hidden in language use" (p. 263).

Conclusions to the conversation study and some implications

The research questions relating to the conversation study asked firstly how international students perceive the linguistic expectations/requirements made of them by their institution and teachers, secondly the effects of the institution's English language policies/practices on their academic identities and self-esteem, and thirdly their effects on home students' intercultural communication skills. To sum up, the finding in relation to the first question is contradictory in that all 34 participants subscribed at least to some extent to the 'native English is best' ideology that permeates much of English medium HE. On the other hand, most of the participants were receptive to ELF. They were also critical of what the institution's native English ideology meant for them in practical terms, and saw its effects on their academic identities and self-esteem (the second question) as harmful in a range of ways relating to their daily academic life and work. This involved criticism of the home students. And although the participants did not link the institution's English language policies/practices directly to their perception of home students' lack of intercultural communication skills (the third question), this came across in much of what they said on the subject.

While there was a certain amount of variation across the participants' experiences and perceptions, there was also a remarkable amount of shared experience despite their differences in nationality, first language, degree level, and prior university education. And even allowing for the possibility of the focus of the analysis being influenced by my own perspective, much of the content of the conversations dwelt on the negative. This is no doubt in part because while I did not encourage the students to focus on such aspects of their university life, I said they should feel free to say whatever they liked with their anonymity guaranteed, and was also frank with them about my own views. It is therefore likely that the various positions and repositions they articulated were affected by the conversation context. However, this is true of all conversations, a point I made earlier in the chapter in relation to Talmy's (2010) argument that interviewers need "heightened reflexivity" in relation to their role. On the other hand, it is doubtful that the students' positions came from nowhere other than my influence. Rather, it seemed to me that many had already been thinking along similar lines in relation to some of the topics we discussed, but in a less formulated manner and/or that they had pushed such thoughts to one side because they did not feel entitled to think of the university, staff, and home students in such ways. If so, the freedom to express their thoughts to someone who openly shared some of them may have acted as a catalyst on this particular occasion. This suggests that what they said in the conversations, notwithstanding my role in eliciting it, provides a reasonably accurate reflection of international students' experience[10] across the institution and possibly in many similar institutions, and that their words cannot be dismissed as typical student 'complaints'.

On the basis of what the conversation participants said, it seems that there is vast room for improvement in terms of how international students are treated English language-wise in this and, quite possibly, other Anglophone HE institutions,[11] and that it will require systemic changes that go far beyond the surface level tinkering that has largely taken place so far, despite endless talk of the 'internationalization' of HE. As Schmitt (2011) points out, the challenge is to find ways of conducting academic life that both take account of universities' international environment and maintain language standards, rather than continuing to conduct 'business as usual', expecting international students (and staff) to fit into the local environment (the language socialization approach discussed in Chapter Five). I will briefly outline those areas in which changes seem to be needed most, at least as I understand it from the participants.

The first area concerns the need for a change of mind-set so that the accommodation of international students' English language needs is not seen as 'dumbing down', but as the incorporation of a genuine international perspective. This means abandoning the notion that international students should fit in with existing (i.e. national) ways of doing English, welcoming what *they* bring, and being far more accepting of their alternative ways. In other words, instead of seeing adaptation as a one-way phenomenon, or what one of my participants called "one-way traffic", home staff and students need to adapt too. This will involve adjusting the way they use English in lingua franca communication (e.g. in seminars and lectures) and making more effort to understand how international students use it in their speech and writing. It will also involve developing an awareness of the difficulties of studying in a foreign language, and of the fact that except when English is a student's major, it is simply a tool for communication to enable them to study something else: the means to an end, not the end itself, as several participants pointed out. It follows that the only criterion should be mutual intelligibility among the relevant international academic community inside and outside the institution instead of blanket conformity to a particular version of native English. And judging from the participants' comments on IELTS and TOEFL, it seems that the same applies to English language entry examinations. To this could be added academic publishing, which my colleague, Rosamond Mitchell, sees as the sine qua non of a change in attitude towards non-native English (personal communication). In this respect, a number of publications on ELF have already adopted 'intelligibility to a wide international readership' rather than conformity to British or American English as their language requirement, though I suspect it may be a while before those of a more traditional frame of mind follow suit.

Secondly, is the time factor. One of the points that came up most frequently in the conversations was a sense of unfairness that international students are required to meet the same deadlines as home students. This, they felt, does not acknowledge the far greater time involved in producing work in a foreign language. Some spoke specifically about deadlines for written assignments such as reports, essays, and dissertations. Several spoke of time limits in examinations. The fact that some universities are now allowing international students to take dictionaries into examinations is a welcome first step. But as the students pointed out, this makes no difference if they do not have time to use the dictionaries. Some also felt they should be given longer than home students to prepare for milestones such as assessed PhD presentations, upgrade vivas, and PhD completion, a position I wholeheartedly endorse from my own supervision experience. Reading more slowly in a foreign language is often part of the problem in all these respects. Schmitt (2011) therefore suggests that library loan periods could be longer for international than home students, and that staff could think more carefully before telling students to 'read widely'. The time factor also came up often in relation to the requirement for native-like English, with the student participants pointing out how much extra time this entailed: time which, as some pointed out, could more productively be spent on their research.

Next, there is a need for more academic support for international students. Many participants felt their lecturers and tutors did not have enough time for them. They attributed this to staff being too busy, some also saying there were insufficient staff on the programme. This of course is not the fault of the teaching staff themselves, but of management who do not employ sufficient staff for the number of international students they accept. Whether or not the participants linked the staff time problem to their high fees (though several did), it would seem reasonable that in fields that recruit large numbers of international students, there should be proportionately more staff to teach them. This would be justified not only in terms of the higher fees they pay, but also the extra help international students may need purely because they are studying in a foreign language, and hence the extra time factor involved for those who teach and supervise them.

Finally, many of the participants' comments about communication on campus demonstrated that home students and staff need educating in order to raise their awareness of what it means to be an international student and study in a foreign language. Baker (2012) talks of three levels of intercultural awareness: basic, advanced, and intercultural. From what the students said about their experiences of communicating with home students and staff, it seems that the vast majority have only a 'basic' level according to Baker's model. By contrast, judging from the participants' descriptions of communicating effectively with each other and finding each other easier to understand than the NESs on campus, it seems that they swiftly reach Baker's 'intercultural' level. This is made possible because, as many participants pointed out, they spend a lot of time in each other's company. Home students and staff, on the other hand, apparently spend little time interacting with international students. Thus, they do not have the opportunity to increase their intercultural communication skills as a matter of course.

A recent UK newspaper interview with a London-based lecturer is telling in this respect (Whitehead 2013). At the time of the interview, the lecturer was teaching in Hong Kong on a partnership scheme. Her Hong Kong teaching experience, she observed, had changed the way she works in her UK institution by making her realize that as half her UK students are international, she needs to alter the way she teaches at home too. In other words, it has taken a stint teaching in East Asia for her to realize the need to make changes in her international UK institution. I suspect the same is true of the vast majority of UK university staff who have not taught recently in English medium in non-Anglophone countries. Even having years of experience teaching international students at home is not sufficient, judging from the findings of my conversation study. In my own case, despite many years of working in close contact with large numbers of international students, I still learned many new things about the international student experience from the 'education' I received from the participants. Courses in intercultural communication for home staff and students are thus urgently needed.

Despite all their criticisms, it nevertheless seemed that most of the participants in the conversation study were reasonably happy with life at the university. They talked of many things that they liked as well as disliked, both at work and at play. Their 'likes', though, tended to relate to their international student networks and – for the lucky ones – to support from supervisors and tutors, and rarely to the institution's English language policies and practices. These were far more likely to be among their 'dislikes'. But I will leave the chapter with the words of a Turkish participant who decided at the end of our conversation to make some recommendations for all international universities in the UK:

> They have to show respect to all accents and all the people the way they speak. They have to respect all the way that they speak, because sometimes the people who are really good in English they might make fun of the others or try to correct them, like they don't be modest at all. This happens, I have seen a few times actually in some places, so this is not really good, and there should maybe be some lessons that can teach some people like classes to communicate for the native speakers to internationals, and yes this would be really helpful actually, yeah, to communicate all together.

Notes

1 As before, I use the term 'international students' in this chapter to refer to all students for whom English is not their first language, that is EU as well as 'overseas', although as before, this should not be taken to imply that I believe international students, however defined, form a monolithic group.

2 The Russell Group is a group of "24 leading UK universities". See www.russellgroup.ac.uk/our-universities/

3 Note that page numbers refer to the 2006 edition, which as far as I can see, differs from the original 1997 version only in pagination.

4 Note that I drew on the framework specifically for its discourse purpose dimension, that is, the speech functions themselves, rather than for their detailed "congruent grammatical realizations" (Eggins and Slade 2006: 192).

5 See Appendix 4 on p. 220 for the transcription conventions. In each exchange, S = the student participant and J = me, the researcher. In order to protect the students' identities, they are identified only by their nationality and, in cases where their nationality is not common in UK HE, by broader region if they say anything of a sensitive nature.

6 The majority of the student participants were not studying among staff or home students whose specialisms were foreign languages. But if they had been, they may have found the situation just as problematic, although for a different reason. That is, among those whose subject of teaching/research or study is a foreign language, there tends to be a belief that the goal of L2 learning should be native or near-native competence such as they themselves have in their own foreign language(s). This means that as well as expecting NNES students to understand the kind of English spoken among NESs, they are also critical of any non-native features that occur in NNES students' English. However, their position fails to take into account either the difference between a lingua franca and a foreign language (see Chapter Two), or the fact that for the majority of NNESs studying in English medium, whether in the UK or elsewhere, English is merely a communication tool to enable them to study something else, a point made by several of my conversation participants; it is not the subject of study itself. On the other hand, Coleman (2013b) notes a recent increase in the number of non-specialist language students (i.e. those majoring in other disciplines) and predicts this will rise further as students become more aware of "the demonstrated employability advantages of acquiring language skills" at a time when "increasingly internationalised campuses provide the glowing example of non-UK students taking full advantage of the courses on offer" (p. 21). Perhaps this development will lead to home students, too, appreciating what it means to use a foreign language as a communication tool.

7 This calls to mind an EAP teacher who told me that if a student said to him in class "I am sinking", he would assume the student was saying s/he was drowning rather than thinking. As I pointed out at the time, the fact that he was able to say he did not know that 'by x the student means y' was a clear demonstration that he did (see Jenkins 2007: 128).

8 Although the institution accepts both IELTS and TOEFL in its English language Entry requirements, it seems that no decision has been made as to how to deal with this in practice, and therefore that acceptance of American English is a matter of individual staff preference. And since, according to their websites, many other universities around the world accept both IELTS and TOEFL (see Chapter Five), arbitrary non-acceptance of either British or American English is likely to be a problem for students elsewhere.

9 As an aside, I wonder how many who rarely notice the frequent NES use of 'criteria' as a singular noun, even in formal writing, would regard it as an error in the informal speech of this NNES!

10 I accept that the chapter presents a one-sided picture in that had I also talked with staff and home students, I would have encountered other perspectives.

11 This is not to suggest that I regard this single study in a single UK institution as generalizable in any traditional sense. Rather, I see it as having 'resonance' (Richards 2003) to the extent that I have created "the conditions under which insights can 'ring true' in the minds of those who encounter them" so that "readers can find through their own experience a means of connecting with the research" and thus "be open to share in [my] understandings and find instantiations of them in their own professional experience" (p. 266).

AFTERWORD

Taking stock and looking ahead

The book began with the single overarching question, 'how do we respond in our teaching to an academic culture that is becoming more and more globalized, and the needs of students with diverse linguistic and cultural backgrounds?', a question that I then set about exploring in relation to the English language. Admittedly, in one sense, I already knew the answer. For as an ELF researcher, I believe, and did from the start, that if English is the language of *international* HE, it is not appropriate for it to be a *national* version of HE's Anglophone minority: in other words, not the kinds of English that North American or British people, academics or otherwise, use among themselves. With so much known about the phenomenon of ELF(A), the time had come, I thought, for HE to start taking account of it. My purpose in carrying out the research was therefore to explore the extent to which traditional orientations to English still permeate HE, whether there was any receptivity to the ways in which English is spoken and written by its NNES ELF majority, and which areas of English language policy and practice were most in need of addressing in these respects. The research questions relating specifically to each empirical study have already been answered in their respective chapters. It is time, now, to take stock.

In order to contextualize HE's orientation to ELF, I begin with a reminder of the current global English language situation as a whole: "the general picture" as Seidlhofer observes, "is one of lack of awareness: we are faced here with a conceptual mismatch between outdated ideas about native-speaker privilege and the overdue acknowledgement of the reality of ELF" (2011: 16). Despite the fact that ELF is used effectively in all kinds of high-stakes settings including HE, "entrenched attitudes and established traditional views of native-speaker authority are still asserted and accepted very widely" (ibid.).

And this is pretty much what I found in my three empirical studies. Around the world, international universities embrace diversity and welcome English lingua franca communities onto their campuses with open arms. But as Coleman (2012a) notes, the reason for this is not a desire for diversity per se, but "to attract fee-paying international students, gifted teachers and researchers, and the most talented postgraduates to enhance the university's reputation" (p. xv). So it is not surprising to find that when it comes to English language use, the fascination with diversity disappears, to be replaced by the "established traditional views of native-speaker authority" to which Seidlhofer refers. That is, a requirement for uniformity according to native English norms, a requirement that, incidentally, is extremely lucrative for international publishers, international English language examination boards, proofreading companies, university pre-sessional courses, and the like. Native English is established as the standard by management, and thence expected (if with varying degrees of tolerance) by staff, and deferred to (if with some ambivalence) by international students. Thus, the overall picture provided by my studies of HE English language policies and practices is one in which native English ideology seems to be pretty much in operation around the entire HE world.[1]

A major reason for this is undoubtedly the marginalization of language issues by those in positions of influence. In recent years there has been an avalanche of published material on the internationalization of HE, while universities have been putting enormous efforts into demonstrating their international credentials on their websites and elsewhere. And yet English – the language in which universities conduct much of, if not all, their international business – is rarely mentioned except in relation to homogenizing practices such as testing, remedial instruction, and proofreading. This means, as Saarinen and Nikula (2012) point out, that EMI is rarely problematized, even though it raises all kinds of complex issues for staff and students as well as, according to some, a potential threat to the local language(s) including domain loss (see Kirkpatrick 2011). Meanwhile in Anglophone contexts, the prime concern is how to help international students 'fit in' better linguistically with the locals rather than how the locals might adapt their own language practices to fit in better with their international student (and staff) population and lingua franca environment. And nowhere in HE, Anglophone or non-Anglophone, does there seem to be any awareness, outside the ELF(A) research community, of what it means to use English as a lingua franca.

This is not to suggest that there are no optimistic signs at all. If my research has demonstrated anything positive, it is that some university staff and international (including EU) students are receptive to ELF and the issues it raises provided their own awareness of these is raised in the first place. It was gratifying to note how many of the staff questionnaire responses and the international student conversation participants expressed an interest in the issues I had brought to their attention, even if they continued to retain their attachment to native English ideology. It was at least a step in the right direction.

As I end the book, I cannot predict what will happen over the next few years. On the one hand, it could be that business will continue more or less as usual, with native English ideology still dominating HE English language policies and practices around the world. After all, as one of my conversation participants said, it could be a couple of generations before ELF takes effect in HE, while another thought it would be difficult to convince NES staff and students about ELF. On the other hand, it is remarkable to think that a little over ten years ago when I published my first empirical book on ELF (2000), it was almost unheard of inside or outside HE. And yet it is now a mainstream area of linguistic research with its own conference series, journal, and book series, vast numbers of academic publications, and more to the point in the current context, is a very popular subject for PhD theses. So it is not beyond the bounds of possibility that during the next ten years, international university managements will gradually become aware of what is happening under their own noses and, as a result, start to act on the English language implications of their international claims, that is, abandon their attachment to native English and start basing their English language requirements on what is appropriate to a lingua franca environment: intercultural communication skills, accommodation skills, familiarity with diverse Englishes, and the need for courses to educate home staff and students in all of these.

Which of these two scenarios it will be, I am not sure. I therefore leave you, in the manner of those novels that allow the reader to select the ending, with two possible outcomes, one pessimistic, the other optimistic. The first concerns a PhD thesis and the second a job advertisement. Both involve mainland European universities, though in the case of the first one, I cannot breach confidentiality by saying which one. The second is Universiteit Gent, or Ghent University, in Belgium, one of the institutions whose websites were explored in Chapter Five.

Scenario one

A PhD candidate whose research was on the subject of ELF wrote at the start of his/her thesis that as the thesis was both about ELF and written and supervised by ELF users, s/he had not done as recommended by the university and had his/her English revised in order to bring it in line with native academic English. S/he cited examples of published edited volumes that had taken the same ELF approach, and argued that the notion of having the thesis revised language-wise, especially by a NES, would have contradicted the entire ethos of ELF. Instead, s/he argued that what was important was whether the text was comprehensible and interesting to its (largely NNES) readership.

As the external examiner, and an ELF researcher myself, I condoned the candidate's position entirely. I also found the text comprehensible regardless of a certain amount of non-native English use (and quite possibly because of it – some of the least clear and comprehensible theses I have read have been written by NES candidates). However, the internal examiner, who was also familiar with ELF research, and who shared the candidate's L1, saw things rather differently. On the one hand, s/he endorsed the use of ELF in academic life. But on the other hand, s/he argued, somewhat paradoxically, that standard (i.e. native) English is still the norm for doctoral theses, and therefore that the candidate should revise the English of the thesis to at least C2 (the highest) level of the CEFR.

In other words, someone familiar with ELF, and who claimed to support its use in academic contexts, still expected conformity to near-native academic English in a doctoral thesis. And this, despite the candidate's reference to published academic works that had provided a precedent. If such is the response of someone who is aware of ELF research, and who supports the use of ELF in academic life, it is not surprising that so many NNES PhD students feel obliged to have their theses proofread. As mentioned in Chapter One, even my own students, whose research is, likewise, on ELF and other areas of global Englishes, feel the need to 'play safe', and have their writing turned into a native English style that they do not endorse and that does not reflect their own academic identities. Others taking part in a focus group study said exactly the same (see Chapter Three).

Scenario two

The optimistic ending involves a change of mind over a job advert and demonstrates that it is possible to influence English related decisions if those in charge have the opportunity to reflect on the issues.

In August 2012, an advertisement for the position of teaching assistant in the Department of Linguistics at Ghent University was posted on the website of the British Association of Applied Linguistics (BAAL). Among the four requirements in the 'Candidate profile' was the following: "Candidates should have near-native (or native) proficiency in the English language". Given that there had recently been a lengthy debate on the BAAL email list and a decision taken that advertisements seeking native speakers of English should no longer be posted, and given that "near-native (or native) proficiency in English" is, to my mind a euphemism for 'native speaker', I sent the following email to the list objecting to the advert:

> I thought BAAL members had agreed not to post any more job adverts asking for "native" English (whatever that is). Or is it okay if the 'n' word is in brackets, preceded by "near native or", and followed by "proficiency"?

Guy Cook, the (then) Chair of BAAL, responded by saying "job adverts posted on BAALmail should not use 'native' English as a criterion". He suggested that the member who had posted the advert should ask the university in question to rephrase the criteria and then repost the advert, and added "there is an important principle at stake". A few days later, the advert reappeared, but now the 'native' criterion had been replaced with "candidates have an expert command of English". In practice, the outcome will have depended on how "expert" was interpreted by the institution in this case. And as I was of course involved in neither the discussions that presumably took place, nor the subsequent job interviews, I have no idea whether the original attachment to 'native' English still lurked beneath the surface and influenced the appointment. But even if that was the case, Ghent's use of the term "expert" was still a vast improvement on 'native', and calls to mind the "expert speaker" of Rampton (1990), which is far more in tune with ELF, and the complete opposite of the perspective of the internal examiner of Scenario one. It was also, to my knowledge, one of the first public signals from a high profile university that the prevailing native English ideology of global HE may finally be starting to give way to a recognition of the diverse English lingua franca nature of the international university. But as I say: you choose.

Note

1 This is not to claim we can be sure that what is engraved in English language policy stone actually reflects what takes place in university classrooms, an observation I made citing Costa and Coleman (2012) in Chapter Five, or that what happens in one institution in a country necessarily happens in another, even within the same region. As pointed out in Chapter Five in line with Doiz et al. (2013b), there is a need for ethnographic studies of each EMI-using institution to be carried out in situ by researchers familiar with the local context.

APPENDIX 1: UNIVERSITIES IN THE WEBSITE STUDY

The websites of the universities listed below were originally accessed in the period November 2011 to July 2012, and again, for the last time, from 15 to 19 October 2012. As mentioned above, the majority were randomly selected, many via the HE search engine, '4 International Colleges & Universities' at http://www.4icu.org/ Even when this was not the case, the selected universities can be found via this search engine or by entering the universities' names into another search engine such as Google. The websites used for information on universities in specific countries that offer programmes or courses in EMI are listed at the end of the Appendix.

East Asia

Beijing Foreign Studies University (BFSU), China
Beijing International Studies University (BISU), China
Beijing Normal University, China
Beijing University of Aeronautics and Astronautics (Beihang University), China
Chukyo University, Japan
Chulalongkorn University, Thailand
Dankook University, South Korea
Dongseo University, South Korea
Fudan University, China
Guangdong University of Foreign Studies, China
Hongik University, South Korea
International Christian University (Tokyo), Japan
International Islamic University of Malaya
Korea University
Kyoto University, Japan

Mahidol University, Thailand
Osaka University, Japan
Paññāsāstra University of Cambodia
Royal University of Phnom Penh, Cambodia
Seoul National University, South Korea
Shanghai International Studies University, China
Shanghai University, China
Shantou University, China
University of Malaya, Malaysia
University of Tokyo, Japan
Waseda University, Japan

Mainland Europe

Bilkent University, Turkey
Budapest University of Technology and Economics, Hungary
Freie Universität Berlin, Germany
Jacobs University (previously International University of Bremen), Germany
KTH University, Sweden
Middle East Technical University (METU), Turkey
Pompeu Fabra University, Spain
Universidad Carlos III de Madrid, Spain
University of Ghent, Belgium
University of Groningen, Netherlands
University of Łódź, Poland
University of Navarra, Spain
University of Tampere, Finland
University of Zagreb, Croatia
Uppsala University, Sweden
Warsaw University of Technology (WUT), Poland

Latin America

Fundação Armando Alvares Penteado (FAAP), Brazil
Tecnológico de Monterrey (TDM), Mexico
Universidad Argentina Austral, Argentina
University of Belgrano, Argentina
University of Fortaleza, Brazil
University of Viña del Mar, Chile

Anglophone

California State University LA (CSULA), US
Imperial College London, UK

Pennsylvania (Penn) State University, US
University of Illinois at Urbana-Champaign, US
University of Queensland, Australia
University of Sheffield, UK
University of Sydney, Australia

Anglophone branches

Lakeland College, Japan
Nottingham-Ningbo University, China
State University New York (SUNY), Korea
Temple University, Japan
Xi'an Jiaotong-Liverpool University (XJTLU), China

Other websites accessed for information about universities offering EMI

Argentina: http://www.menteargentina.com/study-in-argentina/study-abroad-argen
tina.html
China: http://www.china.org.cn/english/LivinginChina/184768.htm
Japan, G30 website: http://www.uni.international.mext.go.jp/
Poland: http://www.studyinpoland.pl/en/nasze_moduly/view_full_guide/univeri
sty_guide.html
Spain: http://aprendemas.com/Guias/Selectividad-elegir-carrera-2010/P5.asp

APPENDIX 2: UNIVERSITY STAFF QUESTIONNAIRE

1. Does your university as a whole and/or your department specifically have any official or unofficial (but usually required) English language policies and practices? If so, could you say how useful (or not) you think they are, and provide some examples?

2. If there are *not* any such policies and practices do you think there should be some? Why, or why not?

3. Are you aware of your university's and/or your department's English language entry requirements for non-native English students? If so, could you briefly explain what they are and give your opinion of them? If there are no language entry requirements, do you think there should be? Why, or why not?

4. When you assess your non-native English-speaking students' *written* work, how far, if at all, do you expect it to conform to native academic English? What are your reasons?

5. Could you say briefly what you expect of your non-native English-speaking students in terms of their *spoken* English.

6. What kinds of support, if any, does your institution offer *both its non-native and its native English students* to help them with their academic work? (e.g. academic writing support, advice on giving presentations). Do you think this support is sufficient or could more be done? If so, what?

7. What effects (positive and/or negative) do you think your university's expectations of its students' English have on its *non-native English* students and (if there are any) on its *native English* students?

8. What, in your view, are the responsibilities of *both non-native and native English staff and students* in achieving effective intercultural communication in universities where English is used as a lingua franca?

9. In your opinion, what are the implications for the kind of English a university should require of its students and staff if it describes itself as 'an international university'?
10. Would you like to make any other comments on the topic or the questionnaire itself?

APPENDIX 3: QUESTIONNAIRE MAIN AND SUB-THEMES

Question 1: Respondent's institution's English language policies and practices

1. Do/don't have an official/stated or unofficial/implicit English language policy.

   - do not have official or unofficial policy, or respondent not aware of one
   - have informal policy/understanding/unwritten rule
   - have policy linked to tests (entry/programme/exit) and/or remedial teaching
   - policy focuses on correctness according to native English
   - policy is flexible regarding kind of English

2. Own institution's English language policies/practices are/are not useful.

   - useful/benefit to NNES/international students
   - useful/benefit to staff
   - useful/benefit to university
   - not useful because …

Question 2: Should there be institutional English language policies?

1. Support for English language policies/more policies.

   - needed in modern universities
   - link between policy and student/staff proficiency
   - need for a standard
   - help international students integrate
   - English is an important communication tool

2. Concerns about English language policies/practices.

- cost to L1 and identity
- many NNES students less able to operate in English than in L1
- dominance of English a bad thing
- because focus on native English
- because decided top down

Question 3: English language entry requirements for NNES students

1. Respondent's institution has English language entry requirements

- various tests named, mainly international, some local
- have entry requirements but flexible
- no entry test or requirements but exit test
- remedial teaching for students who don't match entry requirements

2. Should/should not have English language entry requirements.

- tests useful
- tests unreliable
- ideological and equity issues

Question 4: How far should NNES written work conform to native English?

1. Preference for conformity to native English

- conformity to native academic written English important/desirable
- conformity justified by external factors

2. Variation from native English norms acceptable.

- focus on content/meaning rather than language
- variation in terms of varieties of English
- equity issues
- NNES teacher confidence issues

Question 5: Respondent's expectations about students' spoken English.

1. More normative expectations.

- importance of correctness, good pronunciation
- maintaining non-native English accent unacceptable
- should not mix British and American accents

2. More flexible approaches.

  - communication and intelligibility rather than correctness
  - importance of confidence
  - lower demands of spoken than written English

3. Non-conforming positions.

  - maintaining non-native accent acceptable
  - legitimacy of non-native English

Question 6: English language support for NNES and NES students at respondent's institution

1. Insufficient support

  - mismatch between university's expectations and level of support on offer
  - quality of support inappropriate

2. Support linked to native English

  - assumption that support is to help NNES students conform to Anglo norms
  - need for NES teachers

3. Support focuses on/should focus on areas other than formal language skills

  - importance of teaching communication skills
  - need to help students with confidence
  - should encourage international students to integrate

Question 7: Positive and/or negative effects on students of the institution's expectations of students' English

1. Range of negative effects

  - cause NNES students to struggle
  - reduce students' self confidence
  - time-consuming
  - unreasonable to expect NNES students to achieve same standard as NES
  - too much focus on linguistic forms and exams vs knowledge of discipline

2. Positive effects

  - communication enhancement
  - language abilities

3. University's perceived motivation for expectations about students' English

  - relationship between English and the institution's reputation
  - link between internationalization and English

Question 8: Responsibilities of NES and NNES staff and students for effective intercultural communication (IC)

1. Multilingualism–multiculturalism approach.

   - the aim should be multilingualism
   - all should develop intercultural competence

2. English prioritized within a multicultural approach.

   - English mainly
   - need for tolerance/acceptance of difference
   - divided views of responsibilities for IC
   - familiarity and mutual intelligibility

3. More normative approaches

   - onus on NNESs
   - English only
   - no alternative

Question 9: Implications for an 'international' university for the kind of English it should require

1. Amount/scope of English implied by the term 'international'.
2. Normative approach to the type of English required.
3. More open approach towards English.
4. Multilingual approach to the international university.

Question 10: Any other comments on the topic or questionnaire

1. Importance of the topic.

   - questionnaire raises important ambitious questions
   - enabled respondents to reflect on points previously not considered

2. Language–ideological arguments.
3. Issues relating to the topic that were not covered by the questions.

   - universities should recognize the language needs of international students
   - universities should help NNES staff to teach in English
   - universities should conduct own tests, not use international ones
   - how to distinguish between proficiency level and English variety
   - meaning of 'international university'

4. Complaints about the questionnaire format.

APPENDIX 4: INTERVIEW TRANSCRIPTION CONVENTIONS

In all cases, S is the student participant and J is me. Note that in order to protect the participants' anonymity, the only information I have given in each case is the nationality, and occasionally only the broader geographical origin. Thus, I have not given them an alias or any other means of linking the contributions from any one participant.

CAPS	Stressed word
:	Long syllable (length indicated by number of colons)
@@@	Laughter (length indicated by number of @)
?	Rising intonation
.	Falling intonation
=	Latching
(.)	Pause of one second or less
(2) etc.	Pause of 2 seconds etc.
[	Overlapping speech
[	
(apples and oranges)	Guess at unclear word or words
XXX	Unintelligible word or words
[…]	gaps in transcript because material is sensitive or not relevant

REFERENCES

Adamson, J. & T. Muller 2012. Editorial investigation of roles and responsibilities in academic journal editorial systems. In J. Adamson & R. Nunn (eds.) *Editorial and Authorial Voices in EFL Academic Journal Publishing*. Academic Scholars Publishing House, Australia: Asian EFL Journal Press.

Altbach, P.G. & J. Knight 2007. The internationalization of higher education: motivations and realities. *Journal of Studies in International Education* 3/4: 290–305.

Ammon, U. 2000. Towards more fairness in international English: linguistic rights of non-native speakers. In R. Phillipson (ed.) *Rights to Language. Equity, Power, and Education*. Mahwah, NJ: Lawrence Erlbaum.

Ammon, U. (ed.) 2001. *The Dominance of English as a Language of Science. Effects on Other Languages and Language Communities*. Berlin: Mouton de Gruyter.

Ammon, U. 2003. Global English and the non-native speaker: overcoming disadvantage. In H. Tonkin & T. Reagan (eds.) *Language in the Twenty-First Century*. Amsterdam: John Benjamins.

Ammon, U. 2006. Language planning for international scientific communication.*Current Issues in Language Planning* 7/1: 1–30.

Ammon, U. 2007. Global scientific communication: open questions and policy suggestions. In A. Carli & U. Ammon (eds.) Linguistic Inequality in Scientific Communication Today. *AILA Review* 20. Amsterdam: John Benjamins.

Anderson, A., N. Hargreaves & N. Owtram 2009. Manifesting identity in situated academic writing: institutional factors and individual orientations in writing by post-graduate students in an English as a Lingua Franca context. In M. Gotti (ed.) *Commonality and Individuality in Academic Discourse*. Bern: Peter Lang.

Anderson, B. 2006. *Imagined Communities*. London: Verso.

Anderson, L. 2010. Standards of acceptability in English as an Academic *Lingua Franca*: evidence from a corpus of peer-reviewed working papers by international students. In R. Cagliero & J. Jenkins (eds) *Discourses, Communities, and Global Englishes*. Bern: Peter Lang.

Androutsopoulos, J. 2010. Localizing the global on the participatory web. In N. Coupland (ed.) *The Handbook of Language and Globalization*. Oxford: Blackwell.

Archibald A., A. Cogo & J. Jenkins (eds.) 2011. *Latest Trends in ELF Research*. Newcastle on Tyne: Cambridge Scholars Publishing.

Ates, B. & Z.R. Eslami 2012. An analysis of non-native English-speaking graduate teaching assistants' online journal entries. *Language and Education* 26/6: 537–52.

Auerbach, E. 2000. When pedagogy meets politics: challenging English only in adult education. In E. Duenas Gonzalez & I. Melis (eds.) *Language Ideologies: Critical Perspectives on the Official English Movement*. Mahwah, NJ: Lawrence Erlbaum.

Bailey, S. 2006. *Academic Writing. A Handbook for International Students*. London: Routledge.

Baker, W. 2012. From cultural awareness to intercultural awareness: culture in ELT. *ELT Journal* 66/1: 62–70.

Baker, W. 2013. Interpreting the culture in intercultural rhetoric: a critical perspective from English as a lingua franca studies. In D. Belcher & G. Nelson (eds.) *Critical and Corpus-based Approaches to Intercultural Rhetoric*. Ann Arbor, MI: University of Michigan Press.

Ball, S. 1993. What is policy? Texts, trajectories and toolboxes. *Discourse* 13/2: 10–17.

Bash, L. 2009. Engaging with cross-cultural communication barriers in globalized higher eduation: the case of research-degree students. *Intercultural Education* 20/5: 475–83.

Beebe, L. & H. Giles 1984. Speech-accommodation theories: a discussion in terms of second-language acquisition. In H. Giles (ed.) *International Journal of the Sociology of Language. The dynamics of speech accommodation*. Amsterdam: Mouton.

Belcher, D. 2007. Seeking acceptance in an English-only research world. *Journal of Second Language Writing* 16: 1–22.

Belcher, D. 2009. How research space is created in a diverse research world. *Journal of Second Language Writing* 18: 221–34.

Benesch, S. 2001. *Critical English for Academic Purposes*. Mahwah, NJ: Lawrence Erlbaum.

Benzie, H.J. 2010. Graduating as a "native speaker": international students and English language proficiency in higher education. *Higher Education Research and Development* 29/4: 447–59.

Berg, B.L. 2009. *Qualitative Research Methods for the Social Sciences* 7th ed. Boston: Pearson.

Bex, T. & R. Watts 1999. *Standard English. The Widening Debate*. London: Routledge.

Björkman, B. 2008. So where are we? Spoken lingua franca English at a technical university in Sweden. *English Today* 24/2: 35–41.

Björkman, B. 2009. From code to discourse in spoken ELF. In Mauranen & Ranta (eds) 2009.

Björkman, B. 2010. Spoken lingua franca English at a Swedish technical university. Unpublished PhD dissertation, University of Stockholm.

Björkman, B. 2013. *English as an Academic Lingua Franca. An investigation of form and communicative effectiveness*. Berlin: De Gruyter Mouton.

Blommaert, J. 2006. Languge policy and national identity. In Ricento (ed.) 2006.

Blommaert, J. 2010. *The Sociolinguistics of Globalization*. Cambridge: Cambridge University Press.

Bolton, K. 2011. World Englishes and English as a Lingua Franca: a comparison of approaches with particular reference to English in the Asian context. Keynote speech, 4th International Conference of English as a Lingua Franca, Hong Kong, May 2011.

Bolton, K. & D. Graddol 2012. English in China today. *English Today* 28/3: 3–9.

Bonacina-Pugh, F. 2012. Researching "practiced language policies": insights from conversation analysis. *Language Policy* 11: 213–34.

Bourdieu, P. 1991. *Language and Symbolic Power*. Cambridge, MA: University of Harvard Press.

Bourdieu, P. & J.C. Passeron 1977. *Reproduction in Education, Society and Culture*. London: Sage Publications.

Breiteneder, A. 2005. The naturalness of English as a European lingua franca: the case of the "third person -s". *Vienna English Working PaperS (VIEWS)* 14/2: 3–26.

Breiteneder, A. 2009. English as a lingua franca in Europe: an empirical perspective. *World Englishes* 28/2: 256–69.

Brenn-White, M. & E. van Rest 2012. *English-Taught Master's Programs in Europe: New Findings on Supply and Demand*. Institute of International Education. Available at www.iie.org (accessed 15 March 2013).

Bright, D. & L.H. Phan 2011. Learning to speak like us: identity, discourse and teaching English in Vietnam. In L. Zhang, R. Rubdy & L. Alsagoff (eds.) *Asian Englishes: Changing Perspectives in a Globalised World*. Singapore: Pearson.

Brumfit, C. 2001. *Individual Freedom in Language Teaching*. Oxford: Oxford University Press.

Brunner, B.B. 2006. Student perceptions of diversity on a college campus: scratching the surface to find more. *Intercultural Education* 17/3: 311–17.

Brutt-Griffler, J. 2002. *World English. A study of its development.* Clevedon, UK: Multilingual Matters.

Brutt-Griffler, J. & K.K. Samimy 2001. Transcending the nativeness paradigm. *World Englishes* 20/1: 99–106.

Buripakdi, A. 2012. On professional writing: Thai writers' views on their English. *International Journal of Applied Linguistics* 22/2: 245–64.

Burr, V. 2003. *Social Constructionism* 2nd ed. London: Routledge.

Canagarajah, A.S. 1999. *Resisting Linguistic Imperialism in English Teaching.* Oxford: Oxford University Press.

Canagarajah, A.S. 2002. *Critical Academic Writing and Multilingual Students.* Ann Arbor: University of Michigan Press.

Canagarajah, A.S. 2007. Lingua Franca English, multilingual communities and language acquisition. *Modern Language Journal* 91: 923–39.

Canagarajah, A.S. 2011. Codemeshing in academic writing: identifying teachable strategies of translanguaging. *Modern Language Journal* 95/3: 401–17.

Canagarajah, A.S. 2013. *Translingual Practice. Global Englishes and Cosmopolitan Relations.* London: Routledge.

Carli, A. & U. Ammon (eds.) 2007. Linguistic Inequality in Scientific Communication Today. *AILA Review* 20. Amsterdam: John Benjamins.

Carroll, J. & J. Ryan (eds.) 2005. *Teaching International Students.* London: Routledge.

Carter, S. 2012. English as an additional language (EAL) viva voce: the EAL doctoral oral examination experience. *Assessment & Evaluation in Higher Education* 37/3: 273–84.

Chang, Y-J. & Y. Kanno 2010. NNES doctoral students in English-speaking academe: the nexus between language and discipline. *Applied Linguistics* 31/5: 671–92.

Charles, M.L. & R. Marschan-Piekkari 2002. Language training for enhanced horizontal communication: a challenge for MNCs. *Business Communication Quarterly* 65/2: 9–29.

Charles, M., D. Pecorari & S. Hunston (eds.) 2009. *Academic Writing: At the interface of corpus and discourse.* London: Continuum.

Chiang, S-Y. & H-F. Mi 2011. Reformulation: a verbal display of interlanguage awareness in instructional interactions. *Language Awareness* 20/2: 135–49.

Clifford, V. 2011. Internationalising the home student. *Higher Education Research and Development* 30/5: 555–57.

Clifford, V. & C. Montgomery (eds.) 2011. *Moving towards Internationalisation of the Curriculum for Global Citizenship in Higher Education.* Oxford: Oxford Centre for Staff and Learning Development.

Cogo, A. 2009. Accommodating difference in ELF conversations: a study of pragmatic strategies. In Mauranen & Ranta (eds.) 2009.

Cogo, A. & M. Dewey 2012. *Analysing English as a Lingua Franca: A corpus-driven investigation.* London: Continuum.

Cogo, A. & J. Jenkins 2010. English as a lingua franca in Europe. A mismatch between policy and practice. *European Journal of Language Policy* 2/2: 271–94.

Coleman, J. 2013a. Foreword. Doiz et al. (eds.) 2013a.

Coleman, J. 2012b. Non-specialist linguists in the United Kingdom in the context of the Englishisation of European Higher Education. In C. Gnutzmann, F. Königs & L. Küster (eds.) *Fremdsprachen Lehren und Lernen.* Tübingen: Narr Verlag.

Connor, U. 2004. Intercultural rhetoric research: beyond texts. *Journal of English for Academic Purposes* 3: 291–304.

Connor, U. 2008. Mapping multidimensional aspects of research: reaching to intercultural rhetoric. In U. Connor, E. Nagelhout & W. Rozychi (eds.) *Contrastive Rhetoric: Reaching to intercultural rhetoric.* Amsterdam: John Benjamins.

Connor, U. 2011. *Intercultural Rhetoric in the Writing Classroom.* Ann Arbor: University of Michigan Press.

Copland, F. & S. Garton 2011. "I felt that I do live in the UK now": international students' self-reports of their English language speaking experiences on a pre-sessional programme. *Language and Education* 25/3: 241–55.

Costa, F. & J. Coleman 2012. A survey of English-medium instruction in Italian higher education. *International Journal of Bilingual Education and Bilingualism.* DOI:10.1080/13670050.2012.676621.

Cots, J.M. 2013 Introducing English-medium instruction at the University of Lleida (Spain): intervention, beliefs and practices. In Doiz et al. (eds.) 2013a.

Coverdale-Jones, T. & P. Rastall (eds.) 2009. *Internationalising the University. The Chinese Context.* Houndmills, Basingstoke: Palgrave Macmillan.

Cresswell, J.W. 2011. Controversies in mixed methods research. In N. Denzin & Y. Lincoln (eds.) *The Sage Handbook of Qualitative Research* 4th ed. Thousand Oaks, CA: Sage.

Crystal, D. 2003. *English as a Global Language.* Cambridge: Cambridge University Press.

D'Angelo, J. 2011. What nearby models should Japan consider in the era of globalized higher education? *Journal of the Chukyo University College of World Englishes* 14: 1–14.

Davies, A. 2003. *The Native Speaker in Applied Linguistics* 2nd ed. Edinburgh: Edinburgh University Press.

Denzin, N. & Y. Lincoln 2011. Introduction. The discipline and practice of qualitative research. In N. Denzin & Y. Lincoln (eds.) *The Sage Handbook of Qualitative Research* 4th ed. Thousand Oaks, CA: Sage.

Deterding, D. & A. Kirkpatrick 2006. Intelligibility and an emerging ASEAN English lingua franca. *World Englishes* 25/3: 391–410.

Dewey, M. 2007. English as a lingua franca: an interconnected perspective. *International Journal of Applied Linguistics* 17/3: 332–54.

Dewey, M. 2009. English as a lingua franca: heightened variability and theoretical implications. In Mauranen & Ranta (eds.) 2009.

Dixon, M. 2006. Globalisation and international higher education: contested positionings. *Journal of Studies in International Education* 10/4: 319–33.

Doiz, A., D. Lasagabaster & J.M. Sierra 2011. Internationalisation, multilingualism and English-medium instruction. *World Englishes* 30/3: 345–59.

Doiz, A., D. Lasagabaster & J.M. Sierra (eds.) 2013a. *English-Medium Instruction at Universities Worldwide.* Bristol: Multilingual Matters.

Doiz, A., D. Lasagabaster & J.M. Sierra (eds.) 2013b. Future challenges for English-medium instruction at the tertiary level. In Doiz et al. (eds.) 2013a.

Dörnyei, Z. 2003. *Questionnaires in Second Language Research. Construction, Administration and Processing.* Mahwah, NJ: Lawrence Erlbaum.

Dörnyei, Z. 2007. *Research Methods in Applied Linguistics.* Oxford: Oxford University Press.

Duff, P. 2010. Language socialization into academic discourse communities. *Annual Review of Applied Linguistics* 30: 169–92.

Durant, A. & I. Shepherd 2009. "Culture" and "communication" in intercultural communication. *European Journal of English Studies* 13/2: 147–62.

Duszak, 1997. Cross-cultural academic communication: a discourse-community view. In A. Duszak (ed.) *Culture and Styles of Academic Discourse.* Berlin: DeGruyter Mouton.

Edwards, C. & C. Owen 2002. What should go into an MA TEFL programme? Teachers' evaluations of the taught components of a sample programmme. *ELTED* 7: 54–73.

Eggins, S. & D. Slade 1997. *Analysing Casual Conversation.* London: Cassell.

Eggins, S. & D. Slade 2006. *Analysing Casual Conversation.* London: Equinox.

Ehrenreich, S. 2011. English as a business lingua franca in a German multinational corporation. *Journal of Business Communication* 47/4: 408–31.

Ellingson, L. 2009. *Engaging Crystallization in Qualitative Research.* Thousand Oaks, CA: Sage.

Erling, E. 2007. Local identities, global connections: affinities to English among students at the Freie Universität Berlin. *World Englishes* 26/2: 111–30.

Erling, E. & T. Bartlett 2006. Making English their own: the use of ELF among students of English at the FUB. *Nordic Journal of English Studies* 5/2: 9–40.

Fairclough, N. 2006. *Language and Globalisation.* London: Routledge.

Fairclough, N. 2010. *Critical Discourse Analysis. The critical study of language* 2nd ed. Harlow, UK: Pearson Education.

Feng, Y. 2012. University of Nottingham Ningbo China and Xi'an Jiaotong-Liverpool University: globalization of higher education in China. *Higher Education*. Published online 27 July 2012, DOI: 10.1007/s10734-012-9558-8.

Ferguson, G. 2007. The global spread of English, scientific communication and ESP: questions of equity, access and domain loss. *Ibérica* 13: 7–38.

Ferguson, G., C. Pérez-Llantada & R. Pló 2011. English as an international language of scientific publication: a study of attitudes. *World Englishes* 30/1: 41–59.

Firth, A. 1996. The discursive accomplishment of normality: on "lingua franca" English and conversation analysis. *Journal of Pragmatics* 26: 237–59.

Firth, A. 2009. The lingua franca factor. *Intercultural Pragmatics* 6/2: 147–70.

Firth, A. & J. Wagner 1997. On discourse, communication and (some) fundamental concepts in SLA research. *Modern Language Journal* 81: 285–300.

Fløttum, K. (ed.) 2008. *Language and Discipline Perspectives on Academic Discourse*. Newcastle upon Tyne: Cambridge Scholars Publishing.

Flower, L. 2003. Talking across difference: intercultural rhetoric and the search for situated knowledge. *College Composition and Communication* 55/1: 38–68.

Flowerdew, J. 2001. Attitudes of journal editors to non-native speaker contributions. *TESOL Quarterly* 35/1: 121–50.

Flowerdew, J. 2008. Scholarly writers who use English as an additional language. What can Goffman's *"stigma"* tell us? *Journal of English for Academic Purposes* 7: 77–86.

Flowerdew, J. 2011. Action, content and identity in applied genre analysis for ESP. *Language Teaching* 44/4: 516–28.

Foskett, N. 2010. Global markets, national challenges, local strategies: the strategic challenge of internationalization. In Maringe & Foskett (eds.) 2010.

Fraser, H. 2011. Speaking and listening in the multicultural university: a reflective case study. *Journal of Academic Language & Learning* 5/1: A110–A128.

García, O., M. Pujol-Ferran & P. Reddy 2013. Educating international and immigrant students in US higher education: opportunities and challenges. In Doiz et al. (eds.) 2013a.

Gardezi, S.A. & H. Nesi 2009. Variation in the writing of economics students in Britain and Pakistan. In Charles et al. (eds.) 2009.

Gergen, K. 1985. The social constructionist movement in modern psychology. *American Psychologist* 40: 266–75.

Gibbs, P. 2010. The commoditization and standardization of higher education. In Maringe & Foskett (eds.) 2010.

Gillett, A., A. Hammond & M. Martala 2009. *Inside Track to Successful Academic Writing*. Harlow, UK: Pearson Longman.

Goffman, E. 1963. *Stigma. Notes on the Management of Spoiled Identity*. Upper Saddle River, NJ: Prentice Hall.

Gray, J. 2010. *The Construction of English. Culture, Consumerism and Promotion in the ELT Coursebook*. Houndmills, Basingstoke: Palgrave Macmillan.

Greenall, A.K. 2012. Attracting international students by means of the web: transadaptation, domestication and cultural suppression. *International Journal of the Sociology of Language* 216: 75–85.

Gross, A., J. Harmon & M. Reidy 2002. *Communicating Science. The scientific article from the 17th century to the present*. Oxford: Oxford University Press.

Haberland, H. 1989. Whose English, nobody's business. *Journal of Pragmatics* 13: 927–38.

Haberland, H., J. Mortensen, A. Fabricius, B. Preisler, K. Risager & S. Kjærbeck (eds.) 2008. *Higher Education in the Global Village*. Roskilde, Denmark: University of Roskilde.

Halliday, M.A.K. 1984. Language as code and language as behaviour: a systemic-functional interpretation of the nature and ontogenesis of dialogue. In R. Fawcett, M.A.K. Halliday, S.M. Lamb & A. Makkai (eds.) *The Semiotics of Language and Culture Vol.1: Language as Social Semiotic*. London: Pinter.

Halliday, M.A.K. 1994. *An Introduction to Functional Grammar* 2nd ed. London: Edward Arnold.

Harré, R. & L. van Langenhove 1991. Varieties of positioning. *Journal for the Theory of Social Behaviour* 21/4: 393–407.

Harré, R. & L. van Langenhove (eds.) 1999. *Positioning Theory: Moral Contexts of Intentional Action.* Oxford: Blackwell.

Hashemi, M. 2012. Reflections on mixing methods in applied linguistics research. *Applied Linguistics* 33/2: 206–12.

Haugen, E. 1966. Linguistics and language planning. In W. Bright (ed.) *Sociolinguistics.* The Hague: Mouton.

Held, D., A. McGrew, D. Goldblatt & J. Perraton 1999. *Global Transformations: Politics, economics, and culture.* Cambridge: Polity Press.

Henderson, J. 2011. New and not so new horizons: brief encounters between UK undergraduate native-speaker and non-native-speaker Englishes. *Language and Intercultural Communication* 11/3: 270–84.

Hennebry, M., Y.Y. Lo & E. Macaro 2012. Differing perspectives of non-native speaker students' linguistic experiences on higher degree courses. *Oxford Review of education* 38/2: 209–30.

Hollway, W. 1984. Gender difference and the production of subjectivity. In J. Henriques, W. Hollway, C. Urwin, L. Venn & V. Walkerdine (eds) *Changing the Subject: Psychology, Social Regulation and Subjectivity.* London: Methuen.

Horner, B. 2011. Writing English as a lingua franca. In Archibald et al. (eds.) 2011.

Horner, B., M-Z. Lu, J. Jones Royster & J. Trimbur 2011. Language difference in writing: towards a translingual approach. *College English* 73/1: 303–21.

House, J. 1999. Misunderstanding in intercultural communication: interactions in English as *lingua franca* and the myth of mutual intelligibility. In C. Gnutzmann (ed.) *Teaching and Learning English as a Global Language.* Tübingen: Stauffenburg Verlag.

House, J. 2003. English as a lingua franca: a threat to multilingualism? *Journal of Sociolinguistics* 7/4: 556–78.

House, J. 2006. Unity in diversity: English as a Lingua Franca for Europe. In C. Leung and J. Jenkins (eds.) *Reconfiguring Europe. The contribution of applied linguistics.* London: Equinox.

Hu, G. & S. McKay 2012. English language education in East Asia: some recent developments. *Journal of Multilingual and Multicultural Development* 33/4: 345–62.

Hughes, R. 2008. Internationalisation of higher education and language policy: questions of quality and equity. *Higher Education Management and Policy* 20/1: 111–28.

Hüllen, W. 1982. Teaching a foreign language as "lingua franca". *Grazer Linguistiche Studien* 16: 83–88.

Hülmbauer, C. 2007. The relationship between lexicogrammatical correctness and communicative effectiveness in English as a lingua franca. *Vienna English Working PaperS (VIEWS)* 16/2: 3–35.

Hülmbauer, C. 2009. "We don't understand the right way. We just take the way that we think you will understand" – The shifting relationship between correctness and effectiveness in ELF. In Mauranen & Ranta (eds.) 2009.

Hüttner, J. 2008. The genre(s) of student writing: developing writing models. *International Journal of Applied Linguistics* 18/2: 146–65.

Hyland, F., S. Trahar, J. Anderson & A. Dickens 2008. *A Changing World: The internationalisation experiences of staff and students (home and international) in UK Higher Education.* Subject Centres for Education and Languages, Linguistics and Area Studies. Available at http://escalate.ac.uk/4967 (accessed 15 March 2013).

Hyland, K. 2006. *English for Academic Purposes. An advanced resource book.* London: Routledge.

Hyland, K. 2008a. Academic clusters: text patterning in published and postgraduate writing. *International Journal of Applied Linguistics* 18/1: 41–62.

Hyland, K. 2008b. Different strokes for different folks: disciplinary variation in academic writing. In Fløttum (ed.) 2008.

Hyland, K. 2009. *Academic Discourse. English in a Global Context*. London: Continuum.

Ivanič, R. 1998. *Writing and Identity: The discoursal construction of identity in academic writing*. Amsterdam: John Benjamins.

Ivanič, R. & D. Camps 2001. "I am how I sound": voice as self-representation in L2 writing. *Journal of Second Language Writing* 10: 3–33.

Jackson, J. 2010. *Intercultural Journeys from Study to Residence Abroad*. Houndmills, Basingstoke: Palgrave Macmillan.

Jenkins, J. 1996a. Changing pronunciation priorities for successful communication in international contexts. *Speak Out! Newsletter of the IATEFL Pronunciation Special Interest Group* 17: 15–22.

Jenkins, J. 1996b. Native speaker, non-native speaker and English as a Foreign Language: time for a change. *IATEFL Newsletter* 131: 10–11.

Jenkins, J. 1998. Which pronunciation norms and models for English as an International Language? *ELTJ* 52/2: 119–26.

Jenkins, J. 2000. *The Phonology of English as an International Language*. Oxford: Oxford University Press.

Jenkins, J. 2002. A sociolinguistically based, empirically researched pronunciation syllabus for English as an International Language. *Applied Linguistics* 23/1: 83–103.

Jenkins, J. 2006. Current perspectives on teaching World Englishes and English as a Lingua Franca. *TESOL Quarterly* 40/1: 157–81.

Jenkins, J. 2007. *English as a Lingua Franca: Attitude and Identity*. Oxford: Oxford University Press.

Jenkins, J. 2009. *World Englishes*. A resource book for students 2nd ed. London: Routledge.

Jenkins, J. 2012. English as a Lingua Franca from the classroom to the classroom. *ELT Journal* 66/4: 486–94.

Jenkins, J. & C. Leung 2013. English as a Lingua Franca. In A. Kunnan (ed.) *The Companion to Language Assessment*. Oxford: Wiley-Blackwell.

Jenkins, J. & F. Maringe (in preparation). "It's just in the air". The trouble with academic English.

Jenkins, J. with A. Cogo & M. Dewey 2011. Review of developments in research into English as a lingua franca. *Language Teaching* 44/3: 281–315.

Jin, L. & M. Cortazzi (eds.) 2011. *Researching Chinese Learners. Skills, perceptions and intercultural adaptation*. Houndmills, Basingstoke: Palgrave Macmillan.

John, S. 2009. Using the revision process to help international students understand the linguistic construction of academic identity. In Charles et al. (eds.) 2009.

Johnson, S. & T. Milani (eds.) 2010. *Language Ideologies and Media Discourse*. London: Continuum.

Johnson, S., T. Milani & C. Upton 2010. Language ideological debates on the BBC "Voices" website: hypermodality in theory and practice. In Johnson & Milani (eds.) 2010.

Jordan, R.R. 1999. *Academic Writing Course* 3rd ed. Harlow, UK: Pearson Longman.

Jørgensen, M. & L.J. Phillips 2002. *Discourse Analysis as Theory and Method*. London: Sage Publications.

Kachru, B.B. 1985. Standards, codification and sociolinguistic realism: the English language in the outer circle. In R. Quirk & H.G. Widdowson (eds.) *English in the World: Teaching and Learning the Language and Literatures*. Cambridge: Cambridge University Press.

Kachru, B.B. 1992. Teaching World Englishes. In B.B. Kachru (ed.) *The Other Tongue. English across Cultures*. Urbana: University of Illinois Press.

Kachru, B.B. 1996. English as lingua franca. In H. Goebl, P. Nelde, Z. Starý & W. Wölck (eds.) *Contact Linguistics*, Volume 1. Berlin: Walter de Gruyter.

Kachru, B.B. 2005. *Asian Englishes Beyond the Canon*. Hong Kong: Hong Kong University Press.

Kachru, B.B. 2009. Asian Englishes in the Asian age: contexts and challenges. In Murata & Jenkins (eds.) 2009.

Kachru, Y. 1997. Cultural meaning and contrastive rhetoric in English education. *World Englishes* 16/3: 337–50.

Kachru, Y. 2009. Academic writing in World Englishes: the Asian context. In Murata & Jenkins (eds.) 2009.

Kachru, Y. & C. Nelson 2006. *World Englishes in Asian Contexts.* Hong Kong: Hong Kong University Press.

Kachru, Y. & L. Smith 2008. *Cultures, Contexts, and World Englishes.* New York: Routledge.

Kalocsai, K. 2013. *Communities of Practice and English as a Lingua Franca. A study of Erasmus students in Central European context.* Berlin: De Gruyter Mouton.

Kankaanranta, A. & A. Planken 2010. BELF competence as business knowledge of international operating business professionals. *Journal of Business Communication* 47/3: 380–407.

Kaur, J. 2009. Pre-empting problems of understanding in English as a lingua franca. In Mauranen & Ranta (eds.) 2009.

Kirkpatrick, A. 2010. *English as a Lingua Franca in ASEAN.* Hong Kong: Hong Kong University Press.

Kirkpatrick, A. (ed.) 2010. *The Routledge Handbook of World Englishes.* London: Routledge.

Kirkpatrick, A. 2011. Internationalization or Englishization: medium of instruction in today's universities. *Working Paper Series* 2011/003. Centre for Governance and Citizenship, The Hong Kong Institute of Education.

Klimpfinger, T. 2007. "Mind you, sometimes you have to mix" – the role of code-switching in English as a Lingua Franca. *Vienna English Working PaperS (VIEWS)* 16/1: 36–61.

Klitgård, I. 2011. Plagiarism in the international university: from kidnapping and theft to translation and hybridity. In B. Preisler, I. Klitgård & A. Fabricius (eds.) 2011.

Kloss, H. 1969. *Research Possibilities on Group Bilingualism. A Report.* Quebec: International Center for Research on Bilingualism.

Knapp, K. 1985. Englisch als internationale *lingua franca* und Richtlinien. In K-R. Bausch, H. Christ, W. Hüllen & H-J. Krumm (eds.) *Forschungsgegenstand Richtlinien.* Tübingen: Narr.

Knapp, K. 1987. English as an international lingua franca and the teaching of intercultural competence. In W. Lörsch & R. Schulze (eds.) *Perspectives on Language Performance.* Tübingen: Narr.

Knapp, K. 2002. The fading out of the non-native speaker. Native speaker dominance in lingua-franca situations. In Knapp & Meierkord (eds.) 2002.

Knapp, K. & C. Meierkord 2002. Approaching lingua franca communication. In Knapp & Meierkord (eds.) 2002.

Knapp, K. & C. Meierkord (eds.) 2002. *Lingua Franca Communication.* Frankfurt am Main: Peter Lang.

Knox, J. 2007. Visual-verbal communication on online newspaper homepages. *Visual Communication* 6/1: 19–53.

Kress, G. & T. van Leeuwen 2006. *Reading Images: The Grammar of Visual Design* 2nd ed. London: Routledge.

Kubota, R. 2010. Cross-cultural perspectives on writing: contrastive rhetoric. In N. Hornberger & S. McKay (eds.) *Sociolinguistics and Language Education.* Bristol: Multilingual Matters.

Kubota, R. & A. Lehner 2004. Toward critical contrastive rhetoric. *Journal of Second Language Writing* 13: 7–27.

Kubota, R. & A. Lin 2006. Race and TESOL: Introduction to concepts and theories. *TESOL Quarterly* 40/3: 471–93.

Kvale, S. & S. Brinkmann 2009. *InterViews. Learning the craft of qualitative research interviewing* 2nd ed. London: Sage.

Larsen-Freeman, D. & L. Cameron 2008. *Complex Systems and Applied Linguistics.* Oxford: Oxford University Press.

Lea, M. & B. Street 1998. Student writing in higher education: an academic literacies approach. *Studies in Higher Education* 23/2: 157–72.

Lea, M. & B. Street 2006. The "Academic Literacies" model: theory and applications. *Theory into Practice* 45/4: 368–77.

Lee, H. & M.H. Maguire 2011. International students and identity: Resisting dominant ways of writing and knowing in academe. In D. Starke-Meyerring, A. Paré, N. Artemeva,

M. Horne, & L. Yousoubova (eds.). *Writing in Knowledge Societies*. West Lafayette, IN: Parlor Press and WAC Clearinghouse.

Lee, J.J. & C. Rice 2007. Welcome to America? International student perceptions of discrimination. *Higher Education* 53: 381–409.

Legard, R., J. Keegan & K. Ward 2003. In-depth interviews. In J. Ritchie & J. Lewis (eds.) 2003 *Qualitative Research Practice. A guide for social science students and researchers*. London: Sage Publications.

Lesznyák, A. 2002. From chaos to the smallest common denominator. Topic management in English lingua franca communication. In Knapp & Meierkord (eds.) 2002.

Leung, C. 2005. Convivial communication: recontextualizing communicative competence. *International Journal of Applied Linguistics* 15/2: 119–44.

Leung, C. 2012. English as an Additional Language policy – Rendered theory and classroom interaction. In S. Gardner & M. Martin-Jones (eds.) *Multilingualism, Discourse, and Ethnography*. London: Routledge.

Leung, C., & J. Lewkowicz, J. 2012. Language communication and communicative competence: A view from contemporary classrooms. *Language and Education* 26/6, i-First edition.

Li, T. & S. Wharton 2012. Metadiscourse repertoire of L1 Mandarin undergraduates writing in English: A cross-contextual, cross-disciplinary study. *Journal of English for Academic Purposes* 11/4: 345–56.

Lichtkoppler, J. 2007. "Male, Male" – "Male?" – "The sex is male." – The role of repetition in English as a Lingua Franca conversations. *Vienna English Working PaperS (VIEWS)* 16/1: 39–65.

Liebscher, G. & J. Dailey-O'Cain 2009. Language attitudes in interaction. *Journal of Sociolinguistics* 13/2: 195–222.

Lillis, T. 2001. *Student Writing. Access, regulation, desire*. London: Routledge.

Lillis, T. 2008. Ethnography as method, methodology, and "deep theorizing": closing the gap between text and context in academic writing research. *Written Communication* 23: 3–35.

Lillis, T. & M.J. Curry 2010. *Academic Writing in a Global Context. The politics and practices of publishing in English*. London: Routledge.

Lillis, T. & M. Scott 2007. Defining academic literacies research: issues of epistemology, ideology and strategy. Special issue – New Directions in Academic Literacies, *Journal of Applied Linguistics* 4/1: 5–32.

Lippi-Green, R. 2011. *English with an Accent: Language, ideology and discrimination in the United States* 2nd ed. London: Routledge.

Littlemore, J., P. Trautman Chen, A. Koester & J. Barnden 2011. Difficulties in metaphor comprehension faced by international students whose first language is not English. *Applied Linguistics* 32/4: 408–29.

Lowenberg, P. 2000. Non-native varieties and the sociopolitics of English proficiency assessment. In J. Kelly Hall & W. Eggington (eds.) *The Sociopolitics of English Language Teaching*. Clevedon, UK: Multilingual Matters.

McCarthy, M. & F. O'Dell 2008. *Academic Vocabulary in Use*. Cambridge: Cambridge University Press.

McCabe, L. 2001 Globalization and internationalization: the impact on education abroad programs. *Journal of Studies in International Education* 5/2: 138–45.

McGroarty, M. 2003. Editor's introduction. *Annual Review of Applied Linguistics* 23: vii–xi.

McKay, S. 2009. Pragmatics and EIL pedagogy. In F. Sharifian (ed.) *English as an International Language*. Bristol: Multilingual Matters.

McKenzie, R. under submission. UK university students' folk perceptions of global variation in English: the role of explicit and implicit attitudes.

McNamara, T. 2011. Managing learning: authority and language assessment. *Language Teaching* 44/4: 500–15.

Maley, A. 2009. ELF: a teacher's perspective. *Language and Intercultural Communication* 9/3: 187–200.

Mann, S. 2011. A critical review of qualitative interviews in applied linguistics. *Applied Linguistics* 32/1: 6–24.

Marginson, S., C. Nyland, E. Sawir & H. Forbes-Mewett 2010. *International Student Security*. Cambridge: Cambridge University Press.

Maringe, F. 2010. The meanings of globalization and internationalization in HE: findings from a world survey. In Maringe & Foskett (eds.) 2010.

Maringe, F. & N. Foskett (eds.) 2010. *Globalization and Internationalization in Higher Education*. London: Continuum.

Maringe, F. & N. Foskett 2010. Introduction: Globalization and universities. In Maringe & Foskett (eds.) 2010.

Maringe, F. & J. Jenkins (in preparation). Stigma, tensions and apprehensions: the academic writing experiences of international students.

Marshall, S. 2010. Re-becoming ESL: multilingual university students and a deficit identity. *Language and Education* 24/1: 41–56.

Martinez, R. & N. Schmitt 2012. A phrasal expressions list. *Applied Linguistics* 33/3: 299–320.

Mauranen, A. 2003. The corpus of English as a Lingua Franca in academic settings. *TESOL Quarterly* 37/3: 513–27.

Mauranen, A. 2006a. Signalling and preventing misunderstanding in ELF communication. *International Journal of the Sociology of Language* 177: 123–50.

Mauranen, A. 2006b. Spoken discourse, academics and global English: a corpus perspective. In R. Hughes (ed.) *Spoken English, TESOL and Applied Linguistics*. Houndmills, Basingstoke: Palgrave Macmillan.

Mauranen, A. 2008. Hybrid voices: English as the lingua franca of academics. In Fløttum (ed.) 2008.

Mauranen, A. 2009. Chunking in ELF: Expressions for managing interaction. *Intercultural Pragmatics* 6/2: 217–33.

Mauranen, A. 2012. *Exploring ELF. Academic English shaped by non-native speakers*. Cambridge: Cambridge University Press.

Mauranen, A. & M. Metsä-Ketelä (eds) 2006. Special Issue: English as a Lingua Franca. *Nordic Journal of English Studies* 5/2.

Mauranen, A. & E. Ranta 2008. English as an academic lingua franca – the ELFA project. *Nordic Journal of English Studies* 7/3: 199–202.

Mauranen, A. & E. Ranta (eds) 2009. *English as a Lingua Franca. Studies and Findings*. Newcastle upon Tyne: Cambridge Scholars Publishing.

Mauranen, A., N. Hynninnen & E. Ranta 2010. English as an academic lingua franca: The ELFA project. *English for Specific Purposes* 29: 183–90.

Mauranen, A., C. Pérez-Llantada & J. Swales 2010. Academic Englishes: a standardized knowledge? In Kirkpatrick (ed.) 2010.

Meierkord, C. 1996. *Englisch als Medium der interkulturellen Kommunikation. Untersuchungen zum non-native/non-native speaker Diskurs*. Frankfurt am Main: Peter Lang.

Meierkord, C. 1998. Lingua franca English: characteristics of successful non-native–non-native-speaker discourse. *Erfurt Electronic Studies in English (EESE)*. Available at: http://webdoc.sub.gwdg.de/edoc/ia/eese/rahmen22.html

Metsä-Ketelä, M. 2006. Words are more or less superfluous. *Nordic Journal of English Studies* 5/2: 117–43.

Milani, T. & S. Johnson 2010. Critical intersections: language ideologies and media discourse. In Johnson & Milani (eds.) 2010.

Milroy, J. 2001. Language ideologies and the consequences of standardization. *Journal of Sociolinguistics* 5/4: 530–55.

Mollin, S. 2006. *Euro-English: Assessing Variety Status*. Tübingen: Gunter Narr Verlag.

Montgomery, C. 2008. Global futures, global communities? The role of culture, language and communication in an internationalised university. In Haberland et al. (eds) 2008.

Montgomery, C. 2010. *Understanding the International Student Experience.* Houndmills, Basingstoke: Palgrave Macmillan.

Moore, J. 2007. *Common Mistakes at IELTS Advanced ... and how to avoid them.* Cambridge: Cambridge University Press.

Mortensen, J. in press. Notes on English used as a lingua franca as an object of study. *Journal of English as a Lingua Franca* 2/1.

Mufwene, S. 2001. *The Ecology of Language Evolution.* Cambridge: Cambridge University Press.

Murata, K. & J. Jenkins (eds.) 2009. *Global Englishes in Asian Contexts.* Houndmills, Basingstoke: Palgrave Macmillan.

Nilsson, B. 1999. Internationalisation at home: theory and praxis. *EAIE Forum,* Spring. Available at: www.eaie.nl/pdf/intathome.asp

Nogami, Y. 2011. Japanese L2 users' second language identities and pragmatic use in relations of power and culture. Unpublished PhD thesis, University of Essex.

OECD (Organisation for Economic Co-operation and Development) 2010. *Education at a Glance 2010: OECD Indicators.* Paris: OECD.

Oshima, A. & A. Hogue 2006. *Writing Academic English* 4th ed. New York: Pearson Longman.

Osimk, R. 2009. Decoding sounds: an experimental approach to intelligibility in ELF. *Vienna English Working PaperS (VIEWS)* 18/1: 64–89.

Pauwels, L. 2012. A multimodal framework for analysing websites as cultural expressions. *Journal of Computer-Mediated Communication* 17: 247–65.

Pennycook, A. 1994. *The Cultural Politics of English as an International Language.* London: Longman.

Pennycook, A. 2006. Postmodernism in language policy. In Ricento (ed.) 2006.

Pennycook, A. 2007. *Global Englishes and Transcultural Flows.* London: Routlege.

Pennycook, A. 2009. Plurilithic Englishes: towards a 3D model. In Murata & Jenkins (eds.) 2009.

Pennycook, A. 2010. *Language as Local Practice.* London: Routledge.

Phan, Le Ha 2009. Strategic, passionate, but academic: Am I allowed in my writing? *Journal of English for Academic Purposes* 8: 134–46.

Phillipson, R. 1992. *Linguistic Imperialism.* Oxford: Oxford University Press.

Phillipson, R. 2003. *English-Only Europe? Challenging language policy.* London: Routledge.

Phillipson, R. 2009. *Linguistic Imperialism Continued.* New York: Routledge.

Pickering, L. 2009. Intonation as a pragmatic resource in ELF interactions. *Intercultural Pragmatics* 6/2: 235–55.

Pickering, L. & J. Litzenberg 2012. Intonation as a pragmatic resource in ELF interaction, revisited. In Archibald et al. (eds.) 2011.

Pilcher, N., M. Cortazzi & L. Jin 2011. Different waves crashing into different coastlines? Mainland Chinese learners doing postgraduate dissertations in the UK. In Jin & Cortazzi (eds.) 2011.

Pitzl, M-L. 2005. Non-understanding in English as a Lingua Franca: examples from a business context. *Vienna English Working PaperS (VIEWS)* 14/2: 50–71.

Pitzl, M-L. 2009. "We should not wake up any dogs": idiom and metaphor in ELF. In A. Mauranen & E. Ranta (eds.) 2009.

Pitzl, M-L. 2011. Creativity in English as a lingua franca: idiom and metaphor. Unpublished doctoral thesis, University of Vienna.

Pitzl, M-L. 2012. Creativity meets convention: idiom variation and re-metaphorization in ELF. *Journal of English as a Lingua Franca* 1/1: 27–55.

Potter, J. & D. Edwards 2001. Discursive Social Psychology. In W.P. Robinson & H. Giles (eds.) *The New Handbook of Social Psychology.* Chichester, UK: John Wiley & Sons.

Pratt, M.L. 2010. "You don't understand the system": Reflections on language and globalization. *Sociolinguistics Symposium 18,* Abstracts p.9.

Preece, S. & P. Martin 2010. Guest Editorial. Imagining higher education as a multilingual space. *Language and Education* 24/1: 3–8.

Preisler, B. 2011. Introduction. In Preisler, Klitgård & Fabricius (eds.) 2011.

Preisler, B., I. Klitgård & A. Fabricius (eds) 2011. *Language and Learning in the International University. From English uniformity to diversity and hybridity.* Bristol: Multilingual Matters.

Prodromou, L. 2006. Defining the "successful bilingual speaker" of English. In R. Rubdy & M. Saraceni (eds.) *English in the World. Global rules, global roles.* London: Continuum.

Rajadurai, J. 2007. Intelligibility studies: a consideration of empirical and ideological issues. *World Englishes* 26/1: 87–98.

Rajagopalan, K. 2009. "World English" and the Latin analogy: where we get it wrong. *English Today* 25/2: 49–54.

Rampton, B. 1990. Displacing the "native speaker": expertise, affiliation, and inheritance. *ELT Journal* 44/2: 97–101.

Randall, M. & M. Samimy 2010. The status of English in Dubai. *English Today* 26/1: 43–50.

Ranta, E. 2006. The "attractive" progressive – why use the -*ing* form in English as a Lingua Franca? *Nordic Journal of English Studies* 5/2: 95–116.

Ricento, T. (ed.) 2006. *An Introduction to Language Policy. Theory and Method.* Oxford: Blackwell.

Ricento, T. 2006a. Theoretical perspectives in language policy: an overview. In Ricento (ed.) 2006.

Ricento, T. 2006b. Methodological perspectives in language policy: an overview. In Ricento (ed.) 2006.

Ricento, T. 2006c. Topical areas in language policy: an overview. In Ricento (ed.) 2006.

Richards, K. 2003. *Qualitative Enquiry in TESOL.* Houndmills, Basingstoke: Palgrave Macmillan.

Robertson, R. 1995. Glocalisation: time-space and heterogeneity-homogeneity. In M. Featherstone, S. Lash & R. Robertson (eds.) *Global Modernities.* London: Sage.

Ryan, J. (ed.) 2013. *Cross-Cultural Teaching and Learning for Home and International Students.* London: Routledge.

Ryan, J. & R. Viete 2009. Respectful interactions: learning with international students in the English-speaking academy. *Teaching in Higher Education* 14/3: 303–14.

Saarinen, T. & T. Nikula 2013. Implicit policy, invisible language: policies and practices of international degree programmes in Finnish higher education. In Doiz et al. (eds.) 2013a.

Sanderson, T. 2008. Interaction, identity and culture in academic writing: the case of German, British and American academics in the humanities. In A. Adel & R. Reppen (eds.) *Corpora and Discourse: The challenges of different settings.* Amsterdam: Benjamins.

Schmitt, D. 2006. Writing in the international classroom. In J. Carroll and J. Ryan (eds.) *Teaching International Students: Improving Learning for All.* London: Routledge.

Schmitt, D. 2011. Maintaining standards in TESOL in the face of changing market forces. Keynote talk delivered at the QuiTE 10th Annual Seminar, 22 November 2011, London. Available at: www.quality-tesol-ed.org.uk/seminars/2011/6/2011_Diane.html (accessed 15 March 2013).

Schweisfurth, M. & Q. Gu 2009. Exploring the experiences of international students in UK higher education: possibilities and limits of interculturality in university life. *Intercultural Education* 20/5: 463–73.

Seargeant, P. 2005. "More English than England itself": the simulation of authenticity in foreign language practice in Japan. *International Journal of Applied Linguistics* 15/3: 326–45.

Seidlhofer, B. 2001. Closing a conceptual gap: the case for a description of English as a lingua franca. *International Journal of Applied Linguistics* 11/2: 133–58.

Seidlhofer, B. 2004. Research perspectives on teaching English as a Lingua Franca. *Annual Review of Applied Linguistics* 24: 209–39.

Seidlhofer, B. 2009a. Common ground and different realities: world Englishes and English as a lingua franca. *World Englishes* 28/2: 236–45.

Seidlhofer, B. 2009b. Orientations in ELF research: form and function. In Mauranen & Ranta (eds.) 2009.

Seidlhofer, B. 2011. *Understanding English as a Lingua Franca.* Oxford: Oxford University Press.

Seidlhofer, B. & M. Berns (eds.) 2009. Symposium: Englishes in world contexts. *World Englishes* 28/2: 190–269.

Seidlhofer, B. & H.G. Widdowson 2009. Accommodation and the idiom principle. In Murata & Jenkins (eds.) 2009.

Selinker, L. 1972. Interlanguage. *International Review of Applied Linguistics* 10: 209–31.

Shaw, P. & T. Dahl 2008. Introduction. *Nordic Journal of English Studies* 7/3: 1–8.

Sherry, M., P. Thomas & W.H. Chui 2010. International students: a vulnerable student population. *Higher Education* 60: 33–46.

Shohamy, E. 2006. *Language Policy. Hidden agendas and new approaches*. London: Routledge.

Shohamy, E. 2013. A critical perspective on the use of English as a medium of instruction at universities. In Doiz et al. (eds.) 2013a.

Silverstein, M. 1996. Monoglot "standard" in America. In D. Brenneis & R. Macaulay (eds.) *The Matrix of Language*. Boulder, CO: Westview Press.

Singh, P. & C. Doherty 2004. Global cultural flows and pedagogic dilemmas: teaching in the global university contact zone. *TESOL Quarterly* 38/1: 9–42.

Smit, U. 2010. *English as a Lingua Franca in Higher Education*. Berlin: DeGruyter Mouton.

Spolsky, B. 2004. *Language Policy*. Cambridge: Cambridge University Press.

Spolsky, B. 2009. *Language Management*. Cambridge: Cambridge University Press.

Spolsky, B. 2012. What is language policy? In B. Spolsky (ed.) *The Cambridge Handbook of Language Policy*. Cambridge: Cambridge University Press.

Steger, M.B. 2003. *Globalisation: A very short introduction*. Oxford: Oxford University Press.

Stotesbury, J. 2009. An interview with David Crystal. *The European English Messenger* 18/2, 51–58.

Street, B. 2004. Academic literacies and the new orders: implications for research and practice in student writing in higher education. *Learning and Teaching in the Social Sciences* 1/1: 9–20.

Street, B. 2009. "Hidden" features of academic paper writing. *Working Papers in Educational Linguistics* 24/1: 1–17.

Summers, M. & S. Volet 2008. Students' attitudes towards culturally mixed groups on international campuses: impact of participation in diverse and non-diverse groups. *Studies in Higher Education* 33/4: 357–70.

Swales, J. 1990. *Genre Analysis*. Cambridge: Cambridge University Press.

Swales, J. 1997. English as *Tyrannosaurus rex*. *World Englishes* 16/3: 373–82.

Swales, J. and C. Feak 2004. *Academic Writing for Graduate Students* 2nd ed. Michigan: University of Michigan Press.

Sweeney, E. & H. Zhu 2010. Accommodating toward your audience. Do native speakers of English know how to accommodate their communication strategies toward non-native speakers of English? *Journal of Business Communication* 47/4: 477–504.

Talmy, S. 2010. Qualitative interviews in applied linguistics: from research instrument to social practice. *Annual Review of Applied Linguistics* 30: 128–48.

Talmy, S. 2011. The interview as collaborative achievement: interaction, identity and ideology in a speech event. *Applied Linguistics* 32/1: 25–42.

Talmy, S. & K. Richards 2011. Theorizing qualitative research interviews in applied linguistics. *Applied Linguistics* 32/1: 1–5.

Tange, H. 2012. Organising language at the international university: three principles of linguistic organisation. *Journal of Multilingual and Multicultural Development* 33/3: 287–300.

Tarry, E. 2011. Is west really best? Social and cultural tensions international students experience having studied at British universities. *Journal of Further and Higher Education* 35/1: 69–87.

Tian, M. & J. Lowe 2009. Existentialist internationalisation and the Chinese student experience in English universities. *Compare: A Journal of Comparative and International Education* 39/5: 659–76.

Tollefson, J. (ed.) 2002. *Language Policies in Education: Critical Issues*. Mahwah, NJ: Lawrence Erlbaum.

Tollefson, J. 2006. Critical theory in language policy. In Ricento (ed.) 2006.

Tollefson, J. & A. Tsui (eds.) 2004. *Medium of Instruction Policies. Which agenda? Whose agenda?* London: Routledge.

Trahar, S. 2011. *The Doctorate: international stories of the UK experience.* Bristol: ESCalate.

Trahar, S. & F. Hyland 2011. Experiences and perceptions of internationalisation in higher education in the UK. *Higher Education Research & Development* 30/5: 623–33.

Tribble, C. 2009. Writing academic English – a survey review of current published resources. *ELT Journal* 63/4: 400–17.

Trudgill, P. 2002. *Sociolinguistic Variation and Change.* Edinburgh: Edinburgh University Press.

Trudgill, P. & J. Hannah 2008. *International English* 5th ed. London: Hodder Education.

Turner, J. 2011. *Language in the Academy. Cultural reflexivity and intercultural dynamics.* Bristol, UK: Multilingual Matters.

Turner, J. 2012. Reconfiguring English and pedagogic practices in the "inner circle" international university. Plenary talk delivered at the CALPIU '12 conference, Higher education across borders: Transcultural interaction and linguistic diversity. Roskilde, 1–4 April, 2012.

Turner, Y. & S. Robson 2008. *Internationalizing the University.* London: Continuum.

Van Langenhove, L. & R. Harré 1999. Introducing positioning theory. In Harré & van Langenhove (eds.) 1999.

Wächter, B. & F. Maiworm 2008. *English Taught Programmes in European Higher Education. The Picture in 2007.* Bonn: Lemmens.

Walker, R. 2010. *Teaching the Pronunciation of English as a Lingua Franca.* Oxford: Oxford University Press.

Wang, Y. 2012. Chinese speakers' perceptions of their English in intercultural communication. Unpublished doctoral thesis, University of Southampton.

Wen, Q. 2012. English as a lingua franca: a pedagogical perspective. *Journal of English as a Lingua Franca* 1/2: 371–376.

Wenger, E. 1998. *Communities of Practice. Learning, meaning, identity.* Cambridge: Cambridge University Press.

White, R. & V. Arndt 1991. *Process Writing.* Harlow, UK: Longman.

Whitehead, F. 2013. Lost in translation. *Education Guardian. Eastern Horizons* p. 5. 15 January 2013.

Widdowson, H.G. 1997. EIL, ESL, EFL: global issues and local interests. *World Englishes* 16/1: 135–46.

Wildavsky, B. 2010. *The Great Brain Race. How global universities are reshaping the world.* Princeton, NJ: University of Princeton Press.

Wilkinson, R. 2013. English-medium instruction at a Dutch university: challenge and pitfalls. In Doiz et al. (eds.) 2013a.

Wingate, U. & C. Tribble 2012. The best of both worlds? Towards an English for Academic Purposes/Academic Literacies writing pedagogy. *Studies in Higher Education* 37/4: 481–95.

Wodak, R. 2006. Linguistic analyses in language policies. In Ricento ed. 2006.

Woodfield, S. 2010. Key trends and emerging issues in international student mobility. In Maringe & Foskett (eds.) 2010.

Woolard, K. 2005. Language and identity choice in Catalonia: the interplay of contrasting ideologies of linguistic authority. Paper presented at the Workshop on Language Ideology and Change in Multilingual Communities, UC San Diego February 2005. Available at: http://escholarship.org/uc/item/47n938cp (accessed 15 March 2013).

Woolard, K. & B. Schieffelin 1994. Language ideology. *Annual Review of Anthropology* 23: 55–82.

Wright, S. 2009. The elephant in the room. Language issues in the European Union. *European Journal of Language Policy* 1/2: 93–120.

Wright, S. 2012. Language policy, the nation and nationalism. In B. Spolsky (ed.) *The Cambridge Handbook of Language Policy.* Cambridge: Cambridge University Press.

Wu, W. & M. Hammond 2011. Challenges of university adjustment in the UK: a study of East Asian Master's degree students. *Journal of Further and Higher Education* 35/3: 423–38.

Xiao, Y. 2011 Review of K. Hyland, Academic Discourse: English in a Global Context, London: Continuum. *Journal of English for Academic Purposes* 10/3: 198–99.

Yakhontova, T. 2006. Cultural and disciplinary variation in academic discourse: the issue of influencing factors. *Journal of English for Academic Purposes* 5: 153–67.

Yumei, J. 2010. The role of English language teaching in university internationalization in China. In Maringe & Foskett (eds.) 2010.

Zamel, V. 1997. Toward a model of transculturation. *TESOL Quarterly* 31/2: 341–51.

INDEX

Numbers in **bold** denote tables; numbers in *italics* denote figures.